Towards a New Pedagogy for Teaching Foreign Language Politeness

This book examines how foreign language speakers establish and maintain social and transactional relationships in their target language and how pedagogic intervention can help learners implement practices that will allow them to participate and react in both socially acceptable and individualistically empowering ways.

Arguing that 'doing' foreign-language politeness and culture does not simply involve the indiscriminate and uncritical adoption and implementation of target-language patterns and practices, the author advocates instead for active, judicious and even critical social action. As such, the book presents a dynamic and vibrant dimension to target language politeness and cultural practices, demonstrating that raising learners' critical language awareness in identifying productive communicative resources and assets can lead to successful interpersonal and transactional communication. Building on this notion of a 'positive' pedagogy, Halliday's model of ideational, interpersonal and textual is utilised as a framework for exploring how foreign language users can approach target language politeness in terms of prosocial, interpersonal and contested politeness, with reference to a study of Mexican speakers of English as a foreign language.

Heightening awareness of foreign language politeness patterns and practices, as well as presenting knowledge and resources for overcoming challenges and accentuating benefits of a nuanced learning scheme for politeness in foreign language, this book will appeal to language educators, researchers and bilingual speakers. It will also benefit those working across pragmatics, sociolinguistics, TESOL and cultural studies.

Gerrard Mugford is a lecturer in pragmatics, discourse analysis and sociolinguistics at la Universidad de Guadalajara, Mexico. His current research interests include im/politeness, foreign-language interpersonal language use and critical pedagogy.

Routledge Research in Language Education

The *Routledge Research in Language Education* series provides a platform for established and emerging scholars to present their latest research and discuss key issues in Language Education. This series welcomes books on all areas of language teaching and learning, including but not limited to language education policy and politics, multilingualism, literacy, L1, L2 or foreign language acquisition, curriculum, classroom practice, pedagogy, teaching materials, and language teacher education and development. Books in the series are not limited to the discussion of the teaching and learning of English only.

Books in the series include:

Performed Culture in Action to Teach Chinese as a Foreign Language
Integrating PCA into Curriculum, Pedagogy, and Assessment
Edited by Jianfen Wang and Junqing (Jessie) Jia

Virtual Exchange for Intercultural Language Learning and Teaching
Fostering Communication for the Digital Age
Martine Derivry and Anthippi Potolia

Technology in Second Language Writing
Advances in Composing, Translation, Writing Pedagogy and
Data-Driven Learning
Edited by Jingjing Qin and Paul Stapleton

Teacher Well-being in English Language Teaching
An Ecological Approach
Luis Javier Pentón Herrera, Gilda Martínez-Alba, and Ethan Trinh

For more information about the series, please visit www.routledge.com/ Routledge-Research-in-Language-Education/book-series/RRLE

Towards a New Pedagogy for Teaching Foreign Language Politeness
Halliday's Model and Approaches to Politeness

Gerrard Mugford

Routledge
Taylor & Francis Group
NEW YORK AND LONDON

First published 2023
by Routledge
605 Third Avenue, New York, NY 10158

and by Routledge
4 Park Square, Milton Park, Abingdon, Oxon OX14 4RN

Routledge is an imprint of the Taylor & Francis Group, an informa business

© 2023 Gerrard Mugford

The right of Gerrard Mugford to be identified as author of this work has been asserted in accordance with sections 77 and 78 of the Copyright, Designs and Patents Act 1988.

All rights reserved. No part of this book may be reprinted or reproduced or utilised in any form or by any electronic, mechanical, or other means, now known or hereafter invented, including photocopying and recording, or in any information storage or retrieval system, without permission in writing from the publishers.

Trademark notice: Product or corporate names may be trademarks or registered trademarks, and are used only for identification and explanation without intent to infringe.

British Library Cataloguing-in-Publication Data
A catalogue record for this book is available from the British Library

Library of Congress Cataloging-in-Publication Data
Names: Mugford, Gerrard, author.
Title: Towards a new pedagogy for teaching foreign language politeness : Halliday's model and approaches to politeness / Gerrard Mugford.
Description: Abingdon, Oxon ; New York, NY : Routledge, 2023. | Series: Routledge research in language education | Includes bibliographical references and index.
Identifiers: LCCN 2022025300 (print) | LCCN 2022025301 (ebook) | ISBN 9781032351643 (hardback) | ISBN 9781032352602 (paperback) | ISBN 9781003326052 (ebook)
Subjects: LCSH: Language and languages--Study and teaching--Social aspects. | Politeness (Linguistics)
Classification: LCC P53.8 .M84 2023 (print) | LCC P53.8 (ebook) | DDC 418.0071--dc23/eng/20220727
LC record available at https://lccn.loc.gov/2022025300
LC ebook record available at https://lccn.loc.gov/2022025301

ISBN: 978-1-032-35164-3 (hbk)
ISBN: 978-1-032-35260-2 (pbk)
ISBN: 978-1-003-32605-2 (ebk)

DOI: 10.4324/9781003326052

Typeset in Times New Roman
by SPi Technologies India Pvt Ltd (Straive)

Contents

List of illustrations	vi
Preface	vii
1 Introduction	1
2 Positioning foreign language politeness	31
3 Prosocial politeness	60
4 Interpersonal politeness	89
5 Contested politeness	115
6 Foreign language politeness pedagogy	142
Index	165

Illustrations

Figures

1.1	FL politeness principles, practices and patterns	4
1.2	Different types of FL politeness behaviour	6
4.1	Involvement and commitment pursued in a given relationship	99
4.2	Relational maintenance	101
6.1	Mexican EFL speakers' relational objectives	146
6.2	*Illustration–Interaction–Induction* (i + i + i) mode. (Carter, 2004; Carter & McCarthy, 1995; McCarthy, 1998; McCarthy & Carter, 1995)	151

Table

3.1	Cognitive and Social Strategies	76

Preface

This book examines how foreign language (FL) speakers establish, develop, consolidate and maintain social and transactional relationships in the target language (TL) and how pedagogic intervention can help learners identify, construct and implement practices that will allow them to behave, participate and react in both socially acceptable and individualistically empowering ways. This often-neglected area of FL teaching and learning involves building on students' first-language knowledge, experiences and histories and in helping FL learners employ politeness assets and resources to achieve successful TL interaction. Engaging in TL politeness and understanding cultural behaviour can be a formidable and daunting task but one that can also be stimulating, rewarding and even empowering as FL users celebrate and grapple with wide-ranging communicative challenges and difficulties. Consequently, it is important to establish from the outset that 'doing' FL politeness and culture does not involve the indiscriminate and uncritical adoption and implementation of TL patterns and practices but rather active, judicious and even critical social action.

This book sets out to understand the dynamic and vibrant dimension to TL politeness and cultural practices by raising learners' language consciousness and critical language awareness in identifying productive communicative resources and assets that can lead to successful interpersonal and transactional communication. To achieve this, I outline how Halliday's ideational, interpersonal and textual functions provide a framework for examining how FL users can approach TL politeness in terms of prosocial, interpersonal and contested politeness.

This work stands in close relationship with two previous books: *Addressing Difficult Situations in Foreign-Language Learning: Confusion, Impoliteness, and Hostility* (Mugford, 2019, Routledge) and *Developing Cross-Cultural Relational Ability in Foreign Language Learning: Asset-Based Pedagogy to Enhance Pragmatic Competence* (Mugford, 2022, Routledge). The work *Addressing Difficult Situations in Foreign-Language Learning: Confusion, Impoliteness, and Hostility* examines interpersonal challenges of FL use especially in terms of problematic contexts that may involve dealing with impolite/rude, aggressive and discriminatory viii *Preface*

situations. On a more positive note, *Developing Cross-Cultural Relational Ability in Foreign Language Learning: Asset-Based Pedagogy to Enhance Pragmatic Competence* examines how FL users successfully employ pragmatic resources to achieve speaker goals, celebrate interpersonal encounters, attain communicative intelligibility and interact in their own distinctive ways.

I cannot thank enough all the participants who have helped in this study by providing me with their experiences, insights and suggestions. Their communicative skills and abilities reveal how FL users actually engage in TL politeness practices as they deal with and negotiate everyday situations and contexts. In order to 'pay back' these contributions, I hope that this book helps highlight the need to deal with the teaching/learning of politeness in the FL classroom.

I also need to especially thank Spencer Martin, Josefina Santana, Maria Luisa Arias and Susie Zavala whose critical and analytical comments and suggestions have been extremely helpful, constructive and insightful.

I also want to truly thank the team at Routledge and particularly for all the assistance, reassurance and guidance given by Alice Salt and Katherine Tsamparlis who have helped bring this book to fruition.

It goes without saying that all errors, mistaken beliefs, gaffes and missteps are entirely mine.

1 Introduction

Introduction

Interpersonal communication in a foreign language (FL) involves establishing, developing, consolidating, maintaining and terminating both social and transactional relationships. Such interaction involves linguistic, social and cultural dimensions and entails interrelating first-language (L1) knowledge, experiences and histories with emerging and evolving experiences and encounters in the target language (TL). To achieve meaningful, amicable and functional TL relationships, FL users engage in politeness practices and patterns by selecting the necessary resources and assets to identify, construct and implement practices that will allow them to behave, participate and react in both socially acceptable and individualistically empowering ways.

The challenge for language teachers is to help FL learners employ politeness assets and resources in order to achieve successful TL interaction. Whilst words such as respect, consideration and manners may reflect learners' perceptions, teachers need to also help learners deal with the interpersonal and conflictive dimensions to linguistic politeness. Furthermore, linguistic politeness, in terms of language and culture, can provide structure and order to social, interpersonal and transactional communication (Gumperz, 1987, p. xiii). Achieving TL politeness and understanding cultural behaviour can be a formidable and daunting task but also stimulating, rewarding and even empowering as FL users celebrate and grapple with wide ranging communicative challenges and difficulties. Consequently, it is important to establish from the outset that 'doing' FL politeness and culture does not involve the indiscriminate and uncritical adoption and implementation of TL patterns and practices but rather active and judicious social action.

Instead of reflecting on model speakers' idealised and decontextualised language use, the study of FL politeness and culture needs to focus on how actual language users employ both L1 and FL knowledge, resources and experiences to achieve their communicative aims. FL speakers' objectives will often include group acceptance, integration into society, self-projection,

DOI: 10.4324/9781003326052-1

2 *Introduction*

transactional achievement, etc. Seldom problem-free and smooth-flowing, the enactment of suitable and effective politeness and cultural practices can be challenging. FL speakers may suffer from a lack of knowledge and insights into TL communicative norms, practices and processes. These may be reflected through hesitation, self-doubt and confusion as they strive to interpret and make sense of interactional patterns and procedures. FL teachers and the classroom context have a significant role to play in alerting and preparing learners for TL interpersonal encounters. However, current educational practices do not prime learners for interactional challenges and struggles, as evidenced by extraneous and decontextualised 'polite' and cultural situations so often found presented in language textbooks, which repeatedly fail to reflect TL language realities. For instance, FL users may be expected to reflect on and respond to such unlikely situations as asking a neighbour not to park their car in front of one's house or telling their boss that they cannot work overtime. In everyday interaction, politeness emerges, develops and responds to very real communicative needs and objectives where relationships are just as important considerations as situations and communicative messaging. Realistic communicative challenges involve socialising in new cultural circumstances, trying to participate in ongoing conversations, reacting to awkward situations, interacting in novel settings, asking for help when confused, complaining about poor service, etc. This book sets out to understand the dynamic and vibrant dimension to TL politeness and cultural practices and examine how learners can prepare themselves to cope with a range of communicative eventualities.

This introductory chapter is structured as follows. First of all, I argue for the importance of examining FL politeness. I then position FL politeness and culture within the context of everyday TL interaction and outline their role in establishing and constructing social and transactional relationships. Subsequently, I discuss how raising language awareness and critical language awareness can aid FL users in identifying productive communicative resources and assets that can lead to successful interpersonal and transactional communication. Next, I define politeness in terms of constructing, developing and sustaining interpersonal and transactional relationships. At the same time, I adopt Spencer-Oatey and Kádár's understanding of culture as a 'shared set of artefacts, behavioural patterns and ways of thinking, all of which have meaning for people, affecting their expectations of behaviour and framing their interpretation/ evaluations of behaviour' (2021, p. 346). These discussions are followed by an examination of the features of 'doing' FL politeness behaviour and a justification regarding why it requires special consideration in FL teaching and learning. To achieve this, I outline how Halliday's (1973/1997) ideational, interpersonal and textual functions provide a practical and strategic basis for examining how FL users can approach TL politeness. Indeed, Halliday provides the major framework for examining prosocial

Introduction 3

politeness (Chapter 3), interpersonal politeness (Chapter 4) and contested politeness (Chapter 5). Next, I outline the challenges, difficulties and problems in teaching and learning FL politeness. Finally, I describe the objectives of the book and provide a brief chapter-by-chapter description of the book.

Importance of FL politeness

The underlying purpose of learning and communicating in a FL is to connect with other individuals, relate to other groups and gain insights into other cultures. FL speakers' objectives may be interpersonal or transactional, but, in both cases, interaction involves 'relational work' (Locher & Watts, 2005). This may not be easy in a second or FL as interlocutors interact in new and unfamiliar contexts. First of all, relational work involves the establishment, development, consolidation and maintenance of interpersonal relations and, at the same time, the need to notice, evaluate and respond to other interactants' participation and behaviour. Secondly, relational work also concerns the speakers' expression of their individuality, 'presentation of the self' (Goffman, 1959) and positionality/stance (Englebretson, 2007). Whilst perhaps familiar with these practices in their L1, FL users may find relational work particularly challenging in the TL. The wide scope of relational work is reflected through Halliday's (1973/1997) interpersonal language function, which

> may be understood by the expression of our own personalities and personal feelings on the one hand, and forms of interaction and social interplay with other participants in the communication situation on the other hand.
>
> (p. 36)

It is important to recognise that relational work involves both the interactional and the personal dimensions so that FL users not only relate to others but come across in the TL in the way they desire.

Whilst FL users may be adept at undertaking relational work in their L1, that does not mean that this knowledge and ability is seamlessly transferable to the TL, especially in terms of how they position themselves in TL interaction. Therefore, in this book I make the case that FL politeness deserves special consideration and attention in terms of social contact, individual projection and communicative understandings, given that these aspects provide a communicative foundation for carrying out successful TL interaction. As these arguments are further developed in the book, here I summarise in Figure 1.1 the importance of understanding FL politeness principles, practices and patterns in terms of social contact, individual projection and communicative understandings:

4 Introduction

Figure 1.1 FL politeness principles, practices and patterns.

Social contact

- An awareness of politeness practices helps FL speakers observe and assess key understandings and practices in TL communities, especially since politeness is 'basic to the production of social order, and a precondition of human cooperation' (Gumperz, 1987, p. xiii).
- By understanding the social principles behind TL politeness, FL users are in a stronger position to interact within another community and with individual members of that community in both interpersonal and transactional realms.
- By identifying TL politeness resources, bilingual speakers can recognise which practices and patterns are transferable from their L1. Politeness resources can provide both communicative shortcuts and prefabricated language items with which to engage in relational work.
- By realising that cultures often differ communicatively, FL learners can identify similar and contrasting practices. At the same time, politeness practices should not be seen as binary, i.e. positive in one community and negative in another (Kádár & Haugh, 2013, p. 231).

Individual projection

- People generally want to be seen to be polite, especially in FL interaction. They want to 'give off' (Goffman, 1959) a positive image of themselves as approachable, likeable and friendly.
- An understanding of TL politeness practices allows FL users to position and gauge their own participation within the TL community. By identifying appropriate and acceptable conduct, FL speakers can decide whether they want to adhere to such normative patterns and practices.

Introduction 5

- FL relational work often involves taking a position or a stance and asserting one's individuality. Positionality reflects how interactants express their attitudes, beliefs and assessments in particular interactions.

Communicative understandings

- Given that FL speakers normally seek to achieve 'smooth communication' (Spencer-Oatey & Kádár, 2021, p. 262), politeness resources and assets can help interlocutors choose and maintain their level of participation and involvement in a given encounter.
- Seemingly successful FL communication does not necessarily mean that interactants understand each other in the same way (Bennett, 1976, p. 180). FL users need to be aware that their own (self-perceived) polite behaviour may not be seen as such by other TL interactants.
- Politeness inevitably involves making moral judgements about others' performances, rituals and intentions. An awareness of politeness principles helps FL users understand others' motivations and actions and avoid indiscriminately judging and condemning others.

An awareness and recognition of FL politeness principles, practices and interactional patterns help FL users to tackle their key concerns, doubts and misperceptions as they try to ascertain acceptable conduct, everyday behaviour, common interactional practices and the range of available interpersonal and transactional openings, choices and opportunities in TL interaction.

Positioning FL politeness

All too often linguistic politeness is presented and discussed in potentially abstract and potentially confusing labels (e.g. 'positive' and 'negative' politeness – see Brown & Levinson, 1987). So much so that teachers may find such labels difficult to conceptualise when preparing learners for real-life, day-to-day rough-and-tumble experiences and choices. This book will attempt to interrelate theory with practice so that it is relatable and relevant to FL teaching and learning. However, the focus will be on 'doing' politeness in a FL since politeness cannot be conveniently divided into neatly definable, predictable, formulaic and rigid linguistic categories and dealt with in the FL classroom through presenting and rehearsing prepatterned structures and polite exchanges. In everyday interaction, 'doing' politeness reflects dynamic and vibrant language use as interactants initiate, refocus, resolve and reinforce social and transactional relationships. Such actions require a variety of pragmatic and discursive resources and assets that are often constructed and assembled during localised and focused interaction.

6 Introduction

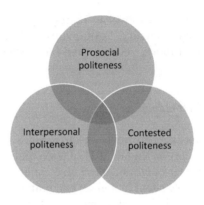

Figure 1.2 Different types of FL politeness behaviour.

FL interlocutors may call upon prepatterned structures and responses to engage in politeness, but, first of all, they need to identify what they want to achieve interpersonally and proceed to construct the necessary resources and assets to accomplish this. Consequently, politeness markers such as *Don't mention it* and *Excuse me* and modals such as *Can I ask you a question?* and *Would you mind...?* need to be understood within the overall communicative context. Rather than just being 'polite,' interactants may also be conveying a communicative message that can range from being humorous and light-hearted to reflecting sarcasm and irony. Therefore, it is a mistake to simply reduce the enactment of FL politeness to mere formulaic expressions and structures when, in fact, it may develop and emerge through unpredictable, evolving and uncharted interactions and encounters. Relevant language teaching has to adopt a more proactive and insightful approach towards explaining and clarifying TL politeness behaviour. Therefore, I describe different 'types' of politeness in which speakers engage at different times and in different contexts:

1 Prosocial politeness – context driven (Chapter 3)
2 Interpersonal politeness – interactant driven (Chapter 4)
3 Contested politeness – power driven (Chapter 5)

The interrelatedness of different 'types' is illustrated in Figure 1.2:
  Before describing different approaches to politeness behaviour, it is important to point out that these are not discrete categories and will often reflect communicative overlaps.

- Prosocial politeness is context-driven and reflects behaving in socially acceptable ways, caring for others and presenting oneself as a 'polite' person. Prosocial politeness embraces both social-norm and addressee-focused politeness.

Introduction 7

- Interpersonal politeness is interactant-driven as interlocutors not only construct, shape, expand and maintain social relationships but also develop personal relationships.
- Contested politeness is power-driven as interactants reflect on, question and challenge relational patterns. They may appropriate politeness practices, create their own way of coming across or even adopt a hybrid approach which intermeshes politeness practices from the L1 and from the TL.

The FL classroom offers opportunities for students to observe, analyse and understand prosocial, interpersonal and contested politeness practices. In doing so, teachers can establish the extent to which politeness can be learnt, enacted and practised as part of the preparation for the real world of everyday TL interaction. At the same time, it is important to recognise that FL classrooms are real-life communicative contexts in their own right, as students establish, develop and consolidate actual relationships with their peers, teachers, school administrators, etc. The classroom represents a hands-on opportunity to rehearse, practise and experiment with social and individual politeness patterns and practices. Furthermore, the classroom provides a relatively safe environment within which to produce, comprehend and evaluate TL politeness behaviour and anticipate potential misunderstandings and misinterpretations. It offers an opportunity to examine critical factors when failing to achieve satisfactory and productive interpersonal and transactional relationships. When learning and understanding TL politeness practices, FL users need opportunities to reflect on and monitor how their politeness practices are received and acted upon by other interlocutors. At the same time, they should examine the approaches, interactions and resources that TL speakers employ and how they achieve satisfactory politeness outcomes. As a first step in this process, it is necessary to develop a level of (critical) language awareness regarding politeness practices.

Developing (critical) language awareness

If the purpose of employing FL politeness practices and strategies is to help bilingual users achieve their own social and personal aims and objectives, adherence to TL norms will not be the overriding concern in FL communication. It is more important that bilingual users develop a language awareness of productive assets and resources that can help them achieve successful interpersonal and transactional communication. Rather than merely studying and practising formulaic, conventional and expected 'polite' structures and expressions, language teaching should focus on the contextualised meaningful use of politeness practices. In this vein, Kramsch (1993) argues:

8 *Introduction*

The teaching of foreign languages must be made relevant to social life, where people need to communicate with each other in order to set the stage for possible mutual understanding. However, the complexity of social contexts will always make social practice variable, unpredictable, open to multiple interpretations.

(p. 240)

Identifying and understanding the relevance of language use involves developing a language awareness that should be the major concern of FL teaching and learning, particularly that of English as an International Language (EIL) (McKay, 2012). EIL reflects the contextual and situational use of English when interlocutors employ both global and local resources, approaches and language varieties in everyday social and business communication. Its use contrasts with employing predominantly Australian, Canadian, United States or United Kingdom varieties [from the so-called 'Inner Circle' countries identified by Kachru (1982, 1985)], which may not be particularly relevant for bilingual speakers who utilise the TL across a variety of global communicative contexts, e.g. in social media and business transactions. In contrast, adherence to Inner Circle varieties calls on bilingual interactants to learn and follow conventional politeness procedures and practices.

In terms of politeness, EIL speakers not only employ a well-established range of interpersonal communicative resources, including direct/indirect language, modal verbs, politeness markers (e.g. *please, thank you*), downtoners and hedges, etc., but they also assess and evaluate contextual clues, participants' stance and their communicative objectives. This process involves

drawing on extralinguistic cues, identifying and building on shared knowledge, gauging and adjusting to interlocutors' linguistic repertoires, supportive listening, signaling noncomprehension in a face-saving way, asking for repetition, paraphrasing, and the like.

(Seidlhofer, 2004, p. 227)

So, rather than simply raising learners' language awareness regarding conventional politeness practices, teachers may want to go further and help students develop critical language awareness (CLA) regarding how language is used to exercise power, control, exclusion and dominance. CLA goes beyond a social focus on language awareness to analyse, question and even criticise discursive practices, including politeness patterns and routines. It aims 'to provide learners with understanding of problems which cannot be resolved just in the schools; and with resources for engaging if they so wish in the long-term, multifaceted struggles ... which are necessary to resolve them' (Fairclough, 1992, p. 13). After examining how to raise FL learners' language awareness, the next step is to define exactly what FL

Introduction 9

politeness involves and then determine whether FL politeness needs special consideration above and beyond L1 concepts and understandings. (Critical language awareness is further explored in Chapters 2 and 5.)

Defining politeness

In preparing FL users to engage in TL politeness practices and patterns of behaviour, it is necessary to at least have a practical definition of politeness – one that can be examined, elaborated on and worked around within the teaching-learning context. In the absence of a definition, politeness is reduced to being seen as being well mannered, saying *please* and *thank you* and generally minding one's Ps and Qs. Any definition of politeness needs to take into consideration interaction patterns, pragmatic behaviour and communicative modes. In other words, polite conduct embraces both socially expected and unanticipated conduct (Watts, 2003), pre-patterned and locally assembled language assets (Kádár & Haugh, 2013) and verbal/ nonverbal behaviour (Eelen, 2001).

Regarding socially expected and unanticipated conduct or prosocial politeness, FL users need to be able to recognise, react to and engage in conventional, appropriate and anticipated behaviour, which Watts (2003) labels 'politic' behaviour. Politic behaviour means being contextually aware of one's surroundings whilst seeking other interactants' cooperation and social acceptance. This involves taking into consideration the addressee(s), other participants (e.g. bystanders), the overall situation, the purpose of the interaction, etc. Pre-patterned language offers FL users ready-to-use interactional structures and practices and thus potentially saves time and effort when engaging with others. By employing appropriate and expected language, FL users can focus on the more communicatively demanding aspects of a given encounter. At the same time, pre-patterned language helps FL users to avoid unintended face threats or 'face threatening acts' (Brown & Levinson, 1987). Furthermore, such formulaic language can reduce stress and anxiety when FL users encounter new and unfamiliar situations and, at the same time, helps them to avoid committing blunders, making slip-ups and just saying the wrong thing. (Politic behaviour, or prosocial politeness, is the focus of Chapter 3.)

On the other hand, Watts's (2003) 'polite' behaviour goes beyond what is expected and anticipated. This means that FL users need to be alert to how politeness is being expressed in a given interaction. In these types of interaction, 'linguistic structures are not, *per definitionem*, inherently polite' (Watts, 2003, p. 21). At the same time, the evolving nature of interaction may reflect that politeness is often not expressed with a single word or phrase but over the course of an interaction. Watts's concept of polite language use can be seen in terms of interpersonal politeness and derives from locally constructed interaction as interlocutors develop relationships according to a specific set of circumstances and participants. Therefore,

10 Introduction

one of the challenges for FL users is to identify polite behaviour that may not initially, or immediately, appear to be inherently polite. (Interpersonal politeness is the focus of Chapter 4.)

Whilst polite verbal behaviour is often afforded some consideration in FL teaching and learning practice, nonverbal behaviour is all too often downplayed or just seen as an add-on, receiving (at best) cursory attention. Importantly, nonverbal behaviour, or body language, may play a crucial role in achieving satisfactory and meaningful relations. Nonverbal conduct embraces the use of physical space, e.g. closeness and distance (proxemics), body movements, e.g. gestures and facial expressions (kinesics), eye contact, e.g. gaze and avoidance, and even touching (haptics). Therefore, FL users should be made aware of the importance of body language in overall communication. (Nonverbal behaviour is discussed in Chapters 2 and 6.)

In order to take into consideration interaction patterns, pragmatic resources and communicative modes, I adhere to Kádár and Haugh's stance that '[p]oliteness is a key means by which humans work out and maintain interpersonal **relationships**' (2013, p. 1, authors' emphasis). Their position emphasises that relationships are constructed, developed and sustained during the course of an interaction. Kádár and Haugh go on to argue that politeness goes beyond conventional acts of linguistic etiquette and

> .... covers something much broader, encompassing all types of interpersonal behaviour through which we take into account the feelings of others as to how they think they should be treated in working out and maintaining our sense of personhood as well as our interpersonal relationships with others.
>
> (2013, p. 1)

This definition underscores three dimensions to politeness behaviour: speaker individuality, interrelatedness and addressee feelings. In the FL context, speaker individuality respects and honours bilingual speakers and underscores that they do not have to be unduly and detrimentally submissive to TL norms. Interrelatedness signals the co-constructed dimension to politeness behaviour even though FL interlocutors may not enjoy a level communicative playing field when engaging with TL speakers. Awareness of hearer susceptibilities, reactions and responses underscore the extent to which interlocutors value other people and that they want to be seen doing so. FL interlocutors need to be constantly evaluating the effectiveness of employing politeness practices and approaches. Speaker individuality, interrelationship and addressee feelings provide a framework for understanding the challenges when engaging FL politeness practices. These understandings will be examined and developed further in Chapter 2 since it might be argued that TL politeness and L1 politeness reflect the same understandings and practices and, therefore, FL politeness patterns and practices do not merit special consideration.

FL politeness

Since linguistic politeness is not solely focused on selecting predetermined resources and enacting them in predictable social situations, FL users need to access a set of skills and abilities that will allow them to: a) project themselves as bona fide language users; b) engage purposively in probable TL interactional encounters; and c) understand and respond to others' communicative objectives. The development of effective FL politeness abilities involves five key components:

1   Raising contextual awareness
2   Establishing common interactional ground
3   Achieving interpersonal convergence and connectedness
4   Developing linguistic and cultural sensitivity
5   Evaluating ongoing interaction

Raising contextual awareness involves being able to both 'feel' and 'read' the room, i.e. to identify others' moods, attitudes and behaviour and to understand a particular communicative environment. Such skills may be transferable from the bilingual user's L1, or they may need to be teased out in the TL context. However, existing knowledge may have to be reviewed, modified or revised as interaction evolves since TL patterns and practices may be different.

Establishing common ground means identifying shared ways of forming and developing relationships. As defined by Clark (1996), common ground embraces 'everything we do with others – from the broadest joint activities … to the smallest joint actions that comprise them' (p. 92). In FL use, interactants need to build on joint assumptions (Levinson, 1983), and it cannot be taken for granted that these are same in the L1 and the TL.

Interpersonal convergence and connectedness may be expressed through supportiveness, consideration and comity. Closer relations may reflect rapport, camaraderie and solidarity. Supportiveness, for instance, may be established through preference organisation as in adjacency pairs (Schegloff & Sacks, 1973), e.g. invitation-acceptance, and through remedial interchanges (Goffman, 1971), e.g. apologising for accidentally making physical contact with someone. Culturally, FL interlocutors also need to be aware of preference organisation. For instance, in Mexico when being offered food, it is often customary to refuse the first offer and subsequently accept after the predictable follow-up offer(s). In an Anglo cultural environment, however, there may not be a follow-up offer, as the first rejection is taken as a definitive refusal.

Linguistic and cultural sensitivity involves taking into consideration the responses and reactions of others. This is often described in terms of face (Goffman, 1967), and interactants can enhance, maintain or protect the face or image that they want to project. This may be carried out in different

12 Introduction

ways in different languages. For instance, face-boosting acts (FBA) (Bayraktaroğlu, 1991, 2001) or face enhancement (Spencer-Oatey, 2008) aim to boost the addressee's self-esteem. This may be achieved through excessive complimenting or manifesting an especially close interest in a hearer's opinions.

Evaluating ongoing interaction means that FL users need to be continually monitoring how a particular social or transactional exchange has been initiated and established and is being maintained. This means identifying those features that indicate an interaction is progressing well, where it is perhaps flagging and where it is perhaps failing to achieve its communicative purpose.

Within FL politeness studies, it is important to acknowledge the role of the cultural dimension as argued by Kádár and Ran:

> Culture has been a central issue in politeness research, as cultural differences tend to entail differences in the production and evaluation of politeness in intercultural interaction.
>
> (2019, pp. 280–281)

Since politeness and culture are intimately interrelated (see, for instance, Kádár & Bargiela-Chiappini, 2011), I shall not unduly separate them in this book except when it is useful to highlight certain individual aspects. However, I do deal with politeness and culture in terms of prosocial, interpersonal and contested politeness practices. Culture will be discussed as follows:

*   Culture and values: beliefs, attitudes and assumptions
*   Culture and convention: routines, patterns and practices
*   Culture and interactional behaviour: skills, action and participation
*   Culture and self-awareness: positionality, feelings and reactions

To interrelate politeness and culture, I analyse in Chapter 2 culture and values by examining cultural capital (Bourdieu, 1972, 1980, 1991) and declarative and procedural cultural knowledge (Block, 2003; Johnson, 1996; Taguchi & Roever, 2017). To examine culture and convention, I review in Chapter 3 cultural norms, practices and expectations and examine whether there are culturally specific or universally applicable norms of behaviour (Brown & Levinson, 1987; Sifianou, 1992). In Chapter 4, I interrelate culture and interactional behaviour by examining research participants' experiences and perceptions in social encounters. To focus culture and self-awareness, in Chapter 5, I study culture in terms of stance, opposition and resistance (Canagarajah, 1999; Giroux, 1983).

FL teaching and learning

Whilst it may be difficult, if not impossible, to 'teach' politeness, teachers still have a role to play in deciding to what extent learners can develop

Introduction 13

pragmatic ability regarding politeness. On the one hand, they may take a universalistic approach and argue that politeness is basically perceived, understood and practised in the same way across languages around the globe with some regional, social and cultural variations. A universalistic approach suggests that politeness practices and patterns are transferable between the L1 and the TL. On the other hand, teachers may decide that politeness is locally positioned, both socially and culturally, as interactants engage in specific communicative encounters. Localised understandings of politeness would suggest that politeness conduct is not always smoothly transferred across languages and cultures. This book explores these contrasting approaches towards teaching and learning FL politeness. (This is paid particular attention in Chapter 6.)

'Teaching' politeness

As the FL learners' world comes into contact with both the TL and the target-language culture (TC), teachers have to ascertain how they can help students either explicitly or implicitly construct, develop and maintain TL relationships. Learners need to determine which courses of action are available to them in order to achieve interpersonal and transactional goals. Different approaches may reflect convergence, concern, affinity, involvement, supportiveness, etc., so FL speakers need to know how to express consideration, likeness, warmness, agreement, etc.

To implement a given communicative plan of action, learners have to recognise the range of resources and assets available. These are often described in terms of pragmalinguistic resources (Leech, 1983; Thomas, 1983), as they reflect 'the resources for conveying communicative acts and relational and interpersonal meanings. Such resources include pragmatic strategies such as directness and indirectness, routines and a large range of linguistic forms which can intensify or soften communicative acts' (Rose & Kasper, 2001, p. 2). With regard to politeness, pragmalinguistic resources may include phatic exchanges, supportive talk, preferred responses, self-disclosure and conventionalised interaction patterns.

Whilst pragmalinguistic knowledge provides a database of resources and practices, FL speakers still need to know which resources in a specific social situation are best suited for establishing and enhancing interpersonal and transactional relations. This involves understanding the nature and purpose of the relationship and taking into account factors such as the desired levels of respect, familiarity and imposition. Consequently, socio-pragmatic knowledge

> gives interlocutors the ability to choose the most suitable way of achieving their communicative purpose taking into consideration factors such as closeness/distance, respect and imposition. For instance, when giving advice, a speaker has a range of ways of showing

14 Introduction

supportiveness, e.g., *If I were you..., Have you thought about...?* and *You should....* In selecting an appropriate structure, the speaker needs to consider, for instance, to whom he/she is talking to (e.g. friend, family member, colleague), the context (e.g. social, professional, personal) and the importance of the advice (e.g. casual, serious, life-changing).

(Mugford, 2022, p. 9)

Whilst pragmalinguistic and sociopragmatic knowledge provides a pragmatic database and appropriateness/suitability indicators, FL users still need to be able to enact politeness practices under real-life communicative conditions and 'participate in quick, on-the-spot, spontaneous and unrehearsed interaction' (Mugford, 2022, p. 10). In pedagogic terms, pragmalinguistic and sociopragmatic knowledge reflects declarative, i.e. 'pragmatically relevant,' resources (Li, 2021, p. 195). However, interactants also require procedural knowledge – the ability to interact in real time, perhaps under stress, whilst also being able to convey their own unique *voice*. Rehearsal and practice can help learners select appropriate pragmatic resources from a range of options as interactants need to communicate under pressure and on the spur of the moment.

Teachers

Preparing learners to engage in FL politeness practices presents teachers with a unique set of challenges. Teachers need to establish a principled position towards the 'teaching' of politeness and avoid improvised and off-the-cuff responses.

First of all, they should realise that learners already count on a wealth of experiences from their L1 from which they have developed their attitudes, beliefs and norms of behaviour. Teachers should ask themselves whether it is practical, rational and beneficial to ask learners to leave such L1 knowledge outside the classroom as promoted in 'English-only' classes. Learner experiences can provide a fruitful and productive starting point for discussing and examining TL politeness practices. For instance, Liddicoat and McConachy argue that 'the learner's emerging sense of the potentiality of linguistic forms and ways of constructing politeness is influenced by their pre-existing notions of politeness, embedded in their L1' (2019, p. 13).

A second challenge for teachers comes from FL users' L1 histories, as they may think that they already know how to be polite and so there is no need to focus on this aspect in the TL. It may be an uphill task to convince some students that politeness practices vary and contrast from culture to culture and from speech community to speech community (Gumperz, 1968).

Thirdly, TL politeness practices may seem 'foreign' to learners as they compare them with their own L1 practices. Learners may need to evaluate

Introduction 15

and consider TL politeness behaviour and adopt a position, e.g. embrace them, modify them, resist them or even reject them. The point is that FL users do not have to indiscriminately accept TL practices, especially since they are not always adhered to by TL speakers themselves. (This aspect is examined in more depth in Chapter 5.)

Fourthly, the learners' own emerging TL experiences may be both positive and negative, and teachers may need to address and explain pleasantly surprising or unexpectedly confusing and perhaps even bewildering practices. For instance, the British fixation with saying *sorry* can cover a myriad of meanings including asking a stranger a question (e.g. *Sorry to bother you*), showing compassion (e.g. *I'm sorry to hear that*), asking for repetition (e.g. *Sorry, can you say that again?*), indicating disagreement (*Sorry, but I don't see it that way*) and conveying a lack of understanding (*Sorry, I'm not with you*), etc.

Fifthly, FL users may find it difficult to express their own L1 politeness practices in the TL. Politeness behaviour may not be conveyed in the same way. For instance, the Mexican interlocutors' focus on sharedness may be hard to express in English. This can be seen when Mexicans provide their home address and finish with *¡Ahí tiene su casa!* (literally meaning 'There is your house'). Another example can be seen when leaving a restaurant: Mexican Spanish-language speakers will often say *¡Buen provecho!* or just *¡Provecho!*, meaning 'Enjoy your meal,' to other diners. Such a comment may sound intrusive in conventional English-language usage.

Teachers face key decisions as to whether TL politeness can indeed be taught and what exactly should be the content of such 'politeness' classes. Watts, for instance, appears to reject the idea that it can be taught:

> no rules can be set up to define what forms of behaviour count as 'polite' in what situations. Native speakers rely very much on the 'feel for the game' that they develop through many years of participation in a wide variety of interactions. The major reason for the ultimate unteachability of politeness is that the 'feel for the game' is culturally determined.
>
> (2003, p. 75)

On the other hand, by not being 'taught' politeness, FL users are faced with the grim task of deciphering and analysing each politeness event as opposed to having an overall grasp and understanding of TL conduct and behaviour. This would be an extremely time-consuming process and, to a certain extent, a hit-or-miss affair as FL speakers would have to grapple with each encountered TL politeness practice and custom. By contrast, Bella, Sifianou and Tzanne argue:

> The need to teach politeness holds particularly true in the context of teaching foreign languages since, unlike native speakers who may be

16   Introduction

> socialised into politeness in their native language, learners of foreign languages will have to learn how to behave politely.
>
> (2015, p. 23)

Teachers need to help FL users observe, familiarise themselves with and appropriate politeness practices and determine how bilingual speakers can best construct their own personalised communicative TL repertoire.

In more operational terms, curriculum designers need to determine whether politeness studies should be fully integrated into FL programmes or given special attention and treatment in their own right. Decisions also have to be made to establish which politeness norms and practices should be highlighted and how learners can be given choices in selecting appropriate and relevant politeness practices. Students need to not only recognise such TL practices but also to select, appropriate and modify those practices that allow them to be themselves, i.e. to express their own *voice*. Therefore, teaching will involve both recognition and production. A key challenge for teachers is to stress the importance of learning TL politeness practices as students may often take it for granted and assume that they are the same in both languages, as pointed out by Leech: 'Naturally it is not an insignificant part of L2 acquisition to learn how to be appropriately polite (or when needed, impolite!) in the second language' (2014, p. xi).

However, just as importantly, FL users may wish to distance themselves from the whole concept of politeness (as traditionally or conventionally understood/perceived) in both their own L1 and the TL. They may feel that politeness practices reflect hypocrisy, dishonesty and deception. Teachers will have to consider this stance to such attitudes and take into consideration the fact that learners have the right to adopt their own positions and attitudes.

Learners

Expressing one's individuality, personality and *voice* are important and often neglected aspects when participating in and negotiating politeness. Whilst adhering to TL practices, FL users should also develop their own ways of interacting. The judicious use of politeness resources allows bilingual speakers to come across in the ways they want to and engage in 'presenting' themselves (Goffman, 1959) as bona fide and authentic interlocutors. They should never be considered deficit language users, even if they make mistakes with respect to fluency and accuracy.

It is important to emphasise that bilingual speakers should not unthinkingly and indiscriminately emulate and conform to TL politeness practices. They also need to develop their own ways of 'doing' politeness which involves employing both individual resources and assets as well as reworking established L1 patterns and practices. Such an approach calls on bilingual speakers to express salient features of their own personality and

Introduction 17

engage in individualistic ways. This allows bilingual speakers to avoid inadvertently coming across as imitation, act-alike 'native' speakers as they establish themselves as legitimate TL speakers in their own right. FL speakers should be encouraged to preserve and express their cultural roots and background whilst adhering to acceptable TL norms of behaviour. Therefore, politeness strategies must allow bilingual speakers, as far as possible, to express their own distinctiveness and particularities, thereby preserving their sociocultural identity. To do so, they need to develop what Watts (2003) calls a 'feel for the game.' On one level this involves understanding what is possible, feasible, appropriate and actually done (Hymes, 1972) so that FL users can conform to TL norms (see Chapter 3 for a fuller discussion). On another level, FL users must determine what they can create, modify and even get away with. As they express themselves in their own ways, students should be aware of pragmatic choices. This position is emphasised by Thomas: 'It is the teacher's job to equip the student to express her/himself in exactly the way s/he chooses to do so – rudely, tactfully, or in an elaborately polite manner' (1983, p. 96).

However, FL users may feel that they are restricted by TL politeness practices and resist conformity and adherence to TL norms and practices. They may particularly object to being stereotyped and expected to perform according to their own national / cultural stereotypes. Within this context, TL linguistic and cultural politeness norms and practices can be used as powerful tools to impose unfamiliar behaviour on FL interactants in expecting them to follow TL conventional language usage, especially in terms of adherence to middle-class politeness norms. This may put FL users at a distinct disadvantage when interacting with other social or professional groups. They may even be expected to observe conventional social and language norms which, meanwhile, may not be adhered to by 'native' speakers themselves. As observed by Harder:

> A foreigner is not permitted to go beyond a certain limited repertoire; if he starts swearing fluently, for instance, he is unlikely to achieve the conventional communicative effect, i.e. underlining the serious objections he has against the situation in question.
>
> (1980, p. 268)

Furthermore, bilingual speakers may find that they are not allowed to fully express themselves interpersonally and are positioned as deficit language users with a reduced personality (Harder, 1980).

Book objectives

To pursue an approach that validates bilingual language users as social individuals with their own experiences, resources and assets that are drawn from two or more languages and cultures, this book identifies key issues

18 Introduction

that teachers and learners have to confront, negotiate and deal with regarding TL politeness. At the same time, this is not a book about how to 'teach' politeness. Rather its purpose is to understand the challenges involved in forming, cultivating, strengthening, preserving and concluding TL relationships. Furthermore, it examines, outlines and discusses guiding principles that allow teachers and students to enhance the learning process and the practice of TL politeness.

The underlying aim of this book is to offer bilingual speakers, language teachers and researchers a practicable way of understanding and 'doing' FL politeness. All too often FL instruction approaches politeness by teaching learners how to be polite by drilling them to employ politeness markers (e.g. *thanks* and *sorry*), modal verbs (e.g. *Could you do me a favour?* and *May I ask you a question?*), direct/indirect speech (e.g. *Lend me a pen* vs. *Could you lend me a pen?*) and hedges (e.g. *kind of* and *sort of*). However, FL politeness practices need to be positioned and developed within FL users' interactional environment. As previously discussed, this means identifying what interlocutors want to express and achieve. It may mean building on the resources and assets that FL users already enjoy and can bring to bear on the TL communicative context. Coequally, bilingual speakers will need to interrelate their existing knowledge with their TL experiences and understandings. The role and importance of existing knowledge can be underscored by the fact that politeness practices are not studied anew when learning another language or when interacting in new linguistic and/or cultural contexts. Learners do not need to learn afresh how to be 'polite' in a second or third language. If this were so, '[s]peakers would have to learn about the particular politeness system of each different hearer before they could ever be polite with any degree of effectiveness' (Eelen, 2001, p. 149). Certain knowledges and assets are transferable across languages. Consequently, there must be a universal dimension to politeness that enables bilingual speakers to negotiate TL politeness. At the same time, being 'polite,' let's say in Spanish, does not always reflect the same conduct as being polite in English. Differences and divergences are underscored in the individually and socially perceived functions of politeness, cultural practices, co-construction of interpersonal relationships, structure of interaction, etc. Importantly, differences and contrasts are not to be found purely in language structures and use but also in social practices, cultural understandings, interpersonal motivations and individualised communicative objectives. Therefore, politeness behaviour needs to be understood not only from individual and societal viewpoints but also as how it is employed to both empower and position other interactants.

In specific terms this book aims to

1   heighten awareness of FL politeness patterns and practices so that teachers and learners appreciate and value how politeness is employed to achieve personal, interpersonal and transactional TL goals;

Introduction 19

2 describe how politeness patterns and practices offer choices for FL interactants to express themselves interpersonally and interact in both individualistic and socially acceptable ways;
3 identify and describe how interrelating and combining L1 and TL resources, knowledge and assets plays an important role in achieving effective and satisfactory TL politeness results;
4 identify the communicative challenges, hurdles and rewards that bilingual speakers encounter when employing, interpreting and evaluating TL politeness patterns and practices;
5 recognise how politeness can be used not only to empower and uplift but also to weaken, subdue and exclude interactants. Therefore, FL users need to be aware of the predetermined and motivated use of politeness; and
6 examine how FL politeness behaviour can be incorporated and integrated into language teaching, especially with regard to syllabus and programme design.

With this strong focus on promoting, encouraging and even celebrating the use of politeness, this book builds on perceived and stated aims of FL users by asking bilingual speakers themselves how they perceive politeness behaviour and building on their expectations and aspirations. So rather than describing how TL politeness can be expressed and outlining available communicative resources, this book aims to help and support teachers and bilingual speakers themselves by pursuing the following objectives:

1 Examine and outline how politeness practices provide bilingual users with choices and opportunities to achieve interpersonal goals socially and individualistically as they build up their levels of self-confidence and the ability to confront new and unexpected situations.
2 Study and discuss the transferability of politeness practices from the L1 to the TL by exploring bilingual speakers' own practices. At the same time, examine how language users' sociocultural environment, histories and background offer a way to construct, convey and develop TL politeness practices.
3 Highlight and underscore diverse language user perceptions and understandings of politeness which result in different views regarding acceptable and suitable individual, social and cultural behaviour. To a large degree, politeness practices will often reflect individual interpretation rather than pre-determined social/cultural patterning.
4 Examine and analyse communicative disparity between apparent and underlying meanings, especially as it relates to FL politeness because 'a great deal of the mismatch between what is "said" and what is "implicated" can be attributed to politeness' (Brown & Levinson, 1987, pp. 2–3).

20   *Introduction*

5   Critically assess and evaluate the extent to which present-day politeness theories and approaches provide productive insights into, and support for, current FL teaching and learning practices. Politeness theory should help explain and provide interactional insights rather than dictate how politeness should be performed and enacted.

6   Analyse key FL users' experiences and reflections as a way of exploring choices, possibilities and limitations when expressing TL politeness. The teaching and learning of politeness must centre on actual experiences rather than contrived and hypothetical situations.

Politeness: critical position

In this book, I question whether politeness practices should be only seen in speaker- or hearer-centred terms. For instance, in classic politeness theory, Brown and Levinson (1987) argue that interactants should protect each other by avoiding face-threatening acts (FTAs). Meanwhile, Lakoff (1973) argues that interactants need to follow certain rules – i.e. do not impose, offer choices and make the hearer feel good – or, otherwise, they will be perceived as impolite. On the other hand, discursive approaches 'focus on the local working out of relations between participants using politeness' (Mills, 2011, p. 73). However, given their communicative reality, FL users may not be able to negotiate politeness behaviour on a level interactional playing field with more experienced and knowledgeable TL interlocutors. Just as importantly, FL users often aim to come across in their own way in the TL, but this may represent a forgotten challenge as participants attempt to interact in another language. A more balanced and nuanced view envisages politeness as both transactional and interpersonal: transactional in achieving personal and joint communicative objectives; interpersonal in enjoying and celebrating relationships with others (Aston, 1988). Especially in the FL context, the successful employment of politeness practices signals that interactants can get along and engage with TL speakers, appreciating and delighting in each other's company and even cementing friendships. Within such a scenario, politeness is not so focused on interactants presenting themselves in a good light but rather on constructing, developing and maintaining relationships.

Justification for book

This book adopts a critical stance towards FL teaching–learning politeness because it builds on lay understandings and perceptions of politeness in L1 and TL and using them as the basis for developing TL interpersonal skills and abilities. This approach contrasts with presenting and explaining TL politeness practices and patterns and teaching learners how to adhere to them. Existing approaches encourage learners to conform to

Introduction 21

conventional politeness patterns and practices and seek to emphasise avoiding making social mistakes and committing faux pas. In contrast, this book examines the knowledge and understandings that FL users bring to the TL context and explores how they can employ existing and emerging politeness assets in their own ways so that they come across at once as socially acceptable and individualistic.

I take the position that FL politeness should be studied in its own right and not as an appendage to general language studies. This is because FL learners and speakers

- interact in the TL with their own understandings, histories and experiences of politeness gained in their L1. This background has to be taken into consideration in any teaching and practice of TL politeness;
- need to decide which TL politeness practices they want to adopt, modify and perhaps even resist and reject. FL users must be helped to identify which practices are socially required and those that provide for interactional flexibility; and
- often confront, negotiate and grapple with TL practices that they find confusing, difficult or even alien. FL users need to be given the opportunity to analyse, consider and reflect on different and contrasting politeness practices.

So rather than telling students what is considered to be TL 'polite' behaviour and presenting them with a list of corresponding structures and resources, this book examines how bilingual speakers can be helped to achieve their interactional goals and what resources and assets are available and can be readily accessed by speakers. Additionally, this book goes beyond studying linguistic politeness to examine TL cultural behaviour regarding politeness. By examining, comparing and contrasting L1 and TL politeness behaviours, learners are placed in a stronger position to understand TL practices and, correspondingly, to interactionally develop acceptable ways of expressing individual politeness.

With its focus on developing politeness assets and practices, this book will not deal with FL impoliteness or rudeness. These themes have, however, been dealt with in detail in Mugford (2019), which describes how bilingual interactants notice, assess and respond to impoliteness and rudeness.

Research approach

In trying to understand 'doing' TL politeness, I look at relational language use rather than examining how politeness theory can illustrate FL communication. This involves examining lay understandings and experiences, personal projection, cooperative understandings and structures. To pursue

22 Introduction

this goal, I adhere to Halliday's ideational, interpersonal and textual functions, which exemplify the structure of TL relational interaction since different strands of meanings are being enacted during politeness behaviour (Eggins & Slade, 1997, p. 48). Halliday's framework offers a coordinated approach to understanding prosocial, interpersonal and contested politeness. Prosocial politeness is examined in terms of the ideational function as speakers construct proper, expected and appropriate ways with which to engage in TL politeness patterns and practices. Interpersonal politeness is discussed in terms of Halliday's interpersonal function, as interactants not only construct, shape, expand and maintain social relationships but also develop more personal relationships. Contested politeness is seen in terms of Halliday's textual function, as interlocutors often reflect on, question and critically challenge TL politeness practices.

The ideational function reflects speakers' communicative experiences and how they view events and interpret both implicit and explicit meanings. With regard to politeness, FL users analyse–question–evaluate relational behaviour as they try to make sense of TL encounters and interaction.

The interpersonal function deals with relationships on both personal and interactional levels. Interactants want to relate to others but also express themselves in their own way. This can be especially challenging for FL users who need to position themselves with TL speakers in terms of closeness/distance, supportiveness/detachment, formality / friendliness, etc. At the same time, FL speakers often want to express their own individuality and personal characteristics in the TL.

The textual function highlights how communication is structured and what aspects are given more prominence, i.e. foregrounded. This may, for instance, be found in frames, which are recurring interactional situations that can give structure to FL users' TL encounters. The textual function may also be highlighted through examining relational behaviour in given text types, such as gossip, small talk and self-disclosure. Consequently, an understanding of genres can help learners recognise how politeness is enacted across different situations and contexts. Whilst often downplayed in FL teaching and learning, the ideational, interpersonal and textual functions can help empower FL users. They need to be seen as 'modes of meaning that are present in every use of language in every social context' (Halliday, 1978, p. 112).

In identifying bilingual speakers' own perceptions and understandings of politeness, research needs to give *voice* and status to interactants. The source of data comes from face-to-face interviews, questionnaires and FL users' narratives. Research follows an emic approach based on participants' experiences, histories and realities and tries to identify important issues for interlocutors in FL politeness practices. To ground investigation within a specific research context, participants are Mexican English-language users whom I refer to as bilingual speakers/interactants/interlocutors. I try to

Introduction 23

avoid potentially demeaning terms such as second-language learners/users as much as possible since such terms seem to undermine and devalue the status of speakers of additional languages and fail to honour their communicative abilities and achievements.

FL speakers should not be considered deficient language users (Mugford, 2022) but rather fully-fledged language users who may suffer from communicative difficulties in expressing themselves in the TL. Problems are more often than not language-based rather than rooted in difficulties participating with other interactants. Building on L2 users' existing abilities and experiences of engagement and assessment, this book adopts both a language awareness viewpoint (Hawkins, 1999) and critical language awareness perspective (Fairclough, 2010), as each builds on bilingual users' existing knowledge to develop a teaching/learning approach that enhances their ability to critically partake in TL politeness practices.

Participants

In examining how interactants approach TL politeness, this book privileges the FL interactants' own experiences, histories and attitudes. This approach underscores the need to view politeness from the speakers' point of view rather than that of the all-knowing 'native speaker' or politeness experts. Any meaningful examination of TL relational work must reflect not only actual interactants' feelings and beliefs but also their relational objectives.

To understand the participants' experiences, attitudes and beliefs, research in the book is focused on three areas:

1 Prosocial politeness (Chapter 3)
2 Interpersonal politeness (Chapter 4)
3 Contested politeness (Chapter 5)

The 52 participants in this research are all middle-class Mexican speakers of English as a FL and enjoy a B2-C1 level of English according to the Common European Framework of Reference for Languages (CEFR). They are aged between 25 and 40, and they all have university degrees. The participants are in full-time employment over a range of professions, often working as customer service executives, IT specialists, administrative managers, teachers and call centre agents, where they use English as part of their daily professional and social lives. They all work in the Guadalajara metropolitan area, which is situated in western Mexico. Many international companies are located in the area, and English is often a key work requirement. This may involve using English as the 'working' language of the company, dealing with English-speaking customers or interacting on a social basis with foreign visitors and tourists. Within this context, these participants are successful foreign-language users since they can effectively

24 *Introduction*

communicate and interact in the TL. Most participants learnt English at school in Mexico and often have limited experience of travelling to English-speaking countries. Therefore, they have developed their pragmatic knowledge and abilities within the Mexican context. Consequently, they provide a rich source for examining and understanding functional and productive politeness practices and strategies. They also offer insights into how FL speakers actually approach and navigate TL politeness practices and how they construct, maintain and consolidate both transactional and interactional relationships in the TL.

To safeguard the anonymity of the participants, respondents have all been given pseudonyms. Furthermore, responses have not been amended or 'corrected' so that the participants' *voices* can be heard.

Procedure

To select the participants I sought out bilingual professionals who employ English in a professional and/or social capacity. By sending out 74 email invitations to current and old contacts (some going back as far as 15 years), I invited potential participants to answer a questionnaire on their experiences of TL politeness at work and/or in social encounters. Subsequently, 52 respondents agreed to participate and were sent a Microsoft Word file. Whilst they could answer in English or Spanish, all participants chose to answer in English. Replies were received over the course of six weeks during the summer of 2021.

The questionnaires are analysed with regard to how interactants sought out conformity, connection and contestation in FL use. Conformity reflects the desire to participate in proper, expected and appropriate ways. Connection examines how interactants looked for opportunities to construct, shape, expand and maintain not only social relationships but also to develop more personal relationships. Meanwhile, a focus on contestation aims to understand how FL speakers reflect on, question and challenge TL politeness practices.

Data collection approach

This book differs substantially from other books on foreign-language politeness studies because it analyses and reflects on actual experiences that FL speakers recall from social encounters, the workplace and when engaged in interpersonal and transactional situations. Through semi-structured questionnaires, Mexican bilingual speakers were invited to reflect on relational work, including any difficulties, obstacles or hurdles they might have faced. Rather than using classroom contexts and teachers' insights and understandings, this book highlights language users' attitudes and beliefs. The data offer key insights into how FL interactants approach pro-social, interpersonal and contested politeness. Given that this book seeks

Introduction 25

to give *voice* to interactants, no attempt will be made to find a common quantitative denominator underlining the answers. The insights provided by the participants offer teachers approaches towards relational work and reflect student-generated understandings. These can be integrated into classroom teaching since they are based on language users' own concerns, observations and understandings.

Chapter layout

The book is structured in the following way, and, to a certain extent, the chapters can be read in any order as they deal with different aspects of FL politeness understandings and behaviour. However, they are interrelated in terms of content, ideas and proposals.

Chapter 2 examines how an understanding of FL politeness and culture can help bilingual speakers achieve personal, interactional and transactional objectives. Politeness as a form of individual and social action helps interlocutors negotiate the rough and tumble of everyday interaction by providing a working framework for relating to others. Meanwhile, culture reflects ways of thinking and acting that in turn reflect societal values and beliefs. FL users need to be aware that politeness and cultural behaviour may be expressed both verbally and nonverbally. Therefore, interlocutors face both verbal and nonverbal choices (and limitations) regarding how they want to establish, develop, consolidate and maintain social and transactional relationships. As a form of social and cultural action, selections emanate from interactants' experiences and attitudes as they determine how they want to construct TL relationships. To understand bilingual interactants' decision-making processes, this chapter examines how politeness theory can inform TL interactional practices and provide insights into prosocial and interactional politeness behaviour. It also underscores the importance of raising bilingual speakers' sense of (critical) language awareness when making personal, interactional and transactional choices.

Chapter 3 examines the concept of prosocial politeness, or what Watts (2003) terms 'politic' behaviour, since it offers FL interlocutors ways through which to gain social integration and acceptance. Very often bilingual interactants want to know what conventional, suitable and customary politeness and cultural behaviour is used in TL interaction. This can be achieved through language awareness, which offers learners an identifiable, convenient and trustworthy way to socialise, adapt and generally get on with others. Prosocial politeness and culture reflect social norms, interactional routines, conventional language use and established behavioural patterns. Furthermore, they offer a degree of social and behavioural security when dealing with the unknown, the unpredictable and even the potentially aggressive. To understand prosocial politeness, this chapter examines relational work through the lens of Halliday's (1978) ideational framework by reflecting on FL speakers' realities, experiences and histories. For

26   Introduction

teachers, prosocial politeness provides an identifiable curriculum that can be taught, rehearsed and reproduced.

However, teachers need to recognise that FL users' concepts of politeness are based on their own understandings of 'polite' people, cultural considerations, the motivation to be polite, conventional behaviour and actual TL experiences. As a consequence, relational behaviour is not just about transferring politeness practices and patterns from the L1 culture to the TL culture. Furthermore, prosocial politeness and culture may not help FL users project and express their individuality and *voice* in the TL. In particular, prosocial politeness can be linked to first-wave politeness theory (Grainger, 2011; Kádár, 2017; Kádár & Haugh, 2013), which reflects a universalistic approach to interpersonal relations and asserts that politeness patterns are parallel across languages. This carries important implications for FL teaching in terms of the pragmatic transfer and enactment of existing knowledge. If politeness develops during social encounters, it may be meaningless to solely teach routine, normative polite language use.

Chapter 4 considers the extent to which politeness is enacted at the individual rather than at the social level (Spencer-Oatey & Kádár, 2021). This may be extremely challenging for FL users as they choose to project, develop and construct their own relational understandings in specific contexts through interpersonal politeness. Interpersonal politeness reflects how interactants relate, engage and position themselves as they express attentiveness, 'consideration, empathy, altruism and helping behavior' (Fukushima, 2019, p. 242). To understand interpersonal politeness, this chapter examines relational work through the lens of Halliday's interpersonal framework, which looks at interactional ability, boosting the face of the other and listenership. Interactional politeness reflects Watts's (2003) 'polite' behaviour as individuals exploit their L1 knowledge and bring it to bear on the TL context, thus helping them project a TL *voice*. By raising their level of language awareness, L2 users can appreciate how interactional politeness helps them deal with communicative challenges, overcome interactional hurdles and be attentive to the needs of others (Fukushima, 2019). Interpersonal politeness is fluid, celebratory, playful and negotiable. It is locally constructed between interactants as they reach common understandings and meaningful relationships, including 'participant interpretations and evaluations of politeness' (Grainger, 2011, p. 170). An understanding of interpersonal politeness helps FL users prepare for improvised, innovative and unplanned ways of seeking connectedness, engagement and involvement between interactants. Interpersonal politeness reflects second-wave politeness theory (Grainger, 2011; Kádár, 2017; Kádár & Haugh, 2013), as it examines the construction of localised contextual language use between interactants. In terms of FL teaching, bilingual interlocutors need to co-construct politeness with other interactants.

Chapter 5 examines contested politeness and meaning making, as interactants often adopt critical positions regarding TL interactional and

Introduction 27

transactional practices. This can be described in terms of opposition, resistance, appropriation and ownership. These critical positions towards politeness reflect personal identity (Kádár & Haugh, 2013). In contesting TL politeness, interactants need to understand the ideologies behind politeness practices, especially as they may clash with their own values and practices, e.g. ways of showing respect and consideration towards others. To understand contested politeness, this chapter examines relational work through the lens of Halliday's textual framework, particularly in terms of activity types, frames and genres. Bilingual interactants may accept, question, resist or even reject behaviour that they are expected to adhere to in the target culture (TC), especially if they find such practices contradictory, overpowering and particularly if they serve to weaken, distance, subdue and exclude them. Bilingual interactants may be notably critical of a mismatch between what is said and actual behaviour. For instance, politeness markers (e.g. *please*) do not always signal politeness as can be seen in *Would you please, please,* please *be quiet?* Given that there is no one way to be polite, FL users should be given the opportunity to explore and construct their own ways of being polite. This may involve constructing a 'third place' (Cohen, 2018; Kramsch, 1993) which allows bilingual speakers to take ownership of politeness as they express their degree of involvement and engagement. Furthermore, FL users can take the opportunity to see how power and dominance may affect interactional and transactional relationships and observe how politeness does not always produce the expected interactional results.

Chapter 6 examines how teachers can offer their students choices regarding how they want to interact interpersonally in the TL. Choices will reflect prosocial, interpersonal or contested politeness behaviour. A critical pedagogy can build on L1 relational practices and raise learners' awareness of TL politeness behaviour. Such an approach offers FL interlocutors an overall strategy rather than purely focusing on the minutiae of politeness, such as politeness markers. By building on interactants' critical language awareness, teachers can provide the necessary resources and assets so that students can engage in prosocial, interpersonal and contested politeness behaviour – and understand the opportunities, implications and risks deriving from following each form of behaviour. Language awareness helps FL users to become aware of communicative contexts and seek out desired relationships, e.g. meaningful / superficial, involved / distant and associative / detached. A pedagogical examination of illustrative events, cultural capsules and key moments can help learners to explore real-life interactional, social and cultural choices, opportunities and constraints. Pedagogical intervention can also help learners to take key interactional decisions when under communicative pressure and when they have little preparation time and/or limited contextual information about other interactants. A structured approach, integrated into the teaching/learning process, can be further developed through identifying learners' wants and

28 Introduction

needs, creating an appropriate language and culture syllabus, designing relevant and meaningful evaluation and appraisal procedures and outlining an appropriate teaching methodology.

References

Aston, G. (1988). *Learning comity: An approach to the description and pedagogy of interaction speech*. Bologna: Cooperativa Libraria Universitaria Editrice Bologna.

Bayraktaroğlu, A. (1991). Politeness and interactional imbalance. *International Journal of the Sociology of Language*, 92, 5–34.

Bayraktaroğlu, A. (2001). Advice-giving in Turkish: "Superiority" or "solidarity"? In A. Bayraktaroğlu & M. Sifianou (Eds.), *Linguistic politeness across boundaries: The case of Greek and Turkish* (pp. 177–208). Amsterdam: John Benjamins.

Bella, Spyridoula, Sifianou, Maria, & Tzanne, Angeliki (2015). Teaching politeness? In Barbara Pizziconi & Miriam Locher (Eds.), *Teaching and learning (im) politeness* (pp. 23–51). Berlin/Boston: De Gruyter.

Bennett, J. (1976). *Linguistic behaviour*. Cambridge: Cambridge University Press.

Block, D. (2003). *The social turn in second language acquisition*. Edinburgh: Edinburgh University Press.

Bourdieu, P. (1972). *Outline of a theory of practice*. Cambridge: Cambridge University Press.

Bourdieu, P. (1980). *The logic of practice*. Stanford: Stanford University Press.

Bourdieu, P. (1991). *Language & symbolic power*. Cambridge: Polity Press.

Brown, P., & Levinson, S. (1987). *Politeness: Some universal in language usage*. Cambridge: Cambridge University Press.

Canagarajah, S. (1999). *Resisting linguistic imperialism in English teaching*. Oxford, UK: Oxford University Press.

Clark, H. (1996). *Using language*. Cambridge: Cambridge University Press.

Cohen, A. D. (2018). *Learning pragmatics from native and nonnative language teachers*. Bristol: Multilingual Matters.

Eelen, G. (2001). *A critique of politeness theories*. Manchester: St. Jerome.

Eggins, S., & Slade, D. (1997). *Analysing casual conversation*. London: Cassell.

Englebretson, R. (2007). Introduction. In R. Englebretson (Ed.), *Stancetaking in discourse: Subjectivity, evaluation, interaction* (pp. 1–25). Amsterdam/ Philadelphia: John Benjamins.

Fairclough, N. (1992). *Critical language awareness*. London: Longman.

Fairclough, N. (2010). *Critical discourse analysis: The critical study of language*. Harlow, England: Pearson.

Fukushima, S. (2019). A metapragmatic aspect of politeness; with a special emphasis on attentiveness in Japanese. In E. Ogiermann & P. Garcés-Conejos Blitvich (Eds.), *From speech acts to lay understandings of politeness* (pp. 226–247). Cambridge: Cambridge University Press.

Giroux, H. A. (1983). *Theory & resistance in education: A pedagogy for the opposition*. New York: Bergin & Garvey.

Goffman, E. (1959). *The presentation of self in everyday life*. London: Penguin.

Goffman, E. (1967). *Interactional ritual: Essays on face-to-face behaviour*. New York: Double Day Books.

Goffman, E. (1971). *Relations in public*. New York: Basic Books.

Introduction 29

Grainger, K. (2011). "First Order" and "Second Order" politeness: Institutional and intercultural contexts. In Linguistic Politeness Research Group (Ed.), *Discursive approaches to politeness* (pp. 167–188). Berlin: Mouton de Gruyter.

Gumperz, J. (1968). The speech community. In Sills, D. L. (Ed.) *International Encyclopaedia of the social sciences* (pp. 381–386). New York: Macmillan.

Gumperz, J. (1987). Foreword. In P. Brown & S. Levinson (Eds.), *Politeness: Some universal in language usage* (pp. xiii–xiv). Cambridge: Cambridge University Press.

Halliday, M. A. K. (1978). *Language as social semiotic*. London: Edward Arnold.

Halliday, M. A. K. (1973/1997). Language in a social perspective. In N. Coupland & A. Jaworski (Eds.), *Sociolinguistics: A reader and coursebook* (pp. 31–38). Basingstoke: Macmillan.

Harder, P. (1980). Discourse as self-expression – on the reduced personality of the second-language learner. *Applied Linguistics, 1*(3), 262–270.

Hawkins, E. (1999). Foreign language study and language awareness. *Language Awareness, 8*(3/4), 124–142.

Hymes, D. H. (1972). On communicative competence. In J. B. Pride & J. Holmes (Eds.), *Sociolinguistics. Selected readings* (pp. 269–293, Part 2). Harmondsworth: Penguin.

Johnson, K. (1996). *Language teaching & skill learning*. Oxford: Blackwell.

Kachru, B. B. (1982). Teaching world Englishes. In B. B. Kachru (Ed.), *The other tongue - English across cultures* (pp. 355–365). Urbana, IL: University of Illinois Press.

Kachru, B. B. (1985). Standards, codification and sociolinguistic realism: The English language in the outer circle. In R. Quirk & H. G. Widdowson (Eds.), *English in the world: Teaching and learning the language and literatures* (pp. 11–30). Cambridge: Cambridge University Press for The British Council.

Kádár, D. Z. (2017). *Politeness, im/politeness and ritual: Maintaining the moral order in interpersonal interaction*. Cambridge: Cambridge University Press.

Kádár, D. Z., & Bargiela-Chiappini, F. (2011). Introduction: Politeness research in and across cultures. In F. Bargiela-Chiappini & D. Z. Kádár (Eds.), *Politeness across cultures* (pp. 1–14). New York: Palgrave Macmillan.

Kádár, D. Z., & Haugh, M. (2013). *Understanding politeness*. Cambridge: Cambridge University Press.

Kádár, D., & Ran, Y. (2019). Globalisation and politeness: A Chinese perspective. In E. Ogiermann & P. Garcés-Conejos Blitvich (Eds.), *From speech acts to lay understandings of politeness* (pp. 280–300). Cambridge: Cambridge University Press.

Kramsch, C. (1993). *Context and culture in language teaching*. Oxford: Oxford University Press.

Lakoff, R. (1973). The logic of politeness; or minding your p's and q's. *Papers from the 9th Regional Meeting of the Chicago Linguistic Society*, Chicago: Chicago Linguistic Society, 292–305.

Leech, G. (1983). *Principles of pragmatics*. London: Longman.

Leech, G. (2014). *Pragmatics of politeness*. Oxford: Oxford University Press.

Levinson, S. C. (1983). *Pragmatics*. Cambridge: Cambridge University Press.

Li, S. (2021). Pragmatics assessment in English as an international language. In Z. Tajeddin, & M. Alemi (Eds.), *Pragmatics pedagogy in English as an international language* (pp. 191–211). Routledge: New York/London.

30 *Introduction*

Liddicoat, A. J., & McConachy, T. (2019). Meta-pragmatic awareness and agency in language learners' constructions of politeness. In T. Szende & G. Alao (Eds.), *Pragmatic and cross-cultural competences: Focus on politeness* (pp. 11–25). Brussels: Peter Lang.

Locher, M. A., & Watts, R. J. (2005). Politeness theory and relational work. *Journal of Politeness Research, 1*, 9–33.

McKay, S. L. (2012). Principles of teaching English as an international language. In L. Alsagoff, S. L. McKay, G. Hu, & W. A. Renandya (Eds.), *Principles and practices for teaching English as an international language* (pp. 28–46). London/New York: Routledge.

Mills, S. (2011). Communities of practice and politeness. In B. L. Davies, M. Haugh, & A. Merrison (Eds.), *Situated politeness* (pp. 73–87). London: Continuum.

Mugford, G. (2019). *Addressing difficult situations in foreign language learning: Confusion, impoliteness, and hostility*. New York/London: Routledge.

Mugford, G. (2022). *Developing cross-cultural relational ability in foreign language learning: Asset-based pedagogy to enhance pragmatic competence*. New York/Abingdon, UK: Routledge.

Rose, K., & Kasper, G. (2001). *Pragmatics in language teaching*. Cambridge: Cambridge University Press.

Schegloff, E. A., & Sacks, H. (1973). Opening up closings. *Semiotica, VIII*(4), 289–327.

Seidlhofer, B. (2004). Research perspectives on teaching English as a Lingua Franca. *Annual Review of Applied Linguistics, 24*, 209–239.

Sifianou, M. (1992). *Politeness phenomena in England Greece*. Oxford: Oxford University Press.

Spencer-Oatey, H. (2008). *Culturally speaking: Culture, communication and politeness theory*. London: Continuum.

Spencer-Oatey, H., & Kádár, D. (2021). *Intercultural politeness*. Cambridge: Cambridge University Press.

Taguchi, N., & Roever, C. (2017). *Second language pragmatics*. Oxford: Oxford University Press.

Thomas, J. (1983). Cross-cultural pragmatic failure. *Applied Linguistics, 4*, 91–112.

Watts, R. J. (2003). *Politeness*. Cambridge: Cambridge University Press.

2 Positioning foreign language politeness

Introduction

When constructing, establishing and maintaining interpersonal and transactional relationships, bilingual interactants are often not aware of the function and importance of politeness resources when negotiating, confronting and overcoming linguistic and cultural challenges. All too often linguistic politeness is seen as a convenient add-on or an accessory that merely serves to soften an interaction so as to make it sound more palatable, cordial and respectful. Meanwhile, culturally-focused politeness is often seen as a matter of imitating TL practices and routines. However, taking a position regarding FL politeness does not mean that bilingual interactants need to follow, reflect or imitate TL practices given that speakers may not even be focused on adopting Inner Circle norms and values (for explanation, see Chapter 1). Rather, they may be seeking acceptable and intelligible ways of engaging in politeness practices which allow them to express themselves in their own ways. For this reason, FL politeness practices cannot be automatically equated with TL norms of behaviour.

However in positioning politeness as a productive social action plan for accomplishing successful TL interaction, I argue that understandings of politeness help bilingual speakers to

a) interact more effectively within the TL cultural context;
b) project a sense of who they are (or personhood);
c) react and respond to others' needs and feelings; and
d) form more meaningful relationships with other interactants.

By positioning politeness as a plan of action centred on the bilingual user and his/her communicative objectives, adherence to TL cultural norms and conforming to the social behaviour of others no longer feature as overriding primary concerns in FL interaction. Politeness is a resource that language users can invest in as they 'are constantly organizing and reorganizing a sense of who they are and how they relate to the social world' (Norton, 2000, p. 10). Investment calls for critical language awareness that enables

DOI: 10.4324/9781003326052-2

32 *Positioning foreign language politeness*

interactants to assess and evaluate how language and cultural patterns and practices are being employed in interpersonal and transactional language use. Bilingual interactants need to be fully aware of the pragmatic assets and resources that are readily available and determine how they can be employed effectively. Such awareness places bilingual interactants in a much stronger position to examine and evaluate meaning and intent behind TL cultural and language practices and subsequently decide whether to adopt, modify or reject them. In assessing the actions of others and reflecting on their own conduct, bilingual interactants can, on the one hand, view politeness as a well-trodden interactional path that allows them to develop, sustain and consolidate relationships, i.e. prosocial politeness which reflects Watts's (2003) 'politic' behaviour (for discussion, see Chapter 1). On the other hand, awareness offers opportunities for bilingual interlocutors to project their individuality with regard to how they wish and aim to interact in the TL context. This may involve searching for, improvising, or even creating the necessary language resources i.e. Watts's (2003) 'polite' behaviour (for discussion, see Chapter 1). Therefore, bilingual learners have choices with respect to how they want to establish relationships whether it be in their own individualistic ways or by conforming to TL societal expectations.

Politeness provides FL users with choices and options along with limitations and restrictions when asserting themselves and/or interpreting and answering to other interactants' needs and concerns. It allows interactants to express, among other communicative factors, a sense of closeness and intimacy and respect for others' autonomy and their right to freedom of action. Tracy and Robles (2013) term these two forms of interpersonal engagement as involvement and independence politeness styles. At the same time, by adhering to established politeness practices, interactants can convey their degree of commitment, support and interest within a given encounter. For instance, politeness may be superficial and purely formulaic as characterised in stereotypical brief transactional encounters (e.g. during a service encounter) or it may be more expressive and substantial as found in evolving social relationships (e.g. with new acquaintances and neighbours). Of course, there is no reason to automatically relegate transactional meetings per se to being superficial and trite with regards to politeness since they too may develop into (or reflect) meaningful and long-lasting relationships.

To position politeness in FL interaction, this chapter is structured in the following way. In order to understand interactional beliefs and attitudes, first of all, I attempt to explore bilingual interlocutors' lay understandings of politeness and subsequently compare and contrast them with possible FL practices. Then I examine FL speakers' understandings of TL culture, especially in terms of negotiating FL communicative norms, attitudes and behavioural patterns. Any serious gulf in understandings between L1 and TL concepts of politeness will call for pedagogic

Positioning foreign language politeness 33

intervention so as to forestall possible misunderstandings and miscommunication. Secondly, I argue that by developing a critical awareness of politeness patterns and practices, bilingual users can study and analyse how politeness is used to empower and enhance or to weaken and undermine. Therefore, I examine how effective use of politeness assets can enable bilingual speakers to come across in their own individualistic ways and interact successfully with others as they deal with any emerging challenges, difficulties and confusions. It is especially important that FL users understand both the cultural and social dimensions to politeness since these reflect different ways of viewing and interacting with the world. At the same time, politeness may be expressed through nonverbal behaviour which is often not afforded due and proper consideration and evaluation in FL teaching and learning contexts. Besides examining patterns and practices, I need to position everyday politeness behaviour within a theoretical framework that informs and illustrates different behaviours and ways of thinking. Given that politeness theory is all too often focused on monolingual native speaker behaviour, little consideration is given to FL users who draw their resources, experiences and values from more than one language and culture. As a conclusion, the chapter offers a tentative outline for teaching/learning politeness that corresponds to learners' needs and wants and builds on their background knowledge, pragmatic resources and interactional capabilities.

Degrees of FL politeness

Politeness does not exist on its own (Spencer-Oatey & Kádár, 2021) and is not self-executing but actively reflects how individuals, social groups and larger communities (e.g. members of a given nationality) engage in conscious decision-making when constructing and maintaining social relationships. FL interactants, consciously or instinctively, decide on their level of engagement during interpersonal and transactional encounters and determine how much time and energy should be given over to expressing politeness. In the FL context, politeness considerations start well before any interaction has begun as speakers bring L1 understandings to bear on TL context. Politeness may be seen as an ongoing concern throughout interaction as speakers may want to communicate in the 'best' way possible (i.e. be on their best behaviour) or, on the other hand, be careful not to say the wrong thing. Therefore, they may consciously engage in minimising face threatening acts (Brown & Levinson, 1987). On the other hand, FL interactants may want to use politeness to manage and augment relationships and are willing to take interactional risks. In between these two courses of action, FL users may decide that politeness is not such an underlying concern as certain TL interactions reflect neither politeness nor impoliteness i.e., they are value free (Leech, 2014).

34 *Positioning foreign language politeness*

False equivalents?

Before engaging in TL interaction, FL users need to reflect on their L1 understandings of polite behaviour and consider whether they align with TL understandings. On the surface, concepts such as politeness, *cortesía* (Spanish) and *politesse* (French) attempt to convey the same notion. However, this does not mean that they are understood in exactly the same way by the interactants themselves. For instance, lay understandings may reflect different emphases: English-language politeness may concentrate on socially correct and appropriate behaviour; Spanish *cortesía* may focus more on demonstrating respect and good manners; and French *politesse* may emphasise the social rules governing correct behaviour. In turn, associated words such as civility, courtesy and etiquette may also carry subtle differences across languages. For instance, respect in English conveys admiration for others while the Spanish-language *respeto* also involves respect for the addressee's personal integrity (Curcó, 2007). Therefore, in FL use, bilingual speakers have to be watchful for possible different interactional manifestations, practices and patterns. At the same time, FL teachers need to careful about imposing Anglo cultural interpretations on others (Mills & Kádár, 2011, p. 28). Therefore, any positioning of politeness should start with the FL learners' own understandings and their interactional practices. As discussed below, the same situation applies to understandings of culture.

Normative politeness

When engaging in the TL, interlocutors may want to present themselves in the best possible way and may want to mirror and adopt relevant norms and practices. If politeness signifies *being on one's best behaviour* and *showing consideration of others*, politeness, as an ongoing concern, may mean that FL users employ prepatterned and conventional resources as they adhere to appropriate, expectable and standard behaviour, i.e. prosocial politeness. At the same time, it is important to acknowledge that prosocial politeness is often contested among TL speakers as there may be fierce disagreement as to what exactly normative behaviour is. Nevertheless, prosocial politeness provides a degree of communicative comfort and self-assuredness. Interactants may want to identify with and understand TL practices and, therefore, they are willing to adopt TL norms and practices even if these may seem strange, bizarre or even clash with their L1 practices. FL users are often concerned with whether they have access to the necessary resources and whether they can actually use them in TL communicative contexts. Besides delivering the requisite quantities of *Yes please* and *No thank you*, FL users may reach for off-the-shelf constructions such as indirect questions e.g. *I was wondering if I could* ... and rely on a heavy use of modal constructions e.g. *May I* ....? To a large extent,

Positioning foreign language politeness 35

such performances reflect the enactment of declarative knowledge as interlocutors call on a data bank of communicative and discourse patterns and practices, grammatical structures and other language assets. Watts (2003) may categorise such knowledge as *politic* behaviour and this may provide very real and tangible means for FL users to come across as polite in the TL language even if it is conventional, predictable and formulaic. *Politic* behaviour is further discussed in Chapter 3.

Risk politeness

Interactants may feel that *politic* behaviour does not allow them to fully express both their individuality as communicators and their L1 ways of coming across as they engage in what Watts (2003) terms *polite* behaviour. By breaking out of predictable, straitjacketed and orthodox conduct, interlocutors take communicative risks as they go beyond the merely appropriate, customary and well mannered and seek out affiliative politeness which may be exploratory, tentative and uncertain. In this way they look to express closeness, involvement, supportiveness, solidarity, etc. and this will involve employing a range of interpersonal language assets such as availability checks (e.g. *Are you really busy?*), disarmers (e.g. *I wonder if you could possibly help me out.*), backchannelling (e.g. *No way!*), appealers (e.g. *So can I count on you?*), etc. as interactants engage in relational talk. Such ability reflects procedural knowledge as interlocutors employ quick and automated conversational openers and responses in unrehearsed and unpredictable communicative situations as they seek to engage in affiliative politeness. Interactants may intertwine *politic* and *polite* behaviour depending on how a given interaction is progressing as expressions of politeness will emerge to varying degrees of intensity/moderation throughout an interaction. Furthermore, *politic* behaviour may represent a fallback position to *polite* behaviour if an interaction is not proceeding smoothly. As interactional/ affiliative politeness, *polite* behaviour is further discussed in Chapter 4.

Nonpoliteness

FL users have to realise that politeness considerations should not unnecessarily dominate TL interaction as FL users are often able to put relational considerations on the back burner. As Leech argues:

> A first point – a fairly obvious one – is that politeness is not obligatory. People can be nonpolite: they normally will not behave politely unless there is a reason to be polite (even if the reason is somewhat vague, such as following convention).... However, there are occasions where rudeness or impoliteness is felt to be desirable – where the recipient of impolite behaviour "had it coming to them".
>
> (2014, p. 4)

36 Positioning foreign language politeness

Therefore, a given utterance may reflect '*nonpoliteness* as excluding not only politeness but also impoliteness. In other words, we define it as a property of utterances that have no politeness value of any kind' (Leech, 2014, p. 216). Routine informative genres (e.g. giving instructions), transactional encounters (e.g. paying at a supermarket) and entertaining speech (e.g. telling jokes) may not demonstrate a pronounced politeness element. Whilst FL interlocutors may evaluate an utterance as polite or impolite, TL interactants may see it as a matter of nonpoliteness and therefore misinterpretation and misunderstanding may result. Again, it is important that teachers help FL learners grasp contrasting cross-cultural understandings of polite behaviour.

'Polite' culture

When preparing to interact with TL speakers, FL learners want to garner information about TL speakers' behaviour, customs and culture. It is only natural to ask what speakers from country X are like and what their daily habits and routines are. FL users want to prepare themselves as best as possible for their first or continuing encounters with TL interlocutors. With little first-hand knowledge or direct contact, speakers will often resort to accepting established stereotypes, generalisations and even listen to anecdotal accounts. Obviously, the danger here is that stereotypes and generalisations can quickly foment myths, falsehoods and slurs and, of course, interactional realities may be quite different (Kramsch, 1993). To study politeness and culture, I adopt Scollon and Scollon's understanding of culture as 'any of the customs, worldview, language, kinship system, social organization, and other taken-for-granted today-to-day practices of a people which set that group apart as a distinctive group' (1995, p. 126). Therefore, in examining politeness and culture, I focus on everyday patterns and practices that the FL interactants might reasonably encounter.

Cultural capital

Insights into politeness and TL culture can be constructed from the bilingual speakers' own knowledge and experience of the world or from what Bourdieu terms cultural capital (Bourdieu, 1972, 1980, 1991). Cultural capital consists of social assets e.g. status, language skills and includes 'discernible traits (for example, accents, styles and ways of expressing oneself)' (Grenfell, 2011, p. 31). FL users will have already built up cultural capital in their L1 and this may provide an important resource in TL interaction. However, bilingual speakers have to decide on the transferability of L1 cultural capital or whether they should submit to TL practices and patterns. Wink lays out the problem as follows:

Positioning foreign language politeness 37

Cultural capital is a process of powerful practices: ways of behaving, talking, acting, thinking, moving, and so on. These practices are determined unconsciously by the dominant culture and are used to promote success for specific groups in our society.

(2011, p. 63)

By bringing their own cultural capital to TL interaction, FL interactants can interact from a position of strength and force, especially with regards to politeness. But this is not a matter of making comparisons between two cultures or languages. Rather it means adopting a cross-cultural approach:

… understanding a foreign culture requires putting that culture in relation to one's own, as we have seen for social interactions as well as for the interaction with written texts, meaning is relational. Thus, for example, an intercultural approach to the teaching of culture is radically different from a transfer of information between cultures. It includes a reflection both on the target and on the native culture.

(Kramsch, 1993, p. 204)

Kramsch goes on to argue that culture is socially constructed as interactants present their values, ways of thinking, ways of coming across:

Traditional thought in foreign language education has limited the teaching of culture to the transmission of information about the people of the target country, and about their general attitudes and world views. The perspective adopted has been largely that of an objective native culture (C1) or target culture (C2). It has usually ignored the fact that a large part of what we call culture is a social construct, the product of self and other perceptions.

(1993, p. 205)

Therefore, in order to understand TL politeness practices, interactants should avoid blunt and decontextualised comparisons. It may be more useful to build up and develop declarative knowledge, automatisation and procedural knowledge.

However, before going further in examining TL culture and politeness, it is important to acknowledge that cultural norms and behaviour are contested within any given language community:

We argue that cultures are not homogeneous and that within each culture there are different views on what constitutes polite and impolite behaviour; therefore, if we use models of politeness which ignore the heterogeneous nature of politeness and impoliteness, those generalisations about culture will be of limited value. They can only tell us about

38　*Positioning foreign language politeness*

the dominant politeness norms and do not reflect the variety of norms and disagreements about politeness and impoliteness which characterise linguistic behaviour within any culture.

(Mills & Kádár, 2011, p. 21)

Declarative cultural knowledge

Declarative knowledge (Block, 2003; Taguchi & Roever, 2017) provides a cultural and linguistic databank of explicit interactional practices, behavioural patterns, social rules, etc. On the other hand, automatisation reflects the transfer of declarative knowledge into useable and practicable language use. Procedural knowledge is the automatised use of declarative knowledge. FL users need to raise their awareness to TL practices and operationalise such knowledge in everyday communicative situations.

Before embarking on a brief description of declarative cultural considerations, it is important to avoid stereotyping nationalities and generalising about specific social groups. As Mills and Kádár argue

> The relationship between culture and politeness can in fact be studied but should be approached with some caution. We believe that it is possible to critically study politeness in [... cultural] settings, provided that one refrains from generalising statements based on the language practices of certain dominant groups or stereotypes of those groups. In other words, the dominant politeness norms of these areas can be faithfully represented as long as it is not claimed that they are absolute norms, and as long as other "norms" are discussed in relation to them.
>
> (2011, p. 44)

Furthermore

> In a sense, cultural norms are mythical; the nation, whatever we take that to mean, cannot speak with one voice, according to one view of what is appropriate or inappropriate. At any one time, there will be a range of different norms or notion of appropriateness circulating within communities of practice within the culture as a whole. Some of these norms will be ones which a large number of communities of practice will draw upon and some of them will be ones which will be recognised as being social rather than individual communities-of-practice norms. However that does not mean that there are no norms or no perceptions of what those norms are. Those norms which are perceived to be social norms are generally ones associated with those who are perceived to be powerful, either economically or culturally, those who have in Bourdieu's (1991) terms 'cultural capital' of some sort and are able to make pronouncements about what is appropriate.
>
> (Mills & Kádár, 2011, p. 43)

Therefore, it is there important not to assume that the traits and practices of one dominant group (e.g. middle class) are adhered to by all other social classes.

At the risk of reflecting politeness and cultural interests of specific groups, I argue that the following British cultural patterns and practices are often the key concerns of FL users:

- Cultural information and facts:
  - Precepts: forms of address; table manners; personal hygiene; formulaic language (e.g. use of *please*, *sorry*, *excuse me* and *thank you*).
  - Proscriptions: speaking loudly; showing overfamiliarity; taboo subjects (e.g. health, death and personal relationships); queue jumping.
- Awareness of customary behaviour and ways of doing things:
  - Precepts: greetings; participating in conversations; discursive styles (e.g. indirectness); relationships with neighbours, acquaintances etc.; small talk topics (e.g. the weather).
  - Proscriptions: asking people how much they earn; invasion of personal space; physical contact; prolonged eye contact.
- Cultural ideas, values, beliefs and attitudes:
  - Precepts: reservedness, independence, modesty / self-deprecation; punctuality / lateness; concepts of humour; respect for individual privacy
  - Proscriptions: avoidance of confrontation; talk about money

A declarative focus provides learners with a potential database of cultural do's and don'ts and offers a prescriptive basis for politeness practices in the TL culture. Obviously, FL speakers themselves need to examine cultural precepts and proscriptions for themselves and identify real-life practices. At the same time, the abovementioned cultural concerns do not in any way attempt to provide a comprehensive survey of politeness culture. Further development could examine macro concepts related to politeness (e.g. social class, tolerance and resignation) or micro concepts (e.g. social invitations and visits, and pub culture). At the same time, it is important to remember that a range of cultures exist within any given language as argued by Culpeper:

> [I]t is all too easy to give the impression that "one language equals one culture", not least of all because the label for the language becomes a convenient label for the culture (e.g., "English and Japanese compliments compared"). But of course we all know that within one language there are many different cultures, however that tricky notion of culture is conceived.
>
> (2012, p. 1128)

40 Positioning foreign language politeness

As a result, FL users should investigate their concerns, experiences and understandings from an ethnographic perspective as opposed to teachers merely providing a prescriptive approach to TL politeness practices in terms of do's and don'ts.

Automatisation and procedural knowledge

In order to convert declarative knowledge into procedural knowledge, FL interactants need to be able to enact knowledge and access resources in real-life communicative contexts. This will involve, first of all, practising and rehearsing linguistic politeness and cultural politeness and examining different courses of action and their consequences. This can be achieved through the use and examination of illustrative events, cultural capsules, critical moments (see Chapter 1). For instance, bilingual learners can examine the polite routines associated when eating out. This may range from ordering food and appropriate conversational topics to complaining and who should pay the bill.

After identifying the different aspects/components of a given interactional event, FL users may find that 'its performance takes up a great deal of conscious attention, or channel capacity' (Johnson, 1996, p. 89). Consequently, FL users seek to achieve automatisation, i.e. 'the ability to get things right when no attention is available for getting them right' (Johnson, 1996, p. 89). This is especially the case when engaging in relational work as FL speakers may want to focus on more challenging interpersonal goals in wanting to express interest, involvement, affinity and supportiveness. Taguchi and Roever describe this as the autonomous stage which 'involves the continuous improvement of a skill to the level that performance becomes fluent and automatic' (2017, p. 44).

To reach the final goal of procedural knowledge, interactants need to be able to access language assets under pressure. They are in a stronger position to achieve this if they practise and participate in TL interactions that are characterised by

- scant preparation time
- restricted contextual clues
- spontaneous and unpremeditated discourse
- unscripted talk
- constantly switching relational talk
- communicative noise and interference

Whilst it may be relatively easy to practise language structures and patterns in the language classroom, FL users may be particularly challenged when they have to engage in quick and coherent relational hustle and bustle in everyday communication. (Chapter 6 examines how FL learners can be helped to access pragmatic resources when under pressure to participate in relational talk.)

Positioning foreign language politeness 41

Automatisation and procedural knowledge place FL users in a much stronger position to negotiate new, emerging and new-found relational contexts. It allows them to concentrate on unfamiliar and unexpected dimensions during an encounter. Furthermore, it puts FL users on much firmer communicative ground when having to overcome possible language shortcomings e.g. not remembering a word or dealing with unaccustomed and perhaps enigmatic TL politeness practices.

(Critical) language awareness

As they transform declarative knowledge to procedural knowledge, bilingual speakers can gain an understanding of everyday relational talk by recognising, examining and assimilating how TL speakers practise and convey relational behaviour. Observation and reflection allow interactants to perceive how politeness is used and, just as importantly, to decide the degree to which they want to adhere to TL patterns and practices. Language awareness can help FL interlocutors to identify and evaluate TL politeness norms, patterns and behaviours from language, social and cultural perspectives. Critical language awareness allows FL users to understand politeness as social practice especially in terms of ideology, subject-positioning and power (Clark & Ivanič, 1999, p. 63).

By raising their level of language awareness, bilingual speakers can examine how other interactants enact politeness especially in terms of expressing supportiveness, interest, empathy, solidarity, involvement, etc. Carter explains that 'language awareness refers to the development in learners of an enhanced consciousness of and sensitivity to the forms and functions of language' (2003, p. 64). Language awareness has important implications for politeness studies that only focus on prescriptive behaviour and norms of conduct as interactants are encouraged to examine interpersonal choices, interactional limitations and pragmatic restrictions in social and transactional encounters. Importantly, language awareness helps 'language learners to gradually gain insights into how languages work' (Bolitho, Carter, Hughes, Ivanič, Masuhara & Tomlinson, 2003, p. 251). In FL learning, politeness structures and practices need to be understood in terms of communicative openings, possibilities and purposes use. Such understandings go beyond students' merely adopting correct behavioural forms and patterns of use. Bolitho et al. further argue: 'Language Awareness offers opportunities for affective engagement, relationships between personal investment, and the raising of self-esteem (Donmall, 1985, p. 7)'. Therefore, language awareness can help students to be more cognizant of their communicative environment and specific interpersonal and transactional contexts.

Going further, critical language awareness examines how 'language is shaped by and shapes values, beliefs and power relations in its sociocultural context' (Clark & Ivanič, 1999, p. 64). Besides employing language assets to

42   *Positioning foreign language politeness*

engage in relational work, interlocutors employ politeness resources to express their view of the world, their position in it and how they want to interact with other interlocutors. For instance, Fairclough (1992) questions the assumption that interactants' behaviour is focused on presenting themselves in the best light possible and protecting the face of other interlocutors as proposed in classical politeness theory. For example, Brown and Levinson (1987), Leech (1983) and Lakoff (1973) argue that interactants usually want to promote a positive image themselves as being caring and attentive to the needs of addressee(s). But Fairclough maintains

> What is missing is a sense of variability of politeness practices across different discourse types within a culture, of links between variable politeness practices and variable social relations, or of producers being constrained by politeness practices.
>
> (1992, p. 162)

Besides seeing how other interactants come across, bilingual speakers also need to take a critical look at their own performance, and both assess and reflect on how they come across when they engage in TL relational work. One way of achieving this is through monitoring the interpersonal responses employed by their addressees. These demonstrate the level of hearer interest and involvement e.g. through backchannelling, uptakes and self-disclosure. Backchanneling and feedback reflect 'the responses that show that the hearer is listening and encourages a speaker to continue talking – such as 'Was it?' and 'Oh really?'... (Cutting & Fordyce, 2021, p. 22). In the same vein, Edmondson and House describe uptakes as 'a speaker's *acknowledgment* of the preceding utterance from the interlocutor' (1981, p. 62, authors' italics). They offer the examples *Really, oh, good heavens* and *Oh my God.* Importantly, from a relational perspective, an uptake 'validates the preceding *move* performed by the previous speaker as a contribution to the ongoing discourse' (Edmondson, 1981, p. 6). With self-disclosure, interlocutors engage in 'sequence of tellings' about themselves that they deem to be newsworthy or are worth telling (Coupland, 2000, p. 17). Meanwhile, Svennevig sees self-disclosure 'as "any information exchange that refers to the self, including personal states, dispositions, events in the past, and plans for the future" (Derlega, Winstead, Wong & Greenspan, 1987, p. 173)' (1999, p. 2–3). Self-disclosure indicates that interactants are willing to open up about themselves as they seek to establish a degree of proximity and familiarity with their addressees. It may even go as far as to indicate that interlocutors are developing a certain amount of togetherness and affinity:

> The degree of self-disclosure has been considered a reliable measure of the depth of a relationship so that, for instance, spouses disclose more intimate information to each other than do strangers.
>
> (Svennevig, 1999, p. 20)

Positioning foreign language politeness 43

Whilst FL speakers may not be seeking close intimate relationships in the TL, meaningful polite discourse needs to go beyond mere pleasantries and talk about the weather.

Noticing

By focusing on (critical) language awareness, one is taking the position that politeness is not merely acquired in TL interaction but needs to be noticed, identified and understood within a specific context. As a first step, bilingual speakers need to notice how language is contextually used to construct and express politeness. Only by being aware of how language is employed can learners hope to notice how politeness is employed in the TL. As Schmidt argues:

> In pragmatics, awareness that on a particular occasion someone says to their interlocutor something like, "I'm terribly sorry to bother you, but if you have time could you look at this problem?" is a matter of noticing. Relating the various forms used to their strategic deployment in the service of politeness and recognizing the cooccurrence with elements of context such as social distance, power, level of imposition and so on, are all matters of understanding.
>
> (1995, p. 29)

However, being aware may not mean that a given politeness practice or process is necessarily understood and fully comprehended. There is a difference between noticing and understanding. As Schmidt argues: 'I use "noticing" to mean conscious registration of the occurrence of some event, whereas "understanding" as I am using the term, implies recognition of a general principle, rule or pattern' (1995, p. 29). FL users may perceive that British people overuse the word *sorry*. However, they may not notice how it is used and more importantly understand why it is used. The same case may be made for indirectness: it is too simplistic to argue that it automatically and unconditionally reflects politeness. For instance, Grainger and Mills argue:

> The assumption in much traditional politeness research tends to be that the more indirect an utterance is, the more polite it is (Brown & Levinson, 1978, 1987). Directness is therefore considered to be in essence impolite. However, this assumption appears to be based on the politeness norms of elite groups of English speakers and turns out to be problematic when one looks at the way indirectness is used, evaluated and understood by interactants in other communities, cultures and contexts.
>
> (2016, p. 2)

Therefore, FL speakers need to evaluate and assess given behaviour and construct their own understandings of TL relational work and politeness

44 *Positioning foreign language politeness*

taking into consideration their own communicative context and not those of Inner Circle norms and values (see Chapter One). As a further step, critical language awareness allows L2 users to observe how politeness can be used to restrain and restrict TL interaction. For instance, FL users may be expected, unnecessarily, to adhere to conventional and prescriptive language usage which may limit their ability of self-expression.

Nonverbal politeness

Just as language awareness examines the motivation behind language choice and language use, studies related to politeness and paralanguage examine not only the expression of nonverbal signs but the motivation behind them. Nonverbal language includes body language (kinesics), physical distancing (proxemics), head movements including eye behaviour (oculesics) and touching (haptics). Nonverbal behaviour can be defined as 'communication that transcends the written or spoken word. This encompasses a number of aspects of body language including facial expression, eye contact, posture, gesture and inter-personal distance' (Gabbott & Hogg, 2001, p. 6). Whilst FL users may be concentrating on the verbal expression of politeness, they make not notice nonverbal dimensions that reinforce (or even contradict) relational work as interactants express supportiveness, empathy, involvement, etc.

Building on Richmond, McCroskey and Payne (1991), Gabbott and Hogg (2001) elaborate on six important functions of nonverbal behaviour, and these have special relevance for the study of FL politeness. They can be summarised as follows:

1 Reinforcement of meaning
2 Substitution of communicative message
3 Emphasis of communicative message
4 Contradiction of apparent meaning
5 Signalling to other interactant(s)
6 Emotional expression of involvement, interest, concern etc.

These can be expanded upon as follows:

- Identification of the reinforcement of meaning through nonverbal language can help FL users confirm, modify or reject their initial understanding and interpretation. For instance, an invitation accompanied by a smile can be seen as genuine and well meaning.
- In contrast an invitation with no eye contact may not be so warm and well intentioned. Meanwhile, a message or an instruction may be substituted by nonverbal language such as by the wave of the arm to signal to an addressee to sit down. With this gesture the interlocutor may be expressing a degree of informality. In this instance, nonverbal

Positioning foreign language politeness 45

communication may be considered to be free-standing and unaccompanied by spoken language.

- Emphasis on nonverbal communication can be reinforced through increased eye contact or reduced physical distance. This may be the case, for instance, when a speaker is pressing the addressee to accept an invitation.
- However, verbal expression may not be matched by a corresponding bodily expression. So, for instance, an apology given with a smile may convey a lack of sincerity.
- At the same time, FL users should be alert to signalling by interactants that encourage other interlocutors to participate (or reduce their participation) in a conversation. Nonverbal communication may be particularly visible in turn-taking, changing conversational topics, seeking clarification, overlapping, interrupting, etc. (Thornbury & Slade, 2006). On the other hand, lack of gaze may mean that a speaker is not ready to yield his turn (Archer, Aijmer & Wichmann, 2012, p. 229).
- Finally, interactants may express emotional interest, involvement and affinity, for instance, through the waving of arms in the air.

It is important to recognise that nonverbal communication is not on add-on to mainstream politeness behaviour. As Gabbott and Hogg point out: 'Unlike the spoken word this form of communication is constant, being projected and received via a large number of different channels' (2001, p. 6). Therefore, FL users should go beyond solely concentrating on understanding the spoken word during a given interaction by also monitoring and evaluating accompanying nonverbal communication. They should be especially alert to possible nonverbal responses which may not be complemented by spoken language. This will allow them to match the TL speakers' nonverbal production with listeners' perceptions and understanding and may, indeed, give added value to an interaction (de Bot & Kroll, 2010, p. 139). However, in the final analysis, as pointed out by Edmondson (1981), FL users may have to choose between accepting linguistic or nonlinguistic responses and indeed nonlinguistic information may be decisive in selecting between two possible interpretations of meaning.

Given the overwhelming difficulty in providing L2 speakers with a glossary of nonverbal signs and their possible meanings, FL users need to undertake their own ethnographic study of politeness behaviour and construct their own understandings of nonverbal communication in a given speech community. For instance, building on Hall (1959, 1969), Scollon and Scollon noted that when Mexicans interact with people from the United States, the use of physical space plays an important interactional role:

One culture, that of Mexicans for example, will have a slightly smaller sphere of intimate space than another culture, such as that of North

46 *Positioning foreign language politeness*

Americans. The result of this difference, which can be measured in just a few inches, is that when a North American and a Mexican stand together to converse, the Mexican will nudge slightly closer to the North American in order to get at the right distance for comfortable interpersonal discourse. The North American, who has a slightly larger intimate sphere, will feel that the Mexican is invading his or her intimate space and will, therefore, step back an inch or two. This will make the Mexican feel uncomfortable because he or she will feel too distant and therefore, he or she will move closer.

The net result of these cultural differences in intimate and personal spaces is that, where norms are different, you will find the person with the smaller sphere constantly moving closer to the other, and the other person constantly moving back a bit to increase the space.

(1995, pp. 145–146)

It is important to recognise that nonverbal communication may be just as structured as spoken language and conveys its own communicative meaning. At the same time, bilingual interactants need to be aware of the nonverbal signs that they *give off* (Goffman, 1967) during relational work which TL speakers may consider to be incomprehensible, confusing and even, in the worse cases, insulting.

Positioning FL politeness

As discussed in Chapter 1, an awareness and understanding of FL politeness principles, practices and patterns needs to answer language learners' basic concerns especially regarding acceptable, permissible and common practice. Furthermore, interactants have to build on critical language awareness and politeness as cultural capital as they access available assets and resources. Therefore, a theoretical framework needs to be adopted/adapted/developed that allows FL users to structure their polite practices in TL interpersonal and transactional contexts. By building on Kádár and Haugh (2013), I discuss these approaches in terms of social-norm, addressee-focused and co-constructed politeness. However, first of all, I need to clarify that a survey of current politeness theory is not attempted here because this has already been successfully carried out by Culpeper (2011), Eelen (2001) and Grainger (2011). Rather, the following discussion highlights how politeness research can provide FL interlocutors with relational insights and communicative understandings.

Social norm politeness

At first glance, an understanding of social-norm politeness fulfils FL speakers' behavioural expectations in their TL objectives. Social norm politeness is reflected in etiquette guides, politeness manuals and self-help

Positioning foreign language politeness 47

books. Fraser states that social norm politeness 'assumes that each society has a particular set of social norms consisting of more or less explicit rules that prescribe a certain behavior, a state of affairs, or a way of thinking in a context' (1990, p. 220). FL interactants want to know how to 'behave' in the TL context and this approach is often adopted by EFL textbooks which issue a list of prescriptive and proscribed behaviours and frequently framed in terms of 'do's' and 'don'ts':

- interactional behaviour (e.g. always say 'please and 'thank you' but don't be too direct in making requests);
- safe topics (e.g. during small talk, do talk about the weather but don't ask people how much they earn);
- body language (e.g. do make eye contact but don't stare); and
- cultural behaviour (e.g. do open the door for other people but do not speak loudly in public).

First of all, a list of 'do's' and 'don'ts' seems to assume that language learners do not know how to be polite in their L1 and therefore need to be taught relational behaviour. Secondly, there is the problem of cultural clashes regarding TL politeness behaviour. Bilingual speakers may not feel comfortable regarding certain practices which may indeed conflict with their understandings of polite conduct. At the same time, there is an equally important problem: Social norm politeness may reflect how people are supposed to behave as opposed to how people actually behave. Furthermore, they may even reflect the imposed norms of one social class. See, for instance, Mills (2017) who argues that English politeness often reflects the perceived middle-class values and behaviour. As sustained by Mills and Kádár: 'At any one time, there will be a range of different norms or notion of appropriateness circulating within communities of practice within the culture as a whole' (2011, p. 43).

To a certain extent, the social norm politeness is reflected in the work of Lakoff (2005) who argues that politeness norms are in a state of flux in the United States as long-standing principles and practices are no longer adhered to. Asserting that 'old versions of "civility" and "politeness" are receding because new styles are more appropriate to current political and interpersonal discourse preference' (2005, p. 38), Lakoff appears to argue that increased incivility is emerging due to: sexual coarseness in public contexts; violence in the media; agonism; uncontrolled displays of hostility (e.g. road rage), negative political advertising, cursing and other bad language, internet "flaming," loss of polite conventions, invasions of privacy and the rise of conventional anti-formality (2005, pp. 30–34). In her conclusion, she argues that '[j]ust as we need to learn to speak to and listen to one another in civil ways despite our diversity, the same is true of discourse between the Number One Superpower and everyone else' (2005, p. 39). Lakoff seems to have positioned herself as the arbitrator of United States

48   *Positioning foreign language politeness*

politeness norms and makes broad generalisations regarding the source of supposedly perceived falling standards across society.

As the above discussion has highlighted, social norm politeness may be dictated by a specific social class, especially one that has status and power or by individuals who feel that that have the authority to speak on social norms. (Social norm politeness is further discussed in Chapter 3.)

Addressee-focused politeness

Addressee-focused politeness studies aim to show how speakers prioritise the relational needs of the hearers, often at considerable communicative expense to themselves. Consequently, so-called classical/traditional politeness theories examine patterns and practices that seek to minimise communicative threats or allay potential hearer unease. Brown and Levinson (1987), for instance, argue that speakers usually try to minimise Face-Threatening Acts (FTAs) which are those actions which undermine and fail to satisfy addressees' desires and wants. Adopting the concept of face from Goffman (1967), Brown and Levinson argue that 'we treat aspects of face as basic wants, which every member knows every other member desires, and which in general it is in the interests of every member to partially satisfy' (1987, p. 62). Meanwhile, Leech's (1983) politeness maxims seek to minimise negative impositions on the hearer and transfer any possible inconvenience onto the speaker. Developing the concept of the Politeness Principle (PP), Leech states:

> In its negative form, the PP might be formulated in a general way: "Minimize (other things being equal) the expression of impolite beliefs", and there is a corresponding positive version ("Maximize (other things being equal) the expression of polite beliefs"), which is somewhat less important.
>
> (1983, p. 81)

Leech later summarises the role of the PP as 'a constraint observed in human communicative behaviour, influencing us to avoid communication discord or offence, and maintain communicative accord' (Leech, 2007, p. 173).

In trying to identify normative behaviour, classical politeness theory can appear attractive to FL users who want to adopt and follow established TL maxims and principles. Often termed first-wave approaches, these theories are appealing because they are:

1   Normative
2   Universal
3   Relatable
4   Expedient

Positioning foreign language politeness 49

Addressee-focused politeness approaches are normative in that they offer standard, rules and principles by which to engage in politeness behaviour. Such guidelines can help FL speakers negotiate novel and unfamiliar situations. For instance, Leech's PP offers the following maxims:

- Tact – Minimize cost to other; Maximize benefit to other.
- Generosity – Minimize cost to self; Maximize cost to self.
- Approbation – Minimize benefit of other; Maximize praise of other.
- Modesty – Minimize praise of self; Maximize dispraise of self.
- Agreement – Minimize disagreement between self and other; Maximize agreement between self and other.
- Sympathy – Minimize antipathy between self and other; Maximize sympathy between self and other.

(1983, p. 132)

By adhering to the PP, FL speakers can follow recognisable and concrete directives when engaging in engage in TL politeness behaviour which may result in conventional successful behaviour.

At the same time, addressee-focused politeness studies claim that principles and maxims have universal application across languages and cultures. For instance, Brown and Levinson claim that politeness and indirect speech acts have a global application since 'the universality of indirect speech acts follows from the basic service they perform with respect to universal strategies of politeness' (1987, p. 142). Such claims may lead FL users to transfer their own L1 understandings and practices onto the TL context. (The use of direct and indirect speech is critiqued in Chapter 4.)

Addressee-focused politeness approaches also appear to be relatable in that FL users often seem to be able to recognise and understand such patterns and practices by referring to their own L1 communicative experiences and histories. For instance, Brown and Levinson's concepts of positive and negative politeness focus on how a speaker (S) interacts with a hearer (H):

Positive politeness is approach-based; it 'anoints' the face of the addressee by indicating that in some respects, S wants H's wants (e.g. treating him as a member of an in-group, a friend, a person whose wants and personality traits are known and liked) ....

Negative politeness, thus, is essentially avoidance-based, and realizations of negative-politeness strategies consist in assurances that the speaker recognizes and respects the addressee's negative-face wants and will not (or will only minimally) interfere with the addressee's freedom of action. Hence negative politeness is characterized by self-effacement, formality and restraint, with attention to very restricted aspects of H's self-image, centring on his want to be unimpeded.

(1987, p. 70)

50 *Positioning foreign language politeness*

Positive and negative politeness behaviour appears to account for how interactants treat intimates, friends, acquaintances and strangers. So, for instance, positive politeness strategies such as showing interest, sympathy and optimism are enacted towards friends whilst negative politeness strategies such as indirectness, hedging and apologising are expressed towards strangers. At the same time, Brown and Levinson also offer more direct 'bald' politeness strategies as well as off-record and avoidance strategies. Bald strategies are employed when expediency or urgency is paramount e.g. shouting *Get out!* when a building is on fire. Off record strategies attempt to conceal the overt communicative purpose and allow the speaker to deny his/her intention if necessary, especially when one's intention has been misinterpreted. For instance, *This is thirsty weather!* may be interpreted as a request for a beer but any negative response from the addressee still allows the speaker to put another spin on the utterance, e.g. How hot it is! Meanwhile an avoidance strategy means not even trying to engage with the potential addressee for fear of giving an offence.

Addressee-focused politeness resources offer expediency to FL interactants since they offer ready-to-use pragmatic resources. They provide short-cuts to achieving social harmony and avoiding interpersonal conflict. As Thomas points out

> ... people employ certain strategies (including the 50+ strategies described by Leech, Brown and Levinson, and others) for reasons of expediency – experience has taught us that particular strategies are likely to succeed in given circumstances, so we use them.
>
> (1995, p. 179)

When under communicative pressure, addressee-focused politeness resources save interlocutors' time and communicative energy when trying to position themselves interactionally and contextually.

However, claims of normativity, universality, relatability and expediency may not hold up in everyday TL interpersonal realities (Eelen, 2001). Relationships are often co-constructed and negotiated on a contextual basis. Furthermore, this approach seems to reinforce FL users' submissiveness in encouraging them to follow established norms and standard behaviour whereas relational work is often locally produced, dynamic and individualistic. The relevance of addressee-focused strategies is further explored in Chapter 3.

Interactional politeness

Interactional or affiliative politeness reflects individual relational work rather than socially focused politeness. Far from being normative, predictable and pre-patterned, interactional politeness is local, emerging and pragmatic – in the sense that it is based on the practical rather than being

Positioning foreign language politeness 51

theoretically based. Interactional politeness is often described in terms of discursive politeness which focuses on lay persons' understandings of politeness and the contextualised constructions of politeness as interlocutors express their individual identities. Emphasising the distinctiveness of discursive politeness, Terkourafi says

> politeness is negotiated at the micro-level and jointly by the speaker and the addressee. Thus, only study of situated exchanges – where active ratification of the politeness potential of any particular utterance can be observed – is warranted, and neither prediction nor generalization can, or should, be aimed at.
>
> (2005, p. 238)

For FL interlocutors, interactional politeness respects their understandings of politeness, allows them to take risks in relational talk and accepts that politeness may reflect challenges and struggles. Therefore, interactional politeness offers FL interactants choices as to how they want to participate in a given encounter. FL users are not expected to perform politeness in a predetermined manner but rather, establish a 'working consensus' (Goffman, 1959) which occurs when

> participants contribute to a single over-all definition of the situation which involves not so much a real agreement as to what exists but rather a real agreement as to whose claims concerning what issues will be temporarily honoured.... It is to be understood that the working consensus established in one interaction setting will be quite different in content from the working consensus established in a different type of setting. Thus, between two friends at lunch, a reciprocal show of affection, respect, and concern for the other is maintained. In service occupations, on the other hand, the specialist often maintains an image of disinterested involvement in the problem of the client, while the client responds with a show of respect for the competence and integrity of the specialist. Regardless of such differences in content, however, the general form of these working arrangements is the same.
>
> (Goffman, 1959, p. 21)

So whereas addressee-focused politeness aims to satisfy the hearer and conform to societal expectations, interactional politeness is more focused on relational work such as building and maintaining relationships and openly embraces participative variability as interactants negotiate common ground and joint understandings.

However, interactional politeness approaches to relational work may leave FL users disoriented and confused when interacting in the TL. This is because, if every interaction is unique, unpredictable and ungeneralisable, FL users may find that they have few relational guidelines to depend

52 *Positioning foreign language politeness*

on or precepts to adhere to. If, in fact, every social encounter is different, FL users are under considerable communicative stress when having to deal with every upcoming situation anew. Haugh appears to position the discursive approach between practice and theory

> ... the ultimate aim of the discursive approach to politeness is not to simply reify *emic* or lay understandings of politeness, thereby elevating them to the level of theory. The aim instead is for the analyst to theorise about politeness so that we may better understand *emic* or lay understandings and *practices* of politeness, the latter not necessarily being synonymous with the former.
>
> (2011, p. 258)

Interactional politeness is further discussed in Chapter 4.

Outline of teaching programme

If FL interaction involves interpersonal and transactional choices in how to participate in the TL context, bilingual speakers should know and understand what politeness can do for them and how they can effectively employ politeness assets rather than examining how they can and need to be polite. The pedagogical challenge is to outline a possible programme for helping learners employ politeness resources to achieve their own interactional goals.

By understanding available choices and accompanying limitations, FL users can assess how they want to engage in relational work. First of all, FL users have to decide how they want to 'present' themselves regarding politeness. Secondly, they have to take a position towards the level of politeness they wish to adopt in a given situation. Thirdly, they need to decide which politeness resources and assets they can access, want to employ and can evaluate regarding their effectiveness.

Presentation of self

Rather than being limited by language, FL users have to take an active decision regarding how they want to 'present' (Goffman, 1959) themselves in the TL. Goffman argues that individuals *give* and *give off* information when coming into contact with other interactants. In the case of FL users, they will *give* or reveal basic information about themselves which will help define their participation in a given encounter and their relationship with other interactants. At the same time, during the course of the encounter, a participant may *give off* or convey information which will affect the way he/she is perceived by others.

> He may wish them to think highly of him, or to think that he thinks highly of them, or to perceive how in fact he feels towards them, or to

Positioning foreign language politeness 53

obtain no clear-cut impression; he may wish to ensure sufficient harmony so that the interaction can be sustained, or to defraud, get rid of, confuse, mislead, antagonize, or insult them.

(Goffman, 1959, p. 15)

So when it comes to relational work, FL interlocutors need to think how they present themselves generally and in specific situations. They may want to project formality/familiarity, respectfulness/casualness, closeness/distance, concern/detachment, attentiveness/disinterest, affection/aversion, etc. These projections may be conveyed through both linguistic and cultural means. Such expressions of politeness may reflect convention, well-manneredness, conformity, assertiveness or even submissiveness. At the same time, specific relationships will determine the level and intensity of relational work that interactants are willing to expend. For instance, expressions of politeness towards family members, friends and intimates may contrast with those shown towards acquaintances, work colleagues and strangers (Eelen, 2001, p. 41).

Politeness commitment

FL users also need to decide the level of interactional commitment they wish to display and convey in a given situation. This can be loosely categorised in terms of pleasantries, comity, solidarity and independence.

*   Pleasantries involve 'polite' conversation which reflects superficial friendliness, adherence to social conventions and manners and inconsequential talk. They offer a safe conversational passage, acknowledging the presence of others whilst avoiding interpersonal commitment. Pleasantries are often to be found in short transactional encounters and reflect the use of stock phrases such as *Pleased to meet you* and *It was a pleasure talking to you*. Whilst such expressions may be sincere in themselves, there is no real indication that the speaker sees the relationship as particularly meaningful. Furthermore, FL users need to be aware that such displays of politeness may reflect obligatory, required or forced social behaviour rather than the desire for any lasting friendly relations or ongoing relational contact. However, such interaction is important for the smooth and uninterrupted functioning of a well ordered and courteous society.
*   Comity reflects convivial and sociable relations and involves 'establishment and maintenance of social relationships' (Aston, 1988, p. 18). When engaging in comity, FL interactants are looking for meaningful relationships as they seek to establish a level of rapport and supportiveness. Comity may be characterised through interpersonal convergence, appreciation of others and affiliation to others' objectives as interactants identify common ground and establish social harmony. Comity means that relational work is focused on constructing relationships with other

54 *Positioning foreign language politeness*

interactants rather than following the dictates of good manners and appropriate behaviour. As argued by Aston, supportive acts often involve making other interactants feel good through face-boosting acts (FBA) (Bayraktaroğlu, 1991, 2001) and endorsing others' wants and celebrating their successes which may be expressed through the use of 'compliments, congratulations, offers, invitations, thanks' (Aston, 1988, p. 107).

- Solidarity sees interactants deepening their relationships as they share common ground/points of view, reciprocal feelings and shared ways of seeing and interacting in the world. Solidarity reflects camaraderie, empathy, likemindedness and 'involves participants sharing similar wants, in the sense that A's wants for A are the same as B's wants for B. … [T] his can be produced by the hearer's finding, as a contextual effect, that he has wants for himself which match those of the speaker for himself' (Aston, 1988, p. 226). It often manifests itself through self-disclosure, troubles telling and gossip as interactants share problems and evaluations of others. Self-disclosure involves divulging personal and perhaps confidential information as interactants build trust and confide in each other. Troubles telling also implies a degree of intimacy as 'people talk about their troubles' (Jefferson, 1984, p. 346). Gossip, on one level, reflects "news about the personal affairs of another" (Bergmann, 1993, p. 45). This allows interactants to construct a degree of trust in one another. However, on another level and with regard to relational talk '[g]ossip transmits information in order to teach and reinforce group norms. Gossip thus contributes to group cohesion, serves as a means to create stronger group identification, and helps to clarify group boundaries ….' (Nevo, Nevo & Derech-Zehavi, 1994, p. 181).
- Independence reflects the objective of bilingual speakers to establish their own identity in the TL and attempt to define their own way of being polite which may reflect both their L1 norms and practices and those of the TL and perhaps creating a 'third place' (Cohen, 2018; Kramsch, 1993) as FL users to take ownership of politeness as they determine the presentation of the self and their degree of relational commitment in a given context. At the same time, independence may involve analysing their position vis-à-vis other TL speakers. Given that they are interacting in a second or third language, FL users may not feel that they are on an equal communicative footing as they struggle to express themselves in another language. They may even feel that they are continually under pressure (or even subdued/subjugated) to conform to prescribed societal standards and constantly evaluated with regard to their language proficiency.

Politeness resources

In a given social/transactional encounter, interactants call upon different politeness assets with which to establish, maintain or conduct a given

Positioning foreign language politeness 55

relationship. FL interactants need to construct and, just as importantly, access a databank of resources which can be retrieved quickly and successfully when under communicative pressure.

Resources are often described in terms of pragmalinguistic and sociopragmatic knowledge and resources (Leech, 1983; Thomas, 1983). Pragmalinguistics relates to 'the resources for conveying communicative acts and relational and interpersonal meanings. Such resources include pragmatic strategies such as directness and indirectness, routines and a large range of linguistic forms which can intensify or soften communicative acts' (Rose & Kasper, 2001, p. 2). Meanwhile, sociopragmatics 'refers to the knowledge of how to select an appropriate choice given a particular goal in a particular setting' (O'Keeffe, Clancy & Adolphs, 2011, p. 137). Pragmalinguistic and sociopragmatic knowledge and resources offer an identifiable and dependable way to interact in the TL as proposed by Leech:

> The learner in the environment of a foreign culture will need to adapt to that culture, albeit partially and gradually, if the pragmatic communication is to be successful. For learning English, this may require pragmalinguistic adjustment – for example, learning to use indirect distinctive formulae such as *Could you give me a cup* rather than relying too heavily on the imperative *Give me a cup*. It can also require sociopragmatic accommodation, such as learning to reply positively rather than negatively to a compliment. The sociopragmatics of politeness in two distinct cultures can be so different that what is normal in one language, if translated into another, may be face-threatening (either for *S* or for *H*). A learner, wishing to communicate like an NS* in English, may feel under pressure to acquire new "face," something that impinges on her/his identity.
>
> (2014, p. 263)

*Native speaker

Whilst the distinction between pragmalinguistic and sociopragmatic knowledge and resources is useful for FL speakers interacting in new and novel situations, there is a risk that bilingual speakers select what is available rather than examining how they want to express/present themselves and convey the desired degree of commitment/involvement. Bilingual speakers may want to express a degree of individuality in the TL context. As argued by van Compernolle (2014), what is more important is sociopragmatic competence which includes production and interpretation of cultural factors:

> As language users, we employ linguistic resources with an objective in mind, and we use our knowledge of sociocultural schemas to choose the resources that can be used to achieve the goals the way we want to

56 *Positioning foreign language politeness*

achieve them…. In other words, we can *choose* to conform or reject conventions of appropriate social behaviour because we know what the consequences of doing one thing or another may be given present circumstances.

(p. 4, author's italics)

FL users must be given choices and opportunities which must be respected in a pedagogical framework. It is important that learners develop socio-pragmatic competence so that they can engage in prosocial politeness as outlined by Leech (2014) or achieve individually defined goals as outlined by van Compernolle. (The concept of sociopragmatic competence is developed in Chapter 6.)

Conclusion

This chapter has demonstrated that politeness gives bilingual speakers choices in how they want to construct, establish and maintain interpersonal and transactional relationships in the TL society. Intercultural interaction is not about selecting an appropriate politeness structure and implementing in an easily identifiable context but, rather, as Janney and Arndt argue:

Being interculturally tactful, we will claim, is a complicated skill that involves much more than simply translating politeness formulas from one language into another.

(2005, p. 21)

Politeness behaviour should reflect what learners need and are looking for rather than displaying imposed politeness from pedagogy. FL users need to position themselves and determine how politeness assets can help them achieve their communicative objectives within a specific community. By positioning politeness as a plan of action, bilingual interactants can invest in politeness assets as they develop a critical language awareness that helps them participate in the TL context in their own way. In the next chapter, I examine how bilingual interactants employ prosocial politeness resources that allow them to participate in expected and conventional ways.

References

Archer, D., Aijmer, K., & Wichmann, A. (2012). *Pragmatics: An advanced resource book for students*. London/New York: Routledge.

Aston, G. (1988). *Learning comity: An approach to the description and pedagogy of interaction speech*. Bologna: Cooperativa Libraria Universitaria Editrice Bologna.

Bayraktaroğlu, A. (1991). Politeness and interactional imbalance. *International Journal of the Sociology of Language*, *92*, 5–34.

Positioning foreign language politeness 57

Bayraktaroğlu, A. (2001). Advice-giving in Turkish: "Superiority" or "solidarity"? In A. Bayraktaroğlu & M. Sifianou (Eds.), *Linguistic politeness across boundaries: The case of Greek and Turkish* (pp. 177–208). Amsterdam: John Benjamins.

Bergmann, J. R. (1993). *Discreet indiscretions: The social organization of gossip.* New Brunswick/London: Aldiner Transaction.

Block, D. (2003). *The social turn in second language acquisition.* Edinburgh: Edinburgh University Press.

Bolitho, R., Carter, R., Hughes, R., Ivanič, R., Masuhara, H., & Tomlinson, B. (2003). Ten questions about language awareness. *ELT Journal, 57*(3), 251–259.

Bourdieu, P. (1972). *Outline of a theory of practice.* Cambridge: Cambridge University Press.

Bourdieu, P. (1980). *The logic of practice.* Stanford: Stanford University Press.

Bourdieu, P. (1991). *Language & symbolic power.* Cambridge: Polity Press.

Brown, P. & Levinson, S. (1978). Universals in language usage: politeness phenomenon. In E. Goody (ed.), *Questions and Politeness Strategies in Social Interaction,* Cambridge: Cambridge University Press.

Brown, P., & Levinson, S. (1987). *Politeness: Some universal in language usage.* Cambridge: Cambridge University Press.

Carter, R. (2003). Key concepts in ELT: Language awareness. *ELT Journal, 57*(1), 64–65.

Clark, R., & Ivanič, R. (1999). Raising critical awareness of language: A curriculum aim for the new millennium. *Language Awareness, 8*(2), 63–70.

Cohen, A. D. (2018). *Learning pragmatics from native and nonnative language teachers.* Bristol: Multilingual Matters.

Coupland, J. (2000). Introduction: Sociolinguistic perspectives on small talk. In J. Coupland (Ed.), *Small talk* (pp. 1–25). Harlow, Essex: Pearson.

Culpeper, J. (2011). Politeness and impoliteness. In G. Andersen & K. Aijmer (Eds.), *Pragmatics of society* (pp. 393–438). Berlin/Boston: De Gruyter Mouton.

Culpeper, J. (2012). (Im)politeness: Three issues. *Journal of Pragmatics, 44,* 1128–1133.

Curcó, C. (2007). Positive face, group face, and affiliation: An overview of politeness studies on Mexican Spanish. In M. E. Placencia & C. García (Eds.), *Research on politeness in the Spanish-speaking world* (pp. 105–120). Mahwah: Laurence Erlbaum.

Cutting, J., & Fordyce, K. (2021). *Pragmatics: A resource book for students.* Abingdon, UK: Routledge.

De Bot, K., & Kroll, J. F. (2010). Psycholinguistics. In Norbert Schmitt (Ed.), *An introduction to applied linguistics* (2nd Edition, pp. 124–142). London: Routledge.

Derlega, V. J., Winstead, B. A., Wong, P. T. P., & Greenspan, M. (1987). Self-disclosure and relationship development: An attributional analysis. In M. E. Roloff & G. R. Miller (Eds.), *Interpersonal processes: New directions in communication research* (pp. 172–187). Newbury Park, CA: Sage Publications, Inc.

Donmall, B. G. (Ed.). (1985). *Language awareness.* NCLE Papers and Reports 6. London: Centre for Information on Language Teaching and Research.

Edmondson, W. (1981). *Spoken discourse: A model for analysis.* Harlow, Essex, UK: Longman.

Edmondson, W., & House, J. (1981). *Let's talk and talk about it.* München-Wien-Baltimore: Urban & Schwarzenberg.

58 Positioning foreign language politeness

Eelen, G. (2001). *A critique of politeness theories*. Manchester: St. Jerome.

Fairclough, N. (1992). *Discourse and social change*. Cambridge, UK: Polity Press.

Fraser, B. (1990). Perspectives on politeness. *Journal of Pragmatics, 14*, 219–236.

Gabbott, M., & Hogg, G. (2001). The role of non-verbal communication in service encounters: A conceptual framework. *Journal of Marketing Management, 17*(1–2), 5–26.

Goffman, E. (1959). *The presentation of self in everyday life*. London: Penguin.

Goffman, E. (1967). *Interactional ritual: Essays on face-to-face behaviour*. New York: Double Day Books.

Grainger, K. (2011). "First Order" and "Second Order" politeness: Institutional and intercultural contexts. In Linguistic Politeness Research Group (Ed.), *Discursive approaches to politeness* (pp. 167–188). Berlin: Mouton de Gruyter.

Grainger, K., & Mills, S. (2016). *Directness and indirectness across cultures*. Basingstoke, Hampshire, UK: Palgrave Macmillan.

Grenfell, M. (2011). *Bourdieu, language and linguistics*. London: Continuum.

Hall, E. (1959). *The silent language*. Garden City, NY: Doubleday.

Hall, E. (1969). *The hidden dimension*. Garden City, NY: Doubleday.

Haugh, M. (2011), Epilogue. In D. Z. Kádár & S. Mills (Eds.), *Politeness in East Asia* (pp. 252–264). Cambridge: Cambridge University Press.

Janney, R., & Arndt, H. (2005). Intracultural tact versus intercultural tact. In R. Watts, S. Ide, & K. Ehlich (Eds.), *Politeness in language: Studies in its history, theory and practice*, Trends in Linguistics, Studies and Monographs, 59. (pp. 21–41). Berlin: Mouton de Gruyter.

Jefferson, G. (1984). On stepwise transition from talk about a trouble to inappropriately next-positioned matters. In M. Atkinson & J. C. Heritage (Eds.), *Structures of social interaction: Studies in conversation analysis* (pp. 191–222). Cambridge: Cambridge University Press.

Johnson, K. (1996). *Language teaching & skill learning*. Oxford: Blackwell.

Kádár, D. Z., & Haugh, M. (2013). *Understanding politeness*. Cambridge: Cambridge University Press.

Kramsch, C. (1993). *Context and culture in language teaching*. Oxford: Oxford University Press.

Lakoff, R. (1973). The logic of politeness; or minding your p's and q's. *Papers from the 9th Regional Meeting of the Chicago Linguistic Society*, Chicago: Chicago Linguistic Society, 292–305.

Lakoff, R. (2005). Civility and its discontents: Or, getting in your face. In R. Lakoff & S. Ide (Eds.), *Broadening the horizon of linguistic politeness* (pp. 23–43). Philadelphia: John Benjamins.

Leech, G. (1983). *Principles of pragmatics*. London: Longman.

Leech, G. (2007). Politeness: Is there an East-West divide? *Wai Guo Yu; Journal of Foreign Languages, 6*, 3–31.

Leech, G. (2014). *Pragmatics of politeness*. Oxford: Oxford University Press.

Mills, S. (2017). *English politeness and class*. Cambridge: Cambridge University Press.

Mills, S., & Kádár, D. (2011). Politeness and culture. In D. Kádár & S. Mills (Eds.), *Politeness in East Asia* (pp. 21–44). Cambridge: Cambridge University Press.

Nevo, O., Nevo, B., & Derech-Zehavi, A. (1994). The tendency to gossip as a psychological disposition: Constructing a measure and validating it. In Robert F. Goodman & Aaron Ben-Ze'ev (Eds.), *Good gossip* (pp. 180–189). Lawrence, Kansas: University Press of Kansas.

Positioning foreign language politeness 59

Norton, B. (2000). *Identity and language learning: Gender, ethnicity and educational change*. Harlow, England: Pearson Education.

O'Keeffe, A., Clancy, B., & Adolphs, S. (2011). *Introducing pragmatics in use*. Abingdon, Oxford: Routledge.

Richmond, V., McCroskey, J., & Payne, S. (1991). *Non-verbal behaviour in interpersonal relations*. Hoboken, NJ: Prentice Hall.

Rose, K., & Kasper, G. (2001). *Pragmatics in language teaching*. Cambridge: Cambridge University Press.

Schmidt, R. (1995). Consciousness and foreign language learning: A tutorial on the role of attention and awareness in learning. In R. Schmidt (Ed.), *Attention and awareness in foreign language learning* (Technical Report 9, pp. 1–63). Honolulu: University of Hawaii, Second Language Teaching and Curriculum Center.

Scollon, R., & Scollon, S. (1995). *Intercultural communication*. Oxford: Blackwell.

Spencer-Oatey, H., & Kádár, D. (2021). *Intercultural politeness*. Cambridge: Cambridge University Press.

Svennevig, J. (1999). *Getting acquainted in conversation: A study of initial interactions*. Amsterdam: John Benjamins.

Taguchi, N., & Roever, C. (2017). *Second language pragmatics*. Oxford: Oxford University Press.

Terkourafi, M. (2005). Beyond the micro-level in politeness research. *Journal of Politeness Research, 1*(2), 237–262.

Thomas, J. (1983). Cross-cultural pragmatic failure. *Applied Linguistics, 4*, 91–112.

Thomas, J. (1995). *Meaning in interaction: An introduction to pragmatics*. Harlow, UK: Routledge.

Thornbury, S., & Slade, D. (2006). *Conversation: From description to pedagogy*. Cambridge: Cambridge University Press.

Tracy, K., & Robles, J. S. (2013). *Everyday talk: Building and reflecting identities*. New York: Guildford Press.

van Compernolle, R. A. (2014). *Sociocultural theory and L2 instructional pragmatics*. Bristol, UL: Multilingual Matters.

Watts, R. J. (2003). *Politeness*. Cambridge: Cambridge University Press.

Wink, J. (2011). *Critical pedagogy: Notes from the real world*. Boston: Pearson.

3 Prosocial politeness

Introduction

When learning and communicating in another language, interactants often want to make sure that they are participating in proper, expected and appropriate ways. In other words, they want to follow societal rules and adhere to social norms of behaviour. At the same time, they want to come across as politely as possible and not commit any faux pas. To achieve these interactional objectives, FL users will often employ *prosocial politeness*. Prosocial politeness involves behaving in socially acceptable ways, caring for others and presenting oneself as a 'polite' person which means having the necessary pragmatic resources and also being able to access them. Prosocial politeness embraces both social norm and addressee-focused politeness. As discussed in Chapter 2, social-norm politeness involves appropriate interactional behaviour, safe topics, appropriate body language and cultural behaviour. Addressee-focused politeness prioritises the hearers' relational needs and downplays speakers' own communicative wants. The concept of prosocial politeness can be understood through Halliday's (1973/1997) ideational function of language as this highlights the content component to politeness. The ideational function reflects interlocutors' understandings, experiences and key events and can help highlight politeness practices and patterns.

The first step to understanding prosocial politeness involves identifying TL understandings of politeness and distinguishing FL users' own concepts and experiences with the aim of comprehending how they approach relational work, i.e. building, developing and maintaining transactional and interpersonal relations. This can be viewed across three overlapping dimensions: linguistic, social and cultural. The linguistic reveals lay people's politeness language whether it be formulaic language, the use of indirectness, appropriate speech acts, etc. The social dimension highlights group and individual interactional behaviour, e.g. showing respect, being attentive to others' needs and demonstrating consideration. Meanwhile, the cultural dimension reflects values, attitudes and beliefs associated with politeness e.g. deference, self-esteem and consideration of others. In FL interaction, the cultural dimension deserves special attention since

DOI: 10.4324/9781003326052-3

Prosocial politeness 61

language users may face politeness behaviour and practices that significantly contrast with their own L1 experiences.

The second step involves identifying what FL users understand by being polite and whether politeness is purely instrumental and self-serving, whether it helps interactants get along with each other or if it aids societal cohesion and wellbeing. Understanding FL users' motivation to be polite should strongly influence pedagogic approaches to presenting, analysing and practising politeness in the language classroom. For instance, a product approach to politeness that focuses on end results offers established patterns of behaviour that help learners achieve communicative objectives. In contrast, a process approach sees politeness as evolving over the course of a given interaction as interlocutors construct and consolidate relationships.

In order to respond to learners' product/process objectives, FL teachers very often focus on teaching prosocial politeness. Such an approach can provide a degree of communicative security. To do so, however, FL teachers face the challenge of having to go beyond identifying interactional routines, conventional language use and established behavioural patterns. They also have to give FL users an element of choice so that they can employ available politeness assets and resources to achieve both transactional and interpersonal goals. Formulaic and overly-restrictive politeness sequences may not help FL users engage in meaningful individual and social action. Furthermore rigid and impersonal politeness structures and practices may hinder FL interlocutors' attempts to navigate day-to-day interactional challenges and barriers found in both transitory and more permanent interpersonal relationships.

To examine prosocial politeness within the context of FL interaction, the chapter is structured in the following way. First of all, I examine more closely the concept of prosocial politeness from lay perspectives in English and highlight which practices are accessible to FL users in terms of language usage, social behaviour and cultural conventions. Secondly, I outline how Halliday's ideational function provides a framework for examining how FL users' approach prosocial politeness. Such an approach privileges FL users' perspectives which are often downplayed in favour of 'native speaker' opinions and assessments. These are often based on intuition, supposition and ethnocentricity and frequently lack a useful and practical framework for FL users. Indeed the label 'native speaker' gives an unsubstantiated air of superiority when set against the term 'nonnative speaker.' Furthermore, the label 'nonnative speaker' undermines and devalues FL users' communicative achievements, language proficiency and linguistic abilities as discussed, for instance in Braine (2010), Mugford (2022) and Mugford and Rubio Michel (2018). Thirdly, I examine 'lay' constructs behind prosocial politeness which offer insights into how FL users engage in TL politeness. These include what it means to be polite, cultural understandings of politeness, the motivation to be polite and established patterns of behaviour. Fourthly, the chapter examines how FL users can be

62 *Prosocial politeness*

helped to engage in conventional, appropriate and customary politeness and cultural behaviour whilst maintaining a degree of choice with regards to how they want to interact with TL interlocutors. Finally, the chapter draws up implications for FL teaching with a focus on how FL users can exploit pertinent histories, relevant experiences and first-hand knowledge of social politeness from their own L1.

Prosocial politeness

To help understand TL lay perceptions of politeness, FL speakers and teachers can examine everyday usage and expressions, displays of social behaviour and ordinary cultural conventions. This may provide more perceptive insights than asking interlocutors for their definitions of politeness which may depict prescriptive norms rather than highlight actual descriptive behaviour. The challenge for FL teachers is to help their students understand TL daily practice which may contrast with their students' L1 performance and behaviour. Rather than subscribe to identifying theoretical behavioural concepts, this section highlights the value and usefulness of observing TL behaviour.

By conducting their own research and investigation, FL users can examine the communicative meanings behind colloquial TL language usage as everyday conventional expressions all too often uncover intended and actual polite behaviour. Expressions may reveal, for instance, how interactants see the role of politeness in trying to maintain harmonious relationships e.g. *I was making polite conversation; I was asking out of politeness*; and *I was being more than polite.* Such expressions disclose attempts to establish common ground and arrive at joint understandings. On the other hand, interlocutors may assert that they are merely adhering to expected normative behaviour, e.g. *I was just trying to be polite; We are so polite; It's just a polite request.* This position reveals interactants' lack of affinity or identification with others whilst perhaps trying to establish an acceptable level of social collaboration. Besides seeking social harmony and following conventional behaviour, utterances may also ask other interactants to respect social norms, e.g. *Can you ask politely?; Didn't your mother ever tell you to say please?; Whatever happened to your manners?* Expressions, therefore, take on a regulatory function and reference expected norms of behaviour. Remarks may even be an overt admission that interactants do not always see themselves as behaving politely e.g. *I'm not always so polite; Excuse/pardon my French; I'm usually very direct.* Colloquial language use may also be judgemental regarding the social behaviour of others, e.g. *They are not our kind of people; He's a bit above his station; It's not the done thing.* To summarise, an examination of on-the-ground colloquial language usage can provide valuable insights into everyday attitudes and commonplace practice and consequently allow FL users to examine TL speakers' stances regarding politeness in actual communicative contexts.

Prosocial politeness 63

The enactment of politeness in social behaviour may be expressed to varying degrees depending on the nature of the interaction and the relationship with other participants. Observation and scrutiny allow FL users to develop contextually based understandings regarding TL politeness patterns and practices. For instance, at a macro level, FL users can examine conversational practices, friendly encounters and business transactions. For example, FL users can explore the structure of conversation, its different purposes and features, turn-taking practices, topic development etc. At a micro level, students can, for instance, uncover the various components of greetings sequences, stages in saying goodbye and thank you routines. For example, in everyday conversation, politeness comes into play when changing the topic (e.g. *I know this wasn't what we were talking about but could I....*), interrupting other interlocutors (e.g. *I'm sorry to butt in but....*) or ending a conversation (e.g. *I mustn't keep you any longer.*). 'Thank you' routines may involve demonstrating appreciation/downplaying the act/ restating gratefulness/offering to reciprocate the action on another occasion or at a later date. Actual social behaviour allows FL users to see politeness as a negotiated process rather than as a series of appropriate utterances.

Cultural conventions reflect perceived normative attitudes towards displays of politeness and how people are expected to behave in 'polite society.' These may emerge from generalisations, stereotypes and societally prescribed behaviour as people are told to *Mind your Ps and Qs* or that *Manners makest the man*. Cultural precepts are often based on actual or perceived cultural conventions with which given community identifies. So, building on Fox's (2004) work for instance, English people may want to display good manners, pursue contrived modesty and emphasise orderliness. These may be expressed verbally and nonverbally. For example, good manners may be expressed verbally through endless streams of *sorry* and *please* or speakers may be told to mind/watch their language or not 'overstep the mark.' Modesty may be seen by not excessively talking about oneself by appearing to be reserved and not appearing to make a fuss by complaining, moaning and whining. Orderliness may be seen through the need to plan/schedule one's daily activity and through the cultural habit of queuing whether it be waiting for a bus, ordering a pint at the pub or waiting to be served at the local shop. Comparisons and contrasts regarding relational behaviour and cultural conventions between the L1 and the TL enable assumptions, conjectures and explanations to be questioned, rejected or confirmed.

Members of a given TL speech community may not identify with the proclaimed politeness conventions, nor even want to do so. For instance, working class interlocutors may reject perceived middle-class norms and practices. FL interactants may, at this point, look for guidance and advice. France argues that '[p]oliteness means learning to accommodate to others within a given social group' (1992, p. 5). Such statements open the way for

64 *Prosocial politeness*

etiquette and politeness 'experts' to enter the stage with pronouncements regarding how they think people ought to behave or fulminate against people who are no longer behaving in the way they should. For instance, Truss (2005) sees an alarming decline in overall civility as conveyed in her book's title: *Talk to the Hand: The Utter Bloody Rudeness of the World Today, or Six Good Reasons to Stay Home and Bolt the Door.* Meanwhile, Lakoff (2005), as discussed in Chapter 2, argues there is an unwelcome shift in everyday politeness norms and behavioural standards.

When it comes to discussing and examining everyday language usage and expressions, displays of social behaviour and ordinary cultural conventions, language teachers face the challenge of trying to convey TL practices and patterns without setting themselves up as explainer-in-chief and final arbitrator of acceptable and appropriate TL relational behaviour. This situation may be even more difficult for teachers who have had limited contact with TL cultures. Nevertheless, lay perceptions of politeness play an important role in FL teaching and learning since students more often than not enter the language classroom with their experiences, perceptions, generalisations and stereotypes regarding the relational behaviour of TL speakers. On a practical level, students want to know what it means to be polite in TL society, how they should view others' politeness practices and convey their own, and what resources are available that will allow them to achieve this goal. In other words, they may want to know what a 'polite person' in such-and-such a culture is and they will more-often-than-not want to come across as this 'polite' person.

Structuring prosocial politeness

Lay perspectives of prosocial politeness provide the groundwork for developing theoretical basis for understanding TL politeness practices and patterns. At the same time, it is important to examine and explore head-on FL users' encounters and experiences with TL relational behaviour and not discount them as merely misunderstood, misinterpreted or unrepresentative events. Real-life events and critical incidents reflect everyday challenges that FL interlocutors face and deal with and decontextualised textbook examples and precepts may offer little practical guidance and direction. In contrast, Halliday's ideational function facilitates the examination, analysis and discussion of actual language use rather than abstract and isolated language patterns and examples. In terms of prosocial politeness, Halliday's ideational function offers a way to examine the content of polite utterances and encounters as interactants employ the 'function as a means of the expression of our experience, both of the external world and of the inner world of our own consciousness' (Halliday, 1973/1997, p. 36). This means analysing events, making sense of activities and understanding what interactants are trying to achieve. As described by Halliday, the ideational function

Prosocial politeness 65

represents the speaker's meaning potential as an observer. It is the content function of language, language as 'about something'. This is the component through which the language encodes the cultural experience, and the speaker encodes his own individual experience as a member of the culture. It expresses the phenomena of the environment: the things – creatures, objects, actions, events, qualities, states and relations – of the world and of our own consciousness, including the phenomena of language itself.

(1978, p. 112)

Reflecting ongoing language use, contact with the TL inevitably causes FL interlocutors to reflect on the actions of other interactants, the meaning(s) behind everyday events and different ways of doing things, especially since relational work may not be performed in the same way. At the same time, the ideational function reflects 'language as expressing the speaker's experience of the external world, and of his own internal world, that of his own consciousness' (Halliday, 1978, p. 45). As argued by Eggins and Slade, this function allows speakers to 'focus on the ideational meanings: this involves looking at what topics get talked about, when, by whom, and how topic transition and closure is achieved, etc.' (1997, p. 49). Within this context, prosocial politeness reflects the 'communication role' (Halliday & Hasan, 1976, p. 240) that interactants are seeking to adopt in a given encounter. Given their experience of both L1 and the TL worlds, FL interlocutors will seek out structure and follow logic which gives them the potential to achieve a range of TL communicative objectives in relational work. This can be provided through prosocial politeness.

Constructs behind prosocial politeness

To engage in prosocial politeness FL users can collect information about polite language, polite actions and polite responses so as to engage in normally appropriate and acceptable ways that are seen as considerate and beneficial to other interactants. These actions can be described in terms of conventional language, accepted practices, rituals, principles, universals, maxims, etc. They provide structured ways to approaching politeness as 'they treat communication as rationalist and objectifiable' (Culpeper, 2008, p. 19). FL users will often seek these out as they provide guidelines with regards to how to participate in given situations and how to interact with others.

Given potential cross-cultural challenges regarding relational behaviour when engaging in with TL interactants, teachers need to explore how FL users can view linguistic politeness, politeness and culture, motivations for being polite. Furthermore, they need to know what the FL users' concepts of conventional behaviour are and analyse the FL users' experiences of politeness. Like Sifianou (1992), I want to see how FL users understand politeness rather than approach the concept from a theoretical viewpoint.

66 *Prosocial politeness*

This will involve what it means to be polite, along with cultural understandings of politeness, the motivation to be polite and what are seen as established patterns of behaviour and FL users' experiences of politeness.

Polite people

FL users approach TL politeness with their own understandings, attitudes and experiences of what politeness looks like. Perceptions and evaluations reflect how FL users 'present' themselves and how they view others. Especially in terms of prosocial politeness, teachers need to understand how students view TL politeness practices so that students can react and interact in socially meaningful ways in TL encounters,

Brown and Levinson approach prosocial politeness through the concept of the Model Person who 'is a wilful fluent speaker of a natural language, further endowed with two special properties – rationality and face' (1987, p. 58). They define rationality as 'a precisely definable mode of reasoning from ends to means that will achieve those ends' (1987, p. 58). As Terkourafi (2005) argues 'rationality' assumes that all interactants approach politeness in the same way. However, this may not be the reality given FL interactants' different sociocultural backgrounds, attitudes, judgements and beliefs. Meanwhile, face consists of two wants: to be given freedom of action and to be accepted and approved of by other interactants. This approach reflects an individualistic approach to politeness and potentially ignores interactants' socially-oriented concept of face (Kasper, 2009). Although they pitch it as tongue in cheek, Brown and Levinson's Model Person would be difficult to construct with regards to foreign language users due to cross-cultural differences regarding rationality and contrasting understandings of face. Therefore, in this chapter I pursue FL users' own understandings of politeness.

Asking FL users to define politeness may not be particularly productive as answers may be more prescriptive and focus on what should happen rather than what actually occurs. Furthermore, answers may be characterised by predictable labelling and classification with words such as *respect*, *consideration* and *manners* – whilst useful – may not provide insights into the workings and enactment of politeness. A more illustrative and revealing approach may emerge by asking FL speakers how they visualise a 'polite' person. Such an approach will hopefully reflect interlocutors' expectations, feelings, experiences, etc. Furthermore, FL users' answers provide the opportunity to analyse how FL speakers view politeness in terms of:

1   Interacting with others e.g. expressions of consideration, attentiveness and solicitousness.
2   Projecting oneself e.g. self-awareness, impression management and strategy avoidance.

Prosocial politeness 67

3   Conforming to society e.g. normative behaviour, accommodation and acculturation.
4   Expressing cultural background and upbringing e.g. expression of social values, forms of participation, interaction practices.

In terms of interacting with others, FL users' politeness practices and patterns can be seen through how interactants express consideration, show attentiveness and demonstrate concern for the needs of others. For instance, whilst consideration takes other needs into account, attentiveness

> means paying attention to others by reading the atmosphere in a situation and anticipating or inferring the other party's feelings, needs and wants through a potential recipient's' verbal and non-verbal cues.
>
> (Fukushima, 2019, p. 229)

Solicitousness goes even further as interactants respond to others' needs without even being asked. Therefore, FL interactants' responses identify how they position themselves with regard to others.

Whilst focusing on others' behaviour, prosocial politeness is also concerned with how one projects oneself and want to come across in the TL. This is expressed in terms of how one is perceived by others and the expressions that interactants *give* and *give off*:

> The first involves verbal symbols or their substitutes which he uses admittedly and solely to convey the information he and the others are known to attach to those symbols. This is communication in the traditional and narrow sense. The second involves a wide range of action that others can treat as symptomatic of the actor, the expectation being that the action was performed for reasons other than the information conveyed in this way.
>
> (Goffman, 1959, p. 14)

Therefore, FL speakers need to be mindful of not only what they say but also how what is said may be inferred or interpreted. With respect to prosocial politeness, verbal and nonverbal language may carry different meanings and understandings. Impression management embraces 'the goal-directed activity of controlling or regulating information in order to influence the impressions formed by an audience' (Schlenker, 2003, p. 492). Interactants often want to present themselves as considerate, concerned and supportive or as being restrained, composed and professional. Meanwhile, strategy avoidance involves employing interactional modes that can overcome potential awkward situations. For instance, Brown and Levinson's (1987) avoidance and off-record strategies (see Chapter 2) can aid TL interaction especially in terms of giving hints, asking rhetorical questions and employing the deliberate use of vague language e.g. the use of words such as *thingamajig* and *thingamabob*.

68 *Prosocial politeness*

Conforming to societal expectations through normative behaviour, accommodation and acculturation can be an enormous challenge for FL users who may have little or no experience of dealing with TL normative behaviour. However, answers can provide insights into whether learners adhere to traditional L1 ways of interacting or whether they follow TL standard practices. Conforming to societal expectations can also be examined through the concept of recipient design as FL users accommodate to TL modes of enacting politeness

> By recipient design we refer to a multitude of respects in which the talk by a party in a conversation is constructed or designed in ways which display an orientation and sensitivity to the particular other(s) who are the co-participants.
>
> (Sacks, Schegloff & Jefferson, 1974, p. 727)

With recipient design, interlocutors try to align themselves with their addressees and achieve a degree of accommodation which reflects 'the extent to which participants adjust to each other's communication and behavioural patterns' (Spencer-Oatey & Kádár, 2021, p. 208). With accommodation, FL users will often try to imitate, replicate or, at least, reflect TL polite conduct and practices. A key aspect of accommodation concerns convergence or 'the adaptation of one or both participants' behaviour to the other participant's behaviour' (Spencer-Oatey & Kádár, 2021, p. 208). Convergence offers one way to develop and maintain relationships with other interactants 'who want to cooperate and who want to be approved of will tend to converge' (Ylänne, 2008, p. 166). Therefore, recipient design and accommodation offer the means by which interactants can conform to societal expectations. From a prosocial politeness perspective, acculturation goes beyond accommodation and reflects interactants' immersion into the TL culture and the adoption of TL cultural beliefs, values and attitudes they integrate themselves into the TL community. Thornbury defines acculturation as 'the process by which a person integrates into a particular culture' (2006, p. 2). As a result, acculturation involves close identification with and adherence to TL norms of relational work especially when trying to attain membership of a specific speech community. However, FL interactants may find that too close an emulation of prosocial politeness may result in potential ridicule and rejection by TL speakers (Ferguson, 2006).

Interactants will often employ existing cultural resources and L1 experiences when engaging in prosocial politeness, whether consciously or not. Interactants will express their cultural background and upbringing especially in terms of social values, forms of participation and interactional practices. For instance, deference to others or social solidarity may be more important than achieving personal relational goals. For instance, Gu (1990) argues that Chinese politeness is both a societal and an individual

Prosocial politeness 69

construct. Therefore, TL politeness practices may focus more on reinforcing communal well-being, achieving social harmony and respecting social positioning or hierarchy. In a similar vein, Mexican politeness practices, for instance, *dar su lugar* (recognising others' social status) and *mostrar respeto* (demonstrate hierarchical respect) are important politeness considerations (Mugford, 2020). Therefore, when it comes to TL politeness behaviour, FL interactants may be at the disadvantage:

> It is not only that people may not know what counts as conventional behaviour in the other's culture, but their own behaviour, evaluations and interactional anticipations may be influenced by both (a) their own underlying perceptions of (in)appropriateness rooted in conventions, as well as (b) their own stereotypical/individual interpretations of the other's conceptions.
>
> (Spencer-Oatey & Kádár, 2021, p. 28)

At the same time, adhering to established forms of TL participation can be a daunting task for FL users when they are attempting to take part in conversations. They have to recognise when an utterance is finishing and take advantage of Turn-Construction Units (TCUs). Wong and Waring define a TCU as 'a word, a phrase, a clause, or a sentence that completes a communicative act' (2010, p. 16). Its importance emerges when interactants are trying to identify a transition-relevance place (TRP) that will allow them to participate in a given interaction.

> Why is the notion of TCU projectability important in language teaching? For one thing, in order to take a turn, one has to know when others are about to stop talking.… Without the ability to project TCU completion, one runs the risk of interrupting others or not getting a word in edgewise. Knowing how to project such completion also allows one to place response tokens (e.g. *uh huh, mm hmm, yeah*) at the right moments, thereby facilitating the back-and-forth flow of natural conversation.
>
> (Wong & Waring, 2010, p. 18)

After identifying TCUs and potential TRP, FL users have to understand turn-taking practices which Sacks et al. (1974) argue is orderly, rule-governed and systematic and allows interactants to achieve relational work with their TL interlocutors:

> It has become obvious that, overwhelmingly, one party talks at a time, though speakers change, and though the size of turns and ordering of turns vary; that transitions are finely coordinated; that techniques are used for allocating turns, whose characterization would be part of any model for describing some turn-taking materials; and that there are

70 *Prosocial politeness*

techniques for the construction of utterances relevant to their turn status, which bear on the coordination of transfer and on the allocation of speakership.

(p. 699)

With respect to prosocial politeness, turn-taking offers an identifiable and structured mode of engaging in relational work through turn-allocation (designation of the next speaker), possible turn transition places (anticipated turn completion) and self-selection (when interactants are able to propose themselves as the next speaker). Sacks et al.'s turn-taking rules can be compressed as follows as interactants try to take advantage of a potential TRP:

1   The current speaker has the right to select the next speaker and a transition may occur. If not ...
2   Self-selection allows the first person who speaks next to assume and acquire the right to speak. If not ...
3   The person speaking at the moment may (but is not required to) continue talking.
4   Interaction proceeds until the next potential TRP becomes available or a change of speaker takes place.

(Sacks et al., 1974)

Besides understanding TRPs and turn-taking practices, FL interlocutors also need to be mindful of other TL participatory practices such as ways of interrupting, changing the topic, returning to a previous topic and ending a conversation, etc. which significantly differ from their L1.

Meanwhile, interpreting and enacting interactional practices which reflect harmonious relational work may present significant communicative challenges for FL users. This are often described in terms of adjacency pairs (Paltridge, 2006) and preferred responses (Schegloff & Sacks, 1973). Adjacency pairs 'are utterances produced between two successive speakers in a way that the second utterance is identified as related to the first one as an expected follow-up to that utterance' (Paltridge, 2006, p. 115). Therefore, with respect to prosocial politeness, FL interactants need to recognise that first utterances may be expected to be followed by a recognisable response, that is

the second part in an adjacency pair may be preferred and others maybe dispreferred. For example, a question may be followed by an expected answer (the preferred second pair part) or an 'unexpected or non-answer' (the dispreferred second pair part). When this happens, the dispreferred pair part is often preceded by a 'delay', a 'preface' and/or an 'account'.

(Paltridge, 2006, p. 117)

Prosocial politeness 71

Politeness and culture

When describing polite people, FL interactants are highlighting values, attitudes and behaviour that are important to them and reflect their view of harmonious and well-organised social relations. From a lay perspective, the cultural dimension to prosocial politeness may be described in terms of education and upbringing, adherence to social norms and rules, consideration for others and presenting oneself in the best possible manner.

A key consideration for FL teachers is whether cultural norms, practices and expectations are culturally specific or whether there are universally applicable norms of behaviour. Brown and Levinson argue that universal principles are compatible with local culture application: 'We wish to emphasize here that our quite specific universal principles can provide the basis for an account of diverse differences in interaction' (1987, p. 242). So, for instance, Brown and Levinson might argue that the closeness/distance and power dimensions are to be found across societies but may be given different emphases by different speech communities.

On the other hand, from the users' point of the view, FL interactants come to the TL context with their own understandings of culture and they may express these at both societal level and at individual level. The task for FL teachers is to help learners understand such expressions of prosocial politeness and help them assess whether they are acceptable and feasible in the TL culture. For instance, in the Mexican culture it is customary to share food to such an extent that if someone is eating a customary lunchtime *lonche* (a bread roll filled with perhaps ham or pork accompanied by cheese and avocado) they may offer a bite to those around them. Whilst enacted as a sign of solidarity, such an intimate display of sharing may be frowned upon in other cultures.

Such reflection provides teachers with the means to encourage students to examine underlying meanings and implications behind their own and also TL politeness practices. For instance, Fox, in her self-examination of English social politeness, claims:

> ... our polite sorries, pleases and thank-yous are not heartfelt or sincere – there is nothing particularly warm or friendly about them. Politeness by definition involves a degree of artifice and hypocrisy, but English courtesy seems to be almost entirely a matter of form, of obedience to a set of rules rather than an expression of genuine concern.
>
> (2004, p. 408)

Such blunt and forthright candour may stimulate and incentivise FL teachers to take a good hard look at identifying, explaining and illustrating different ways in which people can be and are polite. For instance, politeness may not always reflect rapport and caring for others. One can also talk about:

72   *Prosocial politeness*

- forced politeness – being polite because it is socially necessary.
- perfunctory politeness – superficial and formulaic politeness.
- reciprocal politeness – being polite in response to someone else being polite.
- diplomatic politeness – being polite for the sake of being polite.

For instance, in the specific case of English politeness, Fox argues

> We are no more *naturally* modest, courteous or fair than any other culture, but we have more unwritten rules prescribing the *appearance* of these qualities, which are clearly very important to us.
>
> (2004, p. 404, author emphasis)

One way of helping learners examine and contrast prosocial politenesses practices is by presenting Brown and Levinson's concepts of positive and negative politeness in a simplified form. (For a full description, see Chapter 2.)

> **Positive politeness** wants the hearer to feel fully accepted, appreciated and liked as 'one of us', Positive politeness strategies may be expressed through acts of solidarity, supportiveness, sharedness, communality, etc.
>
> **Negative politeness** respects the hearers' desire to be left alone and not imposed upon and enjoy freedom of action. Negative politeness strategies may be expressed by respecting others' space and time, showing interpersonal distance, conveying indirectness, being tentative etc.
>
> (adapted from Brown & Levinson, 1987)

An understanding of positive and negative politeness strategies allows learners to recognise English 'negative politeness' characteristics such as reservedness, a focus on punctuality and acts of self-effacement. Meanwhile, Mexican expressions of closeness and familiarity, unexpected acts of kindness and cooperation reflect positive politeness traits.

Such reflection and analysis can help language learners realise that no country or people are any more polite than any other as recognised by Sifianou:

> ... despite popular stereotypes, no nation may be objectively verified as more or less polite than any other, but only polite in a different, culturally specific way.
>
> (1992, p. 2)

However, it may be a mistake to solely relate politeness to 'national' cultural characteristics, and culture also needs to be seen in terms of speech communities and communities of practice as this may go some way to deconstructing national stereotypes when it comes to describing and analysing politeness and culture.

Prosocial politeness 73

Since values, perceptions and the like appear to vary across cultures, politeness also seems to be a culture-specific phenomenon. This is often used to explain differences in norms of linguistic appropriateness behaviour.

(Kádár & Haugh, 2013, pp. 231–232)

Motivations to be polite

FL teaching has traditionally looked at motivation in terms of extrinsic and intrinsic motivation (Harmer, 2007). Extrinsic motivation would seem to come from external incentives e.g. achieving a job promotion, getting on with other people or having the possibility to travel overseas. In contrast, intrinsic motivation reflects internal incentives including identification with the TL, building up one's CV and success building on success. In terms of extrinsic motivation, politeness includes building and maintaining social relationships and developing rapport with TL speakers. Intrinsic motivational politeness means learners build up their confidence and meaningfulness in pursuing TL relationships as they boost their self-esteem and self-image.

Whilst providing insights into motivation, extrinsic and intrinsic approaches may fail to incentivise students in the day-to-day grind of the language classroom. A perhaps more productive and relevant approach can be gained through Norton's concept of investment:

The construct of investment seeks to make a meaningful connection between a learner's desire and commitment to learn a language, and the language practices of the classroom or community.

(2014, p. 62)

Norton argues that investment relates closely to Bourdieu's (1972, 1980, 1991) concept of cultural capital (See Chapter 2). Development of prosocial politeness can be closely linked to the construction of cultural capital as learners invest in ways of expressing themselves that may help them further develop their economic capital (e.g. monetary wealth and tangible assets) along with their social capital (e.g. network of social connections and relationships). Investment, especially in terms of prosocial politeness, seeks to obtain a 'return':

If learners 'invest' in the target language, they do so with the understanding that they will acquire a wider range of symbolic resources (language, education, friendship) and material resources (capital goods, real estate, money) which will in turn increase the value of their cultural capital and social power.

(Norton, 2013, p. 6)

74   Prosocial politeness

However, Norton stresses that investment is not the same as instrumental motivation:

> It is important to note that the notion of investment I am advocating is not equivalent to instrumental motivation. The conception of instrumental motivation presupposes a unitary, fixed, and a historical language learner who desires access to material resources that are the privilege of target language speakers. The notion of investment, on the other hand, conceives of the language learner as having a complex social history and multiple desires. The notion presupposes that when language learners speak, they are not only exchanging information with target language speakers, but they are constantly organizing and reorganizing a sense of who they are and how they relate to the social world. Thus an investment in the target language is also an investment in a learner's own identity, an identity which is constantly changing across time and space.
>
> (2013, pp. 50–51)

Therefore, investment allows learners to go beyond following societal rules and adhering to social norms of behaviour. It provides them with a framework with which to engage in affiliative and interactional politeness and this allows them to express more of their individuality (see Chapter 4).

Established patterns of behaviour

By engaging in prosocial politeness, FL users normally want a given encounter to run as smoothly as possible in terms of transactional and/or interactional talk. To facilitate successful communication, FL interlocutors are often willing to adopt TL social norms so as to satisfy other interlocutors' needs and wants even at the expense of satisfying other own wishes and requirements. Adherence to established patterns and practices of prosocial behaviour helps FL users to:

1   Achieve a degree of safe communicative ground which reflects standardised and accepted patterns of behaviour;
2   Seek convergence with TL interlocutors through emulating and mirroring their behaviour; and
3   Identify TL concepts and understandings of politeness from which they can engage in more individualised and creative politeness practices.

Safe ground

Whilst often erroneously thinking that TL politeness practices are similar to those in their L1, FL interlocutors need to establish safe 'ground' from which they can reflect on possible parallels and contrasts.

Prosocial politeness 75

An advantage of using a conventional pragmatic pattern to realise an instance of politeness is that the language user can remain on relatively safe grounds. Thus, by realising politeness behaviour in a conventional way, the language user deploys a practice that is shared by other social group members and can anticipate that the other will interpret this behaviour according to his or her intention.

(Spencer-Oatey & Kádár, 2021, p. 27)

Just because it appears to be enacted in similar ways in two languages, a given politeness practice may not convey the same underlying meaning and significance. Therefore, politeness should not necessarily be seen in terms of 'different ways of doing things,' but a given politeness practice or pattern may express a different meaning. Consequently, FL interactants should not be too quick to judge the significance of a given action. For instance, when someone casually runs across an old acquaintance and says *we must get together some time*, there is no real commitment to actually specify a date, time and place for a further encounter. The intention is merely a perfunctory way of saying that one would like to stay in contact. The action should not be interpreted as any deep-rooted desire to reconnect or strengthen a relationship.

Safe ground involves identifying patterns of behaviour that allow FL interlocutors to observe, analyse and reflect on their experiences of TL behaviour. Culpeper has described these in terms of:

* *Personal norms* based on the totality of X's social experiences
* *Cultural norms* based on the totality of X's experiences of a particular culture
* *Situational norms* based on the totality of X's experiences of a particular situation in a particular culture
* *Co-textual norms* based on the totality of X's experience of a particular interaction in a particular situation in a particular culture

(2008, p. 30)

As onlookers and participants, FL interlocutors can identify how politeness is enacted at language and cultural levels in given contexts. Personal norms may be based on previous contact with TL speakers, classroom instruction, EFL textbooks etc. Cultural norms can be identified through observing how communicative objectives are achieved in the TL culture e.g. apologising, complimenting or disagreeing. Situational norms can be garnered from examining communicative events e.g. going through immigration, asking for directions or ordering a meal. Co-textual events examine the overall experience which may be routine or deviate from expectations e.g. a bank clerk who is genuinely interested in where the FL client is from or the immigration officer who asks why the traveller's family is not flying with him/her. Whether there are ulterior motives behind the questioning is another matter.

76 *Prosocial politeness*

By following others and rather than being outside observers, FL users may want to try to integrate themselves into a social group and try and understand prosocial practices as an 'insider.' Such a strategy has a long history in FL learning (Aston, 1988; Fillmore, 1979; Gumperz, 1982). This does not necessarily mean that FL speakers want to be liked but rather that they want to immerse themselves socially and become part of a discourse community. For instance, Fillmore offers the following social and cognitive strategies adopted by young language learners (see Table 3.1):

Filmore's first strategy focuses on attaining membership rather than a full and complete understanding of what is going on interactionally. The cognitive strategy involves looking for connections and making sense of speaker contributions within the overall context. FL users seek to identify politeness practices and patterns. Filmore's second strategy is much more proactive and participative as FL users exploit language chunks and formulaic expressions, which would include prosocial politeness expressions. The third strategy relies on others to be sympathetic and understanding as one tries to participate in more engaging ways. Rather than comparing oneself with the proficiency of others, the communicative focus is on what one can do rather than on what one cannot do, and perhaps on what one can get away with by being a FL user. However, as Aston points out:

> It can however be argued that expecting interlocutors to be sympathetic may not in itself be enough to create conditions for learning: while relying on help may create opportunities for learning, actual learning may not take place unless the learner assumes responsibility for the gap in his knowledge ....
>
> (1988, p. 29)

Table 3.1 Cognitive and Social strategies

Social strategies	Cognitive strategies
S-1: Join a group and act as if you understand what's going on, even if you don't.	C-1: Assume that what people are saying is directly relevant to the situation at hand, or to what they or you are experiencing. Metastrategy: Guess!
S-2: Give the impression –with a few well-chosen words – that you can speak the language.	C-2: Get some expressions you understand and start talking.
S-3: Count on your friends for help.	C-3: Look for recurring parts in the formulas you know.
	C-4: Make the most of what you've got.
	C-5: Work on big things first; save the details for later.

Fillmore (1979, p. 209).

Prosocial politeness 77

Whilst referring to newcomers coming to a country, Gumperz also stresses the importance of networking:

> [L]earning to be effective in everyday communication on the part of culturally and linguistically distinct immigrants, is both a function of actual exposure to the new language and of the networks of associations that speakers form in the new setting.
>
> (1982, p. 57)

Trying to join networks can be an important step in experiencing first-hand everyday language and through which prosocial politeness practices and patterns are adhered to and observed.

Identifying TL concepts and understandings of politeness

Asking people about politeness can be extremely difficult as respondents may claim to do one thing but not actually carry it out in practice. Whilst asking about prosocial politeness norms and practices may be useful, there is no substitute for on the ground observation. On this basis, FL users are in a stronger position to explore their own ways of expressing prosocial politeness that allow a degree of individuality and creativity – hence the importance of ethnographic observation. Hymes identification of communicative competence offers a useful framework with which to observe TL prosocial pattern and practices. Hymes (1972) defined communicative competence as the ability to actively take decisions as to what is feasible, possible, appropriate and actually performed in interaction (pp. 284–286):

- Whether (and to what degree) something is formally possible
- Whether (and to what degree) something is feasible
- Whether (and to what degree) something is appropriate
- Whether (and to what degree) something is in fact done

These modes can help identify actual politeness and cultural practices (formally possible), what can actually be said or performed (in reality, viable), what is contextually suitable (appropriate) and what do TL interactants actually do (in fact done). Such observations can help FL users observe how TL users really engage with other interactants rather than relying on others' self-reports and purported politeness behaviour found in textbooks and politeness guides. As argued by Culpeper and Haugh, 'language use is inherently reflexive' (2021, p. 326) and, therefore, interactants FL users have to examine how others use language and, at the same time, 'we use language bearing in mind how we think others will understand and evaluate how we are using language' (2021, p. 326). From this position FL users can also identify and analyse those practices that they have in common with their L1 and those that differ.

78 *Prosocial politeness*

Experiences of prosocial politeness

Playing safe, examining motivation, following others, identifying concepts and understandings of politeness all help to appreciate how FL users approach TL politeness. However, in the final analysis greater insights can be gained from examining the experiences of FL users themselves especially in terms of how they conceive of politeness, engage in polite activity and how they see its relationship with culture. Therefore, the following section reports on the reflections of 52 Mexican FL users who evaluated TL interactional experiences which led them to form their attitudes and beliefs on everyday TL conduct. (For full details of the research approach, participants and procedure, see Chapter 1.)

Methodology

In order to understand prosocial politeness practices and patterns, I asked participants to respond to the following questions:

1   What is a polite person? Can you describe the characteristics of a polite person?
2   Is being polite closely related to both language and culture? If so, how?
3   Why are people generally polite and what do they want to achieve by being polite? Please explain your answer.
4   Does being polite involve following established patterns of behaviour? Please explain your answer.
5   Describe your experiences of politeness when speaking in English. Please give details of any incidents that you found to be significant.

(For full details of the research approach, participants and procedure, see Chapter 1.) As also mentioned in Chapter 1, responses have not been amended or 'corrected' so that the participants' 'voices' can be heard.

Results

The results reflect how FL speakers approach prosocial politeness practices in terms of what they want to achieve and their desire to participate in proper, expected and appropriate ways. The answers reveal that L1 considerations and practices appear to strongly influence TL conduct.

Question 1 attempts to understand how FL speakers view politeness practices by asking participants to characterise a 'polite person.' In doing so, interactants focused on the importance of how to interact with others, project oneself and conform to societal expectations. With respect to interacting with others, respondents emphasised the need to show respect and consideration. For instance, Fabiola stated that 'a polite person is considerate of other people, tactful and cares about the comfort of others' (1.7). She has an underlying

Prosocial politeness 79

concern for others' wellbeing. A similar attitude is conveyed by Delia who said 'A polite person is an individual that considers the other in his interactions. He or she doesn't impose on others nor makes them feel upset' (1.12). Therefore, interactants convey an identifiable interactive purpose behind politeness i.e. making other interactants feel good and putting them at ease. At the same time, participants also saw politeness as a means of self-projection. For example, Claudia said that a 'polite' person 'is someone who cares about giving a good impression, but not hypocritically. Also, is someone who understands that being polite is a way to show amicability, and a way to welcome people into their own activities and customs' (1.5). Meanwhile, Silvia emphasised the concept of image: 'A polite person is someone who can conduct himself/herself in an appropriate manner when interacting in a social environment, considering and respecting other people. A polite person to me is respectful, punctual, kind, generous and considerate' (1.20). Concurrently, interactants were well aware of the need to conform to societal expectations. For instance, Julieta said that 'In my opinion, a polite person is one who addresses people according to social rules. The characteristics would be respectful, kind and not self-centred' (1.1). Meanwhile, Angelica said,

A polite person is someone who follows certain sociocultural rules, such as greeting others when you arrive to a place, or saying, "thank you" and "you're welcome". Moreover, this person is a good listener, is respectful, approachable, and easy going.

(1.8)

A polite person who appears to be someone who follows the social rules, puts others first and conforms to societal norms.

Question 2 sought to find out whether participants related politeness with culture. Besides making comparisons between L1 and TL cultures, the answers revealed numerous instances of stereotyping and users' insights into the problematic nature of politeness. Respondents were more than aware of differences between the L1 and TL. For instance, Pedro noted that 'since polite practices are different between countries, so polite words and polite habits are determined by each culture' (2.14).

Meanwhile, Susana went further and argued that different people see the world differently:

Yes, politeness can be shown differently depending on cultures because people behave based on values, what they see and their environment. All that may influence as well as if the language they speak has a large variety of utterances that can be used to show politeness.

(2.31)

There was little focus on similarities or commonality between languages although Pablo noted: 'Yes, as every culture has its own customs politeness

80 Prosocial politeness

it's tied to it. However, some may share similar values such as respect, tolerance, etc.' (2.46). Similarities may offer opportunities for learners to make comparisons besides merely contrasting politeness practices between different cultures. Furthermore, numerous replies reflected stereotypical attitudes towards TL behaviour. For instance, Roberta states that

> For instance, in Mexico, we are used to greeting people when entering a room; the people in the room greet us back and this is considered a polite behavior. In the US, this does not seem to be a common practice. People who enter a room are not expected to greet other people in the room, and they do not interpret this as lack of politeness. I think this has to do with their culture, which, generally speaking, is considered to be less friendly and warm than Latin American cultures.
>
> (2.23)

Meanwhile, Eva contrasts her L1 compatriots with British speakers:

> I think that being polite is closely related to culture and language. There are some cultures that are considered to be politer. As a generalization I consider that British people are politer than Mexicans. I think we consider a culture to be politer than other based on language usage, use of gestures and culture norms.
>
> (2.27)

Such generalisations present teachers with an opportunity to examine the concept of positive and negative stereotyping (see Chapter 6). On a more constructive note, respondents were well aware of the problematic nature of politeness. For instance, Esmeralda recognises the problem of potentially confusing politeness practices: 'What is polite in some places for some people may not be polite in other places. It may actually be even the opposite. So, I think language and culture are really tied to politeness' (2.18). Going even further, Esteban argued that social politeness practices may be very different as, for instance, in time keeping:

> I can tell that punctuality is considered to be extremely polite and important in Germany, whereas in Mexico, punctuality does not play an important role, it can even be seen as weird or unusual to arrive punctual to a party. Not being punctual in Germany means not caring for the other person's time and it is seen as wasting valuable time that was previously and carefully planned, sometimes even with weeks in advance.
>
> (2.22)

Question 3 asked participants to reflect on the motivation behind being polite. Answers centred on upbringing, socialisation and self-interest. With respect to upbringing and parenting, Tomas maintains that:

Prosocial politeness 81

Most people are polite because that the way they were raise to be, it is a thing that is thought to children as a show of respect/good manners, however, when someone is being overly-polite it can come off as conceited or that they have something in mind.

(3.13)

This view is supported by Francesca who says:

I think people are generally polite because that's how we were raised and we like respect. As a Mexican, I also think it has to do with social practice, but it really depends. I have been close to different cultures and what is polite for me is not polite for them or it might just seem different.

(3.2)

These explanations may lead to examining concepts of politeness at the family, and perhaps more intimate, level and revealing their influence on the FL speakers' everyday lives. Socialisation was also considered to be an important motivation for polite conduct. For instance, Pablo noted that 'People are generally polite to be accepted in the community they are trying to fit in as this may help them achieve their personal goals' (3.46). Meanwhile, Daniel said that politeness is a way of trying to fit in: 'Personally, I believe that whilst we live in a society, we must be polite as much as possible, so we can get along and somehow have better relationships among us' (3.17). Answers revealed that interactants were well aware of the social function of politeness. Finally, self-interest was also seen as a key motivational factor as expressed by Cristina:

Well, here in Mexico being polite is a mean to get something you want. That is to convince someone that you are well intended, harmless even. It could also be used to show that one is educated in order to be treated with respect.

(3.52)

This self-serving impulse is often ignored in FL teaching. However, the respondents were well aware of this reason as asserted by Diana: 'They're polite because that's the way they were raised or maybe because they want something in return. It can depend on the context, situation or person' (3.41). Silvia went even further and said: 'Most of the people I would say are polite in order to obtain something' (3.20). These answers reveal the importance of understanding why FL users engage in politeness practices.

Question 4 examined whether polite behaviour reflected established patterns of behaviour which is a fundamental characteristic of prosocial politeness. Respondents described polite behaviour in terms of adhering to rules/patterns, following others' behaviour interactants and reading the

82 *Prosocial politeness*

room i.e. being aware of situational/contextual factors. Established norms and rules strongly influenced participants' politeness behaviour. For instance, Bernardo said that 'politeness can be seen as a set of rules established by people in society, and language is a vehicle for this behavioural patterns to be shown or not shown' (4.6). Therefore, Bernardo considered politeness to be mainly conveyed through language. This view is also supported by Alberto who maintains that 'Yes, being polite is tied to following the pre establish rules in society and one knows that they have to follow them to be accepted by the society' (4.37). Respondents noted that they often followed others established patterns when trying to be polite. For instance, Felipe maintained that:

> being polite is not something we learn through our own experience, but by following examples of people before us. In my case, it was because my grandparents showed me and taught me how to be polite. This is why I think being polite involves following established patterns we live and see in our family, community, or society.
>
> (4.11)

Imitating others' conduct was an important tool in adhering to prosocial politeness patterns. This view was echoed by Dafne: 'Familiar patterns are the most common when talking about being polite. Normally when there are polite parents, children grow-up watching this and they follow it' (4.29). However, interactants cannot just rely on observed behaviour and need to take into consideration contextual factors as argued by Teresa:

> Yes, there are re-established behavioural patterns that are expected to be followed in certain situations, that are considered polite, for example offering beverages to the visitors, or sitting or talking in a certain way. One can imprint one's own personality to such patterns, but if we deviate much from them, it is no longer considered politeness.
>
> (4.9)

Paloma agrees with this assessment as she 'reads the room':

> I think that certain situations do involve a pattern, for example when you arrive at a meeting you always greet the people in the room, sometimes you even do it in a hierarchy order to avoid disrespecting someone, we offer a beverage, a snack, etc. Generally, culturally, not greeting others when arriving at a reunion, a house that isn't yours, etc. it's a lack of respect.
>
> (4.35)

Respondents' adherence to perceived established patterns of behaviour offers teachers a way of structurally approaching TL politeness and offering a framework with which to engage in relational work.

Prosocial politeness 83

Question 5 offered an opportunity for respondents to reflect on their own experiences with TL politeness. Respondents often saw politeness an investment and they often made a conscious effort to be polite in everyday social encounters. Perhaps surprisingly, some interactants found it easier to be polite in English than in their L1. That politeness pays an interactional dividend was reported by José: 'Whenever I travel (travelled before the pandemy) and used English I always had a positive reaction from the listeners and I've always assumed that politeness has had a lot to do with it' (5.3). ('Pandemy' refers to Covid-19.) His observation was also echoed by Sandra: 'Politeness has always given me advantages in English. People treat you better. (5.48). Meanwhile, Guillermo was more explicit:

Being polite is very useful. Definitely, it can help you to deal with people in a simple way, effortlessly. I worked as a customer service advisor in a car dealership, I had to interact with different kinds of people in diverse circumstances. I learned that politeness has a tremendous weight value and sets the tone when communicating for the first time with others.

(5.21)

Reaping the rewards seems to come from making a conscious effort to be polite. For instance, Julia said: I always try my best to find the appropriate words to use in English to be 'I polite to whomever I'm talking to. I will admit that for me writing is easier than talking most of the times' (5.50). Paula said that she was more conscious of the need to be polite when interacting in the TL:

I think that when I speak in English I am even more aware of being polite because it is a second language for me and I believe I am a bit more careful when I talk to strangers. For example when I was in New York, I would approach people no matter their age by saying "Excuse me sir" and I noticed that they looked at me like thinking it was odd. Later on I learned that in New York it is ok to speak informally even to strangers or elders.

(5.10)

It is remarkable that interactants commented that they often found it easier to be polite in English. Eva reflected on the structural dimension to be being polite in the TL:

I think it is easier for me to be polite in English than in Spanish. I think there are specific words or phrases in English such as would, could, do you mind if… that already show politeness and that makes it easier to express it. On the other hand, I think it's hard to know when to show certain level of formality without sounding unnatural or like a book.

84 *Prosocial politeness*

> I like the fact that in English I do not have to change my register to talk to someone "de tú" or "de usted", however, that makes it more difficult to show politeness being necessary to use specific words to express it.
>
> (5.27)

[*Tú* and *usted* are different ways of expressing 'you' in Spanish, especially with respect to politeness.]

Delia was equally effusive:

> I find politeness in English to be simpler than the politeness in Spanish. Greetings and farewell in English are shorter, for instance. Most of my interactions in English nowadays are through email communications. I exchange many emails in English to multilingual speakers, and in Spanish with both monolingual and multilingual speakers. It is usually the case that emails in English are briefer in their greeting and farewell in comparison with Spanish.
>
> (5.12)

Respondents' observations provide important insights into how they feel about using politeness in the TL. These understandings offer meaningful opportunities with which to discuss with students their perceptions and attitudes and, therefore, allow teachers to respond more effectively to learners' needs.

Discussion

Question 1 reflects lay persons' L1 perceptions and expectations regarding how to interact in the TL community. Catering to the needs of others may be seen as particularly a Mexican concern to make others feel welcome and at ease. But there is also an underlying interest regarding how one is seen by others. It may be important to maintain one's image as an involved, educated and well-mannered person. Therefore, interactants will look for resources that take into consideration others' feelings and allow them to come across in the best light possible. This may be especially important for FL speakers interacting in a language that is not their own so that language mistakes can be offset by 'polite' behaviour. At the same time, interactants are keen to identify polite rules. Therefore, prosocial politeness has an important role to play in reassuring FL interactants in the way that they treat others, promote themselves and confirm to societal expectations and norms.

Question 2 attempted to understand respondents' perspectives on politeness and culture. Answers offer considerable grounds for examining why interactants focus on differences rather than on universal dimensions. Respondents' politeness concerns reflect consideration for others, respect

Prosocial politeness 85

and cordiality. Differences expressed through stereotyping and generalisations do not help interactants negotiate politeness on an individual basis nor does it promote interpersonal understandings. Stereotyping and generalisations potentially undermine cultural tolerance and understanding. Meanwhile the problematic nature of politeness and culture reveals that certain practices, on one hand, can open up unexpected ways of expressing politeness whilst, on the other, underscore confusion and complications.

Question 3 revealed that FL speakers were well aware of the motivations behind employing politeness resources. Given that upbringing and social pressure to conform were important motivational factors, teachers need to consider how speakers can express their own attitudes, values and beliefs within the prosocial politeness context. The self-serving aspects of politeness behaviour underline the fact that interactants are not often polite in order to be polite but rather they have ulterior, and perhaps exploitative, motives. Consequently, FL users need to be aware of others' motivation to be polite which may be self-serving and purely transactional.

Question 4 focused on the conventional expression of politeness which was often achieved through implicit learning e.g. following others. As to be discussed in Chapter 6, implicit learning may not be sufficient in helping FL learners achieve successful politeness behaviour. Little reference was made in the responses to nonlinguistic means of expressing prosocial politeness. This provides a teaching opportunity so that learners can be made aware of nonverbal expressions of polite conduct. However, conventional expressions offer a socially approved means for FL learners to observe and participate in TL norms and practices.

Answers to question 5 demonstrated that respondents appear to actively reflect on their use of politeness in the TL. They do not see politeness merely as employing formulaic expressions and conventional language use but rather as an investment in what they are trying to achieve. They appear to be more than aware of their surroundings and the interactive context. Such moments appear to underline the importance of making learners aware of how politeness can be employed so as to achieve their goals and objectives.

Conclusion

This chapter has attempted to privilege FL interactants and understand how prosocial politeness can provide a structured, predictable and relatively comfortable way to conduct TL relationships on both social and personal levels.

It has identified what FL users seek to achieve by engaging in prosocial politeness practices. This has been accomplished by asking respondents to describe and characterise a 'polite person' from their own point of view. This information enables teachers to recognise where learners are coming from and how they approach TL interaction. As a consequence, FL pedagogy is in a position to distance itself from solely relying on 'native speaker'

86 *Prosocial politeness*

concepts of politeness. Furthermore, by relating politeness to culture, teachers are also in a stronger position to make relational comparisons and contrasts, and subsequently build on the learners' existing and evolving knowledge and experience. Meanwhile, FL users' motivation to be polite may reflect their own background, personal histories and upbringing and the communal desire to interrelate with other people rather than adhering to an individualistic approach and pursuing self-centred goals and objectives. Furthermore, research in this chapter has highlighted the degree to which FL interlocutors adhere to TL politeness rules/patterns, follow others interactants' behaviour and 'read the room' since these practices offer interactants a structural approach to employing TL politeness and engaging in relational work. Just as importantly, the research offered respondents the opportunity to reflect on their own experiences with TL politeness. Any meaningful 'teaching' of politeness must be based on learners' attitudes, values and experiences of politeness rather than on promoting prescriptive and doctrinaire pronouncements regarding suitable and appropriate conduct and manners.

However, prosocial politeness is not without its limitations since there is an emphasis on the speaker. However, as argued by Culpeper and Haugh, a focus on the speaker may not consider what the hearer does 'or indeed the interaction between the two' (2021, p. 324). Any study of FL politeness patterns and practices needs to examine the intertwined interactional dimension to politeness as interlocutors seek to establish, structure, develop and sustain interpersonal relationships. Therefore, the interpersonal and contested dimensions of politeness will be examined in the two following chapters.

References

Aston, G. (1988). *Learning comity: An approach to the description and pedagogy of interaction speech.* Bologna: Cooperativa Libraria Universitaria Editrice Bologna.
Bourdieu, P. (1972). *Outline of a theory of practice.* Cambridge: Cambridge University Press.
Bourdieu, P. (1980). *The logic of practice.* Stanford: Stanford University Press.
Bourdieu, P. (1991). *Language & symbolic power.* Cambridge: Polity Press.
Braine, G. (2010). *Nonnative speaker English teachers: Research, pedagogy, and professional growth.* New York: Routledge.
Brown, P., & Levinson, S. (1987). *Politeness: Some universal in language usage.* Cambridge: Cambridge University Press.
Culpeper, J. (2008). Reflections on impoliteness. In D. Bousfield & M. Locher (Eds.), *Impoliteness in language: Studies on its interplay with power in theory and practice* (pp. 17–44). Berlin: Mouton de Gruyter.
Culpeper, J., & Haugh, M. (2021). (Im)Politeness and sociopragmatics. In M. Kádár Haugh, Z. Dániel, & M. Terkourafi (Eds.), *The Cambridge Handbook of sociopragmatics* (pp. 313–339). Cambridge: Cambridge University Press.
Eggins, S., & Slade, D. (1997). *Analysing casual conversation.* London: Cassell.

Prosocial politeness 87

Ferguson, G. (2006). *Language planning and education*. Edinburgh: Edinburgh University Press.

Fillmore, L. W. (1979). Individual differences in second language acquisition. In C. J. Fillmore, D. Kempler, & W. Wang (Eds.), *Individual differences in language ability and language behavior* (pp. 203–228). New York: Academic Press.

Fox, K. (2004). *Watching the English: The hidden rules of English behaviour*. London: Hodder.

France, P. (1992). *Politeness and its discontents: Problems in French classical culture*. Cambridge: Cambridge University Press.

Fukushima, S. (2019). A metapragmatic aspect of politeness; with a special emphasis on attentiveness in Japanese. In E. Ogiermann & P. Garcés-Conejos Blitvich (Eds.), *From speech acts to lay understandings of politeness* (pp. 226–247). Cambridge: Cambridge University Press.

Goffman, E. (1959). *The presentation of self in everyday life*. London: Penguin.

Gu, Y. (1990). Politeness phenomena in modern Chinese. *Journal of Pragmatics, 14*, 237–257.

Gumperz, J. J. (1982). *Discourse strategies*. Cambridge: Cambridge University Press.

Halliday, M. A. K. (1973/1997). Language in a social perspective. In N. Coupland & A. Jaworski (Eds.), *Sociolinguistics: A reader and coursebook* (pp. 31–38). Basingstoke: Macmillan.

Halliday, M. A. K. (1978). *Language as social semiotic*. London: Edward Arnold.

Halliday, M. A. K., & Hasan, R. (1976). *Cohesion in English*. Harlow, UK: Longman.

Harmer, J. (2007). *The practice of English language teaching*. Harlow, Essex: Pearson Longman.

Hymes, D. H. (1972). On communicative competence. In J. B. Pride & J. Holmes (Eds.), *Sociolinguistics. Selected readings* (pp. 269–293). Harmondsworth: Penguin.

Kádár, D. Z., & Haugh, M. (2013). *Understanding politeness*. Cambridge: Cambridge University Press.

Kasper, G. (2009). Politeness. In S. D'hondt, J.-O. Östman, & J. Verschueren (Eds.), *The pragmatics of interaction* (pp. 155–173). Amsterdam/Philadelphia: John Benjamins.

Lakoff, R. (2005). Civility and its discontents: Or, getting in your face. In R. Lakoff & S. Ide (Eds.), *Broadening the horizon of linguistic politeness* (pp. 23–43). Philadelphia: John Benjamins.

Mugford, G. (2020). Mexican politeness: An empirical study on the reasons underlying/motivating practices to construct local interpersonal relationships. *Russian Journal of Linguistics, 24*(1), 31–55.

Mugford, G. (2022). *Developing cross-cultural relational ability in Foreign language learning: Asset-based pedagogy to enhance pragmatic competence*. New York/Abingdon, UK: Routledge.

Mugford, G., & Rubio Michel, C. (2018). Racial, linguistic and professional discrimination towards teachers of English as a foreign language: Mexican context. *Journal of Language and Discrimination, 2*(1), 32–57.

Norton, B. (2013). *Identity and language learning* (2nd Edition). Bristol: Multilingual Matters.

Norton, B. (2014). Identity and poststructuralist theory in SLA. In S. Mercer & M. Williams (Eds.), *Multiple perspectives on the self in SLA* (pp. 59–74). Bristol: Multilingual.

88 *Prosocial politeness*

Paltridge, B. (2006). *Discourse analysis*. London: Continuum.

Sacks, H., Schegloff, E., & Jefferson, G. (1974). A simplest systematics for the organization of turn-taking for conversation. *Language, 50,* 697–735.

Schegloff, E. A., & Sacks, H. (1973). Opening up closings. *Semiotica, VIII*(4), 289–327.

Schlenker, B. R. (2003). Self-presentation. In M. R. Leary & J. P. Tangney (Eds.), *Handbook of self and identity* (pp. 492–518). New York: Guilford.

Sifianou, M. (1992). *Politeness phenomena in England greece*. Oxford: Oxford University Press.

Spencer-Oatey, H., & Kádár, D. (2021). *Intercultural politeness*. Cambridge: Cambridge University Press.

Terkourafi, M. (2005). Beyond the micro-level in politeness research. *Journal of Politeness Research, 1*(2), 237–262.

Thornbury, S. (2006). *An A-Z of ELT*. Oxford: Macmillan.

Truss, L. (2005). *Talk to the hand: The utter bloody rudeness of the world today, or six good reasons to stay home and bolt the door*. New York: Gothan Books.

Wong, J., & Waring, H. Z. (2010). *Conversation analysis and second language pedagogy*. New York: Routledge.

Ylänne, V. (2008). Communication accommodation theory. In H. Spencer-Oatey (Ed.), *Culturally speaking: Managing rapport through talk across cultures* (2nd Edition, pp. 164–188). London: Continuum.

4 Interpersonal politeness

Introduction

Foreign language (FL) interaction provides speakers with opportunities to construct, shape, expand and maintain not only social relationships but also to develop more personal relationships. Whether interactants want to take advantage of such opportunities depends on the nature and purpose of target language (TL) interaction. In transactional and fleeting encounters there may be little interest or motivation in furthering more personal relationships. However, in interpersonal encounters, FL users may seek more meaningful and productive interaction. This will mean, however, that interlocutors must be willing to take communicative risks as they explore interpersonal possibilities, attempt to co-construct joint understandings and take up individual positions regarding ongoing interaction. By taking risks, FL speakers are in a position to reap anticipated communicative rewards as they employ interpersonal politeness strategies and practices that allow them to proactively engage in camaraderie, supportiveness, empathy, solidarity, etc. Vibrant, celebratory, playful and negotiable, interpersonal politeness reflects how interactants relate, engage and position themselves with respect to others. *Relating* involves exploring, establishing, creating, connecting and sustaining interpersonal relationships (Arundale, 2010, 2020). *Engagement* reveals the degree, extent and intensity of involvement, responsiveness, commitment invested by the different parties in a given interaction. This may be expressed through connectedness, rapport and comity (Aston, 1988, 1993). *Positionality* or stance (Englebretson, 2007) reflects how interactants align themselves with others as they express and display (or perhaps reveal) their beliefs, attitudes and feelings. Therefore, interpersonal politeness reflects a dynamic, vigorous and unpredictable dimension to linguistic and cultural politeness.

Engaging in interpersonal politeness presents unique challenges for the FL interlocutors as there are no ideally structured ways through which to engage interactionally with other TL participants: speakers are individuals, and each context is different and there are never predictable outcomes. There is no formulaic means by which to connect to others, achieve

DOI: 10.4324/9781003326052-4

90 *Interpersonal politeness*

rapport and establish one's positionality. However, relating, engaging and positioning can be described in terms of investment, doing politeness and relational maintenance. Investment reflects the actions taken when establishing and exploring TL relations. This involves aligning with others, developing trust and assessing and evaluating developing relationships. Doing politeness reflects actions taken to achieve workable relationships such as affiliation, supportiveness and empathy. Relational maintenance calls for attentiveness, synchronisation and responding to others' ongoing wishes and needs in order to preserve and sustain interpersonal relationships. As a consequence, FL speakers have to develop a critical awareness of the possibilities and opportunities with which to engage in interpersonal politeness and subsequently identify how pragmatic assets and resources can be employed to achieve communicative objectives. Furthermore, FL interlocutors need to develop cultural sensitivity towards target language use and assess probable, possible and permissible interactional behaviour and conduct. This does not mean blindly and indiscriminately adhering to societal norms but rather FL interlocutors should assess group norms, try to integrate and blend in and accommodate to others whilst expressing their individuality and personal understanding of particular situations.

To examine interpersonal politeness within the context of FL interaction, the chapter is structured in the following way. First of all, I examine how Halliday's (1973/1997) interpersonal language function can provide insights into the interactional and personal dimensions of interpersonal politeness. Secondly, I explore how the interactional and personal language functions are reflected through relating, engaging and positioning as FL interactants seek to establish, structure, develop and sustain interpersonal relationships. Thirdly, I position interpersonal politeness within politeness theory by briefly examining insights and drawbacks provided by discursive approaches. Fourthly, I examine the specific actions FL speakers take when engaging in TL interpersonal politeness. These are discussed in terms of investment, doing politeness and relational maintenance. Whilst the use of such assets may not be unique to FL speakers, they do represent specific challenges that need to be taken into account when engaging in TL interpersonal politeness. Finally, I examine the adult Mexican EFL users' own perspectives regarding interpersonal politeness. An emic perspective provides greater insights into how FL users themselves approach interpersonal politeness and seek to express supportiveness, achieve rapport and perhaps even celebrate togetherness in the TL.

Interpersonal language function

As outlined in Chapter 1, I argue that Halliday's (1973/1997) ideational, interpersonal and textual functions can help exemplify the structure of TL relational interaction. In Chapter 3, I argued that the ideational function provides insights into prosocial politeness. I maintained that the ideational function reflects interlocutors' understandings, experiences and key events

Interpersonal politeness 91

and can help highlight TL politeness practices and patterns. In this chapter, I sustain that the interpersonal function offers a way of understanding interpersonal politeness.

The interpersonal language function

> may be understood by the expression of our own personalities and personal feelings on the one hand, and forms of interaction and social interplay with other participants in the communication situation on the other hand.
>
> (Halliday, 1973/1997, p. 36)

Halliday's interpersonal function highlights twin objectives of interpersonal politeness: the need to relate to others e.g. through companionship, comity and supportiveness and the need to express one's own qualities e.g. understanding, considerateness and respectfulness. Given that Halliday (1978) sees language as meaning potential, the interpersonal function represents what the FL speakers seek and are able to achieve in the TL. At the same time, Halliday sees the speaker as an intruder in a given context, a role that the FL user may easily identify with when he/she attempts to interact in a TL social encounter:

> The interpersonal component represents the speaker's meaning potential as an intruder. It is the participatory function of language, language as doing something, this is the component through which the speaker intrudes himself into the context of the situation, both existing his own attitudes and judgements and seeking to influence the attitudes and behaviour of others. It expresses the role relationships associated with the situation, including those that are defined by language itself, relationships of questioner-respondent, informer-doubter and the like. These constitute the interpersonal meaning of language.
>
> (1978, p. 112)

FL users may often feel like intruders especially when they are unfairly cast as deficit language users, as 'foreigners' and as projecting a 'reduced personality' (Harder, 1980). This positioning may put the FL interactants at a clear disadvantage when engaging in interpersonal speech. Furthermore, as FL interlocutors attempt to engage in interpersonal talk, '[g]rammatical mistakes/linguistic variation, creative vocabulary and accented speech may lead TL interlocutors to rush to judgement and regard FL speakers as deficient communicators' (Mugford, 2022, p. 108).

Understandings of interpersonal politeness

Interpersonal politeness reflects relational management at localised and interactional levels as interlocutors pursue both social and personal goals

92 *Interpersonal politeness*

when interrelating with others and projecting their own individuality. Rather than generalising about socially acceptable and appropriate politeness practices and patterns of interaction, interpersonal politeness studies focus on the assets and resources that interlocutors draw on when establishing, consolidating and maintaining interpersonal relationships. As discussed in Halliday's (1973/1997) interpersonal function of language, speakers pursue the twin goals of expressing their own personalities and relating to others.

Interpersonal politeness is reflected to a key extent through discursive approaches to politeness. Rather than focusing on prosocial politeness's individual speaker, discursive politeness concentrates on understanding evolving and local constructed interaction within a social context (Grainger & Mills, 2016, p. 154). Furthermore, the discursive approach moves away from making categorical and universalistic judgements regarding politeness and impoliteness:

> The discursive approach does not hold that utterances are inherently polite or impolite, but rather examines ways in which individuals draw on what they assume to be the resources available, simultaneously both to fashion an individual, community, regional and cultural identity and to manage relationships with others in the group, displaying and contesting statuses (Kasper, 2006; Linguistic Politeness Group, 2011; Locher, 2004; Mills, 2011). In this way, a discursive approach examines the way that politeness serves both the relational function but also a social function in terms of identity and relationship maintenance.
>
> (Mills, 2017, p. 15)

Therefore, politeness is seen as a resource for achieving relational objectives and needs to be understood and evaluated within a specific context. However, discursive approaches have come into a certain amount of criticism because they fail to offer a structured approach to understanding politeness since every case is seen as unique given that 'minute descriptions of individual encounters ... do not in any way add up to an explanatory theory of the phenomena under study' (Terkourafi, 2005, p. 245). Whereas discursive approaches are context-based with an interactional focus, interpersonal politeness studies also recognise prosocial practices but, importantly, on a much more individualised and nuanced basis than prosocial politeness approaches.

Interpersonal politeness can also be understood in terms of 'proactive' and 'reactive' behaviour as interactants are engaged in 'producing politeness' (Spencer-Oatey & Kádár, 2021, p. 3). As Spencer-Oatey and Kádár explain:

> Within interaction, politeness may come into existence in the form of proactive behaviour as people seek to maintain smooth relationships

Interpersonal politeness 93

(e.g. engage in a chit-chat with someone they know) or establish new relationships. It may also come into existence through reactive behaviour, as interactants react to offence including instances when they perceive that they have offended others or that someone else has offended them.

(2021, pp. 3–4)

Discursive approaches and proactive and reactive behaviour provide important insights into the enactment of interpersonal politeness where there is an emphasis on constructing, developing, maintaining and sustaining relationships. They also examine behaviour from the language users' or emic point of view rather than from a hypothetical stance or by following an 'ends driven explanation' (Grundy, 2000, p. 186). An examination of FL interpersonal politeness is data driven as it explores how speakers establish, connect and sustain interpersonal bonds. Nevertheless, it needs to be supported by a theoretical framework so that it provides 'a coherent framework for studying politeness' (Ogiermann & Garcés-Conejos Blitvich, 2019, p. 3). I approach the goal of appreciating FL politeness practices by seeking to understand how FL users actively engage in interpersonal politeness through relating, engaging and positioning.

Interpersonal politeness actions

Relating, engaging and positioning reflect the active dimension to interpersonal politeness. These actions allow FL speakers to adopt a more functional position in achieving satisfactory interpersonal relationships rather than just relying on predetermined conventional language. Unlike a good deal of prosocial politeness practices, interpersonal politeness is evolutionary, transitional and productive as relationships develop, grow and perhaps flourish.

Relating

Relating involves probing, constructing, crafting, linking and continuing interpersonal relationships (Arundale, 2010, 2020). FL interactants may want to relate to others by employing L1 linguistic and cultural knowledge and assets or adopt TL resources. In contrast to the focus by prosocial politeness practices on the single interactant, the dyad is the basic unit of analysis in relating (Arundale, 2020). The dyad, as a unit of analysis, highlights the dynamic and potentially ever augmenting dimension to interpersonal politeness. In everyday social interaction, the process of communication reflects ongoing change, creativeness and improvising. This can be especially challenging for FL speakers who often have to work spontaneously, under pressure and in real time as they interpret other participants' points of view, process utterances rapidly, produce adequate and coherent

94 Interpersonal politeness

responses, work with inadequate information and keep track of everchanging nature of everyday talk (Mugford, 2022). Highlighting the fluid and constantly evolving nature of relational talk, Arundale argues: 'As persons create, sustain, and change a social system, however, they at the same time configure, maintain, and reconfigure their resources for interacting with one another' (2020, p. 39). A further important aspect that FL users have to take into consideration with respect to relating is that interpersonal politeness may need to be reconstructed with each subsequent encounter given that 'social systems terminate when communication ceases, but that they can be re-created on future occasions if communicating resumes' (Arundale, 2020, p. 39). Therefore, FL users need to be aware of the reconstructive dimension to interpersonal politeness in each and every continuing interaction or as Arundale argues:

> Relating in everyday interacting generates operative interpretings of "our relationship-at-this-moment" that may or may not be compatible with the interpretings that the participants have created either in the immediately preceding moments, or over multiple moments across prior episodes of inter-action.
>
> (2020, p. 251)

This may be especially challenging for FL users who do not feel, or perceive themselves to be, on an equal communicative footing with TL speakers. So whilst an interaction may develop concurrently and synchronously, it may be going too far to state that it is co-constituted given the possible (and perhaps highly probable) communicative and discursive power differences between the FL speakers and TL interlocutors. This theme is further explored in detail in Chapter 5.

Engaging

When relating to other interactants, FL participants need to decide on the level of involvement they wish to pursue. Far from being a fixed or predetermined course of action, speaker involvement may be established before and/or during an encounter and, at the same time, may increase, stabilise or even diminish as the interaction evolves. Engagement reflects the intensity and force of attentiveness, involvement and commitment. This may be expressed through affinity, congruence and comity (Aston, 1988, 1993). FL interactants may want to engage by employing L1 linguistic and cultural patterns and practices or adopt and embrace TL behaviour.

Engagement during interpersonal politeness is highlighted through interactional practices, patterns and styles. For instance, Tracy and Robles argue that interactants can engage with others through expressing their involvement or respecting addressee independence:

An **involvement politeness style** is one that puts a premium on recognizing others' positive face wants. Speakers using an involvement style will emphasize friendliness and building connection to others. In contrast, an **independence politeness style** puts a premium on recognizing others' negative face wants; this style "respects the rights of others to their own autonomy and freedom of choice."

(authors' emphasis, 2013, p. 187)

Since Tracy and Robles appear to place involvement and independence on a continuum, intermediate points can be found between (and beyond) the two poles. These may range, for instance, from positions of alignment, interest and concern to those of disinterest, indifference and apathy. At the same time, successful engagement reflects coordinated speaker and hearer interaction as they both try to understand what each other is trying to achieve. However, when this goes wrong, a speaker who expresses involvement may not be appreciated by the addressee who seeks independence. The challenge for FL users is to understand whether their addressees perceive the context/situation in the same way that they do. To help promote such understanding, FL interlocutors need to identify and recognise how everyday pragmatic devices and practices are employed to reflect closeness/ involvement, distance/considerateness, etc. As argued by Tannen (1984), involvement means joint sense making and

> [b]ecause of the paradoxical nature of closeness (and consequently of communication), speakers must constantly observe both the need for involvement and the need not to impose or, expressed positively, for considerateness.

(p. 27)

Engaging calls for a balance between showing affiliation and interest and respecting the others' wish to be unconstrained and left alone. Where to position oneself will often emerge during the course of an interaction itself as interlocutors identify and respond to each other's needs and wants. At the same time engagement offers FL users choices with respect to how they want to interact with TL interlocutors and their degree of commitment and participation.

Positionality

Whilst engagement practices reflect the level of involvement with others, FL users still need to determine how they want to project themselves and how they want to be perceived. The concept of positionality or stance covers concepts of interpersonal behaviour such as personal beliefs, points of view, feelings and subjectiveness, i.e. the expression of oneself. As argued by Johnstone, 'stancetaking involves the mutual orientation of two (or more)

96 *Interpersonal politeness*

social actors, it is always interactive; speakers position themselves, with respect to attitude or affiliation, relative to other speakers' (2009, p. 49). Just as engagement reflects others' level of involvement on a dyadic basis, stance reflects dialogic positioning since when 'one speaker's subjectivity reacts to another's subjectivity, we will have a real opportunity to witness the dialogic emergence of intersubjectivity' (Du Bois, 2007, p. 159). Intersubjectivity reflects convergence or divergence as interactants align themselves with, or distance themselves from, other points of view (Jaworski & Thurlow, 2009, p. 229). It does not always reflect shared ideas, histories, emotions, evaluations and aspirations. Stance is 'only implied, and that its accomplishment is based on the combination of the ongoing activity, sequential position, language and body' (Keisanen & Kärkkäinen, 2014, p. 314). However, intersubjectivity can acknowledge difference and diversity and show respect for others' views and positions. Consequently, positionality must always be seen in reference to other interactants and cannot stand alone.

Stance offers FL users discursive choices regarding how they want to express themselves, gauge their contributions and identify themselves with other TL users. For instance, modality and hedges allow interactants to downgrade their contributions with less assertive stances such as *I could* and *probably* to non-committal positionality such as *I might* and *perhaps*. Stance can reflect the cultural dimension as interactants may decide to openly take a position or limit their participation. For instance, Mexicans do not generally like to participate in overt criticism of others (Mugford, 2011). Therefore, it is important to state that stance maybe only the public display regarding how interlocutors align as they convey their beliefs, opinions and emotions.

Enacting interpersonal politeness

Whilst relating, engaging and positioning convey interpersonal politeness, consideration will now be given to how FL speakers pursue their relational goals. Interpersonal politeness strategies are focused on the process of achieving satisfactory relationships, understanding others' points of view and coming across in one's own way in the TL. Engaging in interpersonal politeness can be especially challenging for FL learners as they interact in a language other than their own, come to terms with different and contrasting cultural practices and try to find and establish their own voice. Locher and Watts (2005) rightly call this process 'relational work' and FL speakers may have to work especially hard at identifying those with whom they want to develop meaningful relationships, deciding what is feasible and achievable in TL interaction and determining how far they want to go in a given relationship in terms of connectedness, closeness and perhaps intimacy. Therefore, interpersonal politeness must be seen as negotiable, ongoing, with no guaranteed outcomes and may reflect 'weak' or 'strong' relationships (Arundale, 2010).

Interpersonal politeness 97

By employing prosocial politeness assets and resources, FL users seek to achieve their communicative goals by adopting standardised and recognisable discursive patterns and practices. They adhere to socially acceptable practices, engage in *politic* behaviour (Watts, 2003) and present themselves as 'polite' persons. As discussed in Chapter 3, prosocial politeness reflects adherence to social norms and maxims and reflect addressee-focused practices. In contrast, the process of engaging in interpersonal politeness can be described in terms of investment (Locher & Watts, 2005), practising or 'doing' politeness and maintenance (Spencer-Oatey, 2008). Investing in TL relationships means that FL speakers have to dedicate time and effort to cultivating these relationships. Such a process may not achieve the sought-after goals but may produce unanticipated and perhaps, on occasions, surprisingly, even more satisfactory results. Doing so means intentionally and knowingly adopting and implementing politeness practices and strategies aimed at developing and strengthening TL relationships. FL speakers' L1 resources and assets may not necessarily be applicable and effective in TL encounters and may need to be constructed anew. Relationship maintenance means evaluating and monitoring their status because interpersonal relationships need constant scrutinising and adjustment. In summary, interpersonal politeness involves sustained effort and sometimes hard graft.

However, it is important to emphasise that the same resources and strategies employed in prosocial politeness may also be found in interpersonal politeness but with an important difference. In prosocial politeness they are used to achieve acceptance, appropriateness and conformity. In interpersonal politeness they are employed to relate to others and to develop and strengthen interactional and transactional relationships.

Investing

In order to successfully relate to others, engage with other interactants and position themselves, FL interlocutors have to invest in interactional and transactional processes so that they can assess and evaluate whether they are achieving the desired results. Far from reflecting the impetus or a 'motivation' to be polite, investment allows bilingual users to build on their knowledge and experience of the world especially in terms of capital (see Chapter 2). Therefore, investment aims to achieve interpersonal objectives and reap the hoped-for rewards:

> ... investment carries connotations of hopes of returns and benefits; it accentuates the role of human agency and identity in engaging with the task at hand, in accumulating economic and symbolic capital, in having stakes in the endeavor and in perceiving that endeavor.
>
> (Kramsch, 2013, p. 195)

98 *Interpersonal politeness*

Kramsch argues that investing is closely associated with agency which Norton and Toohey define as 'the possibility to take action in social settings' (2011, p. 417). Agency allows FL speakers to decide the stance/position they want to adopt in a determined encounter as they build up symbolic capital (Bourdieu, 1972, 1980, 1991). Symbolic capital represents 'the *value* and *power* of speech' (Bourdieu, 1977, p. 646. author's italics). FL interactants want to be taken as bona fide communicators who actively express their own identities and resist and contest being designated by other interlocutors as merely deficient language users trying to express themselves in a foreign language. An understanding of interpersonal politeness can help FL interactants enhance their value and power as TL participants. Furthermore, it allows FL interactants, as legitimate language users, to take up and defend their interpersonal and transactional positions. In relational work, interpersonal politeness strategies offer such opportunities, and choices and to achieve this

> [t]he notion of investment recognizes that learners often have variable desires to engage in the range of social interactions and community practices in which they are situated.
>
> (Norton & Toohey, 2011, p. 420)

Investment represents both a personal and dialogic commitment and risk in the TL as FL interlocutors engage in relational work that allows them to connect with others e.g. through companionship, comity and supportiveness and to express their own qualities such as understanding, considerateness and respectfulness. As argued by Norton, investment

> presupposes that when language learners speak, they are not only exchanging information with target language speakers, but they are constantly organizing and reorganizing a sense of who they are and how they relate to the social world. Thus an investment in the target language is also an investment in a learner's own identity, an identity which is constantly changing across time and space.
>
> (2013, pp. 50–51)

Investment in interpersonal politeness affords FL speakers the opportunity to go beyond participating on a prosocial plane and actively engage with other interlocutors and promote a sense of self.

Doing politeness

Doing politeness contrasts with prosocial politeness since FL interactants identify and determine what they want to achieve rather than being constrained by contextual and situational factors. Rather than automatically adhering to pre-packaged and pre-determined language structures and

Interpersonal politeness 99

'having to be polite,' doing politeness means that FL interlocutors actively relate, engage and position themselves and which Arundale (2020, p. 291) also discusses in terms of 'doing face.' This involves imaginatively and dynamically establishing, developing, maintaining and consolidating TL relationships. This can be described in terms of affiliation, supportiveness or empathy (Aston, 1988; Mugford, 2014). The desired level of doing politeness will depend on the desired degree, extent and intensity of interpersonal involvement and commitment pursed in a given relationship. This can be broadly categorised as follows (as seen in Figure 4.1):

- affiliation: identifying common interests, accommodating to others' wishes, seeking togetherness and companionship and complementing others' assessments.
- supportiveness: reacting to others' feelings and concerns, demonstrating appreciation and encouragement and caring about others' doubts, unease and anxieties.
- empathy: sharing the same experiences, histories, showing likemindedness, engaging in troubles talk and sharing gossip.

Affiliation demonstrates a deliberate effort to move closer to, and associate with, other interactants. This may be reflected through building on others' contributions, recognising common interests, aligning with others' points of view, participating in joint activities or even sharing dislikes and negative attitudes. Affiliation can be understood in terms of alignment, collaboration and reciprocity.

Supportiveness involves showing considerateness, understanding others' situations and predicaments and expressing concern and compassion. This means responding and reacting to others' feelings and emotions in meaningful ways and even prioritising their wants and needs over one's own. Supportiveness can be understood in terms of closeness, comity and connectedness.

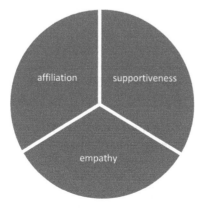

Figure 4.1 Involvement and commitment pursued in a given relationship.

100 *Interpersonal politeness*

Empathy involves bonding with other interactants and creating camaraderie. This can be expressed as feeling *with* others (as opposed to *for others*), sharing the same experiences and developing mutual trust. It may be seen in extremely positive terms as interactants encourage and motivate one another. Empathy may be understood in terms of solidarity, rapport and sharedness.

Doing politeness involves taking a stance as FL interlocutors position themselves vis-à-vis other interactants. It reflects an active and ongoing choice with regards to the extent that FL speakers want to construct, develop and express TL interpersonal relationships.

Relational maintenance

Whilst rewarding and more than worthwhile, interpersonal relationships are usually unpredictable, uncertain and often changeable since they either progress, flourish, strengthen and consolidate or weaken, deteriorate, decline and perhaps terminate (Knapp, 1978). Engaged in a perhaps unconscious but nevertheless ongoing and evolving process, interactants will often monitor, reassess and rework existing ties and associations. This will be expressed through interpersonal politeness. Interlocutors may decide to renew, bolster and reinforce existing bonds. This can be achieved through attentiveness (Fukushima, 2019), face boosting acts (Bayraktaroğlu, 1991, 2001) and endorsing others' wants (Mugford, 2020) and celebrating interactional successes (Aston, 1993). However, FL interactants may employ interpersonal politeness to extricate themselves from unfulfilling, unproductive and inactive relationships. Assuming that interlocutors want to terminate a relationship as amicably as possible, interactants will aim to use thoughtfulness, tact and sensitivity in terminating such relationships as smoothly as possible.

All too often interaction is treated in terms of nervousness, worries, doubts, anxieties and difficulties. However, FL users may often adopt a more positive and risk-taking attitude and concentrate much more on what can be gained.

To conserve and sustain social connections, participants should recognise the focus of relational maintenance. In carrying out relational maintenance, interactants may focus on the rapport (relationship itself), enhancement (addressee focus) or benefit (speaker) (as seen in Figure 4.2):

Before describing different approaches to relational maintenance, it is important to point out that these are not discrete categories and will often suggest communicative overlaps.

Rapport: enriching friendly relations, reinforcing interpersonal bonds, celebrating convergence and communion.

Enhancement: demonstrating supportiveness; respecting others needs and rights and boosting others' self-image.

Achievement: accomplishing successful outcomes, engaging in satisfactory relationships, gaining social acceptance and integration.

Interpersonal politeness 101

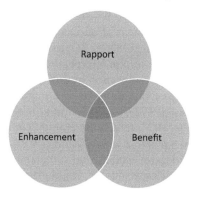

Figure 4.2 Relational maintenance.

The rapport focus of relational maintenance involves the personal assessment regarding the quality of a relationship and the accrued benefits. In an ideal relationship, rapport reflects 'the lovely satisfaction of being understood without explaining oneself, of getting what one wants without asking for it' (Tannen, 1981, p. 224). Such communication probably does not accurately reflect the realities of TL interaction as FL interlocutors may struggle to explain themselves and find the right words to convey their feelings and emotions. In their study of intercultural politeness, Spencer-Oatey and Kádár offer a more grounded definition, defining rapport as 'the formation of interconnectedness between the participants of an interaction, which can be changed or decreased' (2021, p. 348). Spencer-Oatey and Kádár capture the dynamic nature of rapport as interactants attempt to strengthen friendly relations and bolster interpersonal bonds. In an earlier work, Spencer-Oatey defines rapport as 'people's subjective perceptions of (dis)harmony or smoothness-turbulence in interpersonal relations' (2008, p. 335). Here she underscores the subjective dimension to rapport which may not be apparent to outsiders. In evaluating how a relationship is going, Spencer-Oatey describes four orientations:

1   Rapport-enhancement orientation: a desire to strengthen or enhance harmonious relations between the interlocutors;
2   Rapport-maintenance orientation: a desire to maintain or protect harmonious relations between the interlocutors;
3   Rapport-neglect orientation: a lack of concern or interest in the quality of relations between the interlocutors (perhaps because of a focus on self);
4   Rapport-challenge orientation: a desire to challenge or impair harmonious relations between the interlocutors.

(2008, p. 32)

102 Interpersonal politeness

On the other hand rapport can go beyond enhancement and embrace celebration and the accomplishment of successful communication i.e. "look we can talk together" (Aston, 1988, p. 387). The fact that FL interactants can establish, develop and maintain interpersonal relationships in a foreign language may be cause for celebration and consequently they may enjoy talking just for the sake of talking as seen through the concept of phatic communion (Malinowski, 1923/1969). Aston argues, for instance, that to 'celebrate ordinary success' interactants employ comity 'as a manner of enhancing relations in a positive sense (Aston, 1989)' (1993, p. 230). Aston uses the word comity to mean establishing and maintaining social relationships. Consequently, and especially in transactional encounters, celebration reflects 'displayed pleasure in each other's company in the here-and-now, with positive attitudes to the interaction' (Aston, 1988, p. 319). In terms of FL interpersonal politeness, celebration indicates a mutual recognition of successful relational talk.

Enhancement involves a deliberate attempt to make the addressee feel good about him/herself and consequently boost their self-confidence and self-esteem. This practice has been variously labelled as face-boosting acts (Bayraktaroğlu, 1991, 2001), face enhancement (Sifianou, 1995; Spencer-Oatey & Kádár, 2021) and rapport enhancement (Spencer-Oatey, 2000). For instance in the following mealtime encounter at a London university hall of residence, Celia, a Mexican PhD student, has been talking to fellow students at a table when they are joined by Francesca, a Spanish MA student:

> FRANCESCA: ¡*Buenos días!*
> CELIA: ¿*Buenos días! guapa guapa* means lovely *guapa*
> [good morning beautiful, guapa means lovely, beautiful].
> (Mugford, 2009, p. 80)

In the interaction, Celia not only greets Francesca with the formulaic ¡*Buenos días!* but adds the compliment which repeats *guapa* three times with an explanation for the English-speaking audience. Not only does Celia directly boost Francesca's face but she also acts out a public display. Face-boosting acts may be particularly prevalent in the FL interlocutors' L1, and they may attempt to employ them in the TL. Such actions can further enhance interpersonal relations. Such practices demonstrate supportiveness and acknowledge others' needs and rights to be appreciated and underscore individualised goals as FL speakers interrelate with others and project their own individuality. Therefore, relational maintenance need not be considered in purely preventative terms. It may mean valuing and celebrating relationships.

Relational achievement involves examining the current state of interpersonal relationships. FL users may assess and evaluate what has been (or is being) achieved relationally. They may reflect on whether interactional

Interpersonal politeness   103

outcomes have been successful. Depending on their interpersonal goals, FL interactants may consider such factors as involvement, social acceptance and social integration. As argued by Eggins and Slade '[a]s we take turns in any interaction, we negotiate meanings about what we think is going on in the world, how we feel about it, and how we feel about the people we interact with' (1997, p. 6). Achievement may involve relational work since interpersonal politeness is not guaranteed and may need extra effort and concentration.

As discussed in Chapter 1, relational work reflects the effort that interlocutors exert in establishing, developing, consolidating and maintaining interpersonal relations as they also express their individuality and positionality/stance: 'Relational work refers to the "work" individuals invest in negotiating relationships with others' (Locher & Watts, 2005, p. 10). However in the case of FL use, speakers often have to do double the work in confronting and figuring situatedness (i.e. relating their experiences, personal histories and responses to TL contexts) as they shape and cope with TL language use. Teachers have a key role to play in helping students grapple with FL patterns and practices:

This situatedness comes in many forms. It can involve considering contrasts (across cultural groups, languages, dialects or genres), but this is not essential. The in-depth study of politeness phenomena within a particular setting – such as educational, medical, or legal settings – can also deepen … knowledge of how im/politeness functions.
(Kádár & Haugh, 2013, p. 48)

It is important to recognise relational work as an ongoing process and one that is constantly and continually present in all interpersonal encounters (Watts, 2008).

In conclusion, in enacting interpersonal politeness, politeness emerges and is not preplanned. Interlocutors are not subservient to politeness patterns and practices. Politeness can be constructive and reactive and the strategies interlocutors employ may be on-the-spur of-the-moment rather than taken from a language toolkit. As argued by Culpeper and Haugh:

There is also, whilst acknowledging that there is always directedness (or 'intentionality') underpinning communication, increasing realisation in pragmatics that speakers do not make plans and then speak, but that plans emerge through the course of interaction….
(2021, p. 324)

Methodology

In order to understand how FL interactants integrate their own degree of politeness practices into TL interaction, I asked participants to respond to the following questions:

104 *Interpersonal politeness*

1   Does politeness reflect convention and routine, or does it develop during the conversation? Please explain your answer.
2   Do you think you have to be polite following English-language ways/customs, or can you be polite in your way as well? Please explain your answer.
3   Do you think politeness is expressed in the same way in Mexican Spanish and English in terms of language and culture? Please explain your answer.
4   Are you ever polite in English using Mexican politeness expressions/behaviour? Please explain your answer.
5   Do you notice when people are not polite in English? Please give details of any incidents that you found to be significant.

(For full details of the research approach, participants and procedure, see Chapter 1.) As also mentioned in Chapter 1, responses have not been amended or 'corrected' so that the participants' *voices* can be heard.

Results

The results reflect how FL speakers approach interpersonal politeness practices as they explore interpersonal possibilities, attempt to co-construct joint understandings and take up individual positions regarding ongoing interaction.

Question 1 attempted to go beyond the structured framework of prosocial politeness (see Chapter 3) and examined the evolving nature of interpersonal politeness. At the same time, respondents saw interpersonal politeness on a personal dimension which develops from prosocial politeness but is subject to 'negotiation.' Indeed, respondents largely saw interpersonal politeness as developing from prosocial politeness. For instance, Fabiola said: 'Usually when upon first meeting a person, we tend to show politeness in the expected way, but as the familiarity with the person grows, it can take different forms' (6.7). This sentiment was echoed by Tomas who stated that politeness 'starts as part of routine/convention but it develops mid conversation via the interaction of the parties involved' (6.13). Individual relationships appeared to play an important role in the development of interpersonal politeness. For instance, Bernardo viewed politeness patterns and practices as

> depending on the chemistry with the people you are speaking with, politeness can take the form of small talk when the speakers interact for the first time or only for a short period of time. Whereas in deeper conversations it is easier to see politeness developing (or failing to develop) more naturally.
>
> (6.6)

Therefore, interpersonal politeness is an indication of how relationships are ongoing, emerging and evolving. The same stance was adopted by Silvia who claimed that 'among our closest friends or family there is room

Interpersonal politeness 105

for some improvisation on politeness or expressions of support and love because there is no "fixed way" of acting, and these could be more openly received here than in another type of social interaction' (6.20). At the same time, respondents acknowledged a degree of 'negotiation' in interpersonal politeness. For instance, Delia claimed that 'politeness is frequently negotiated with the persons involved. In these cases, politeness is achieved through agreement, mostly' (6.12). Meanwhile, Eva asserted that 'in some other situations it is necessary to be polite due to how the conversation develops and specially if being polite has a purpose; to convince, to be friendly, etc.' (6.27). Eva has introduced a much more transactional dimension to interpersonal politeness.

Question 2 further explored interpersonal ways of engaging in relational work by asking interactants if they could be polite in their own way in the TL. Whilst generally agreeing that there is room for an individual dimension in FL talk, respondents said that they still needed to be aware of TL cultural practices, judiciously combining L1 and TL practices and always be aware of others' feelings and attitudes. Aware of TL patterns and practices, Eva sought to blend politeness patterns: 'I think everyone can be polite in their own way; however, it is important to know what it's not acceptable in a specific culture and that should be avoided in order to respect people's customs and to avoid misunderstandings' (7.27). So rather than interrelating polite conduct, Eva tried to maintain both practices on parallel tracks. This was also the view of Alberto:

> Well, of course the idea is to try and use as much as possible the English ways, however not being a native of that language I would occasionally be polite in my own natural way, which in any case I don't think differs a lot from the English ways.

Alberto accepted that he wanted to be polite in TL ways but would, at the same time, resort to his L1 behavioural patterns. A bolder position was taken by Esteban who argued that there was room for a more personalised dimension:

> Certainly you have to adapt or at least adjust to the conventions established by target language in order to be perceived as polite: nonetheless, you can also add your distinctive "touch" to the language ways, which still come into play within the range of the target language.
>
> (7.22)

Similarly, Monserrat shared:

> I believe you can be polite in your way as well, but you have to be very cautious that your way is not disrespectful the English-language ways/ customs. Although, I believe they are very similar.
>
> (7.24)

106 *Interpersonal politeness*

Combining L1 and TL leads to the possibility of constructing a 'third way' which allows bilingual speakers to take resources from the L1 and the TL and construct their own forms of involvement, engagement and participation (see Chapter 5). However, in the final analysis, respondents stated that they needed to take into consideration others' practices, feelings and attitudes. For instance, Pablo argued that

> in order to be polite in your way the other person needs to be aware of what is polite for you for not being rude or offensive to each other. If the other person is not aware of that then following English-language ways is better to avoid any misunderstanding.
>
> (7.46)

A similar view was held by Miguel who stated:

> I think you can be polite on your own way but you have to develop a cultural literacy in order to comprehend what is going on around you, particularly when you visit a different country. Sometimes you might get a reaction that you didn't expect, especially when you try to follow the "rules" that apply in your own country. It's always important to learn the "rules" that are followed in the country where you are.
>
> (7.34)

Miguel made an important point regarding 'cultural literacy' – the need to be sensitive to TL communicative practices and patterns whilst maintaining one's own ways of interacting with others.

Question 3 examined whether there are similarities between Mexican Spanish and English expressions of politeness with respect to language and culture. Respondents identified common approaches towards expressing politeness, different ways of viewing relational work and even asserting that English and Mexican politeness should not be seen as the same concepts. Respondents largely identified commonality between Spanish and English politeness practices, and this was voiced by Soledad who reflected on her own personal situation:

> This makes me think about my family in Mexico and the United States. I see that we are culturally educated/raised in a very similar way, with certain cultural differences but whether they speak English or Spanish I believe politeness can be expressed the same.
>
> (8.35)

The same view was held by Blanca who felt that politeness could be translated between the two languages:

Interpersonal politeness 107

In my opinion, in terms of language can be similar because there exists a translation of the phrases used to show politeness, such as 'May I...' 'Could I...' 'Would you mind...' and we used them for the same purpose.

(8.16)

However, respondents were quick to point out differences between Spanish and English. Rocio, for instance, said that

because I have personally noticed that the Mexican culture and the English one are different. The first one being warmer and full of contact and the second one being colder. Hence, there are going to be different ways to express those traits.

(8.30)

The emotional dimension to politeness appeared to be an underlying difference as also asserted by Fabiola:

No, I don't think they are expressed in the same way. As I've said on a previous question, generally speaking, in Mexican Spanish, there is a certain familiarity with which you interact with a person even upon meeting them for the first time. For example, in Mexico, to show politeness, you might ask about the person's family. In English, you might be more mindful of respecting personal boundaries.

(8.7)

However, many interactants went beyond comparing politeness practices and contended that they were different concepts. For instance, Anahi stated:

In my opinion, the most significant difference is in culture because in Mexican Spanish sometimes we tend to be nosy for English speaking people since we ask a lot of questions and they might not be used to know that much information about people.

(8.39)

Therefore, Anahi viewed Mexican politeness as showing inquisitiveness and in wanting to relate to others. Meanwhile, Carmen said that Mexican politeness is unique:

Definitely Mexican people have their "own" way to be polite. Starting from the vocabulary we use to express politeness. In Mexico people say "God bless you, God will pay this favour", expressions like these to say thanks and in English I haven't heard a person saying this. They say thanks, thanks a lot, I really appreciate it, etc.

(8.19)

108   *Interpersonal politeness*

The answers reveal that politeness may not be viewed in the same way between different languages even if there appears to be universals such as concern for others and showing respect.

In question 4, respondents were asked whether they employed Mexican politeness resources in English. The question sought to explore whether interactants focused more on expressing politeness rather than keeping to determined language structure. Respondents said that expressing Mexican politeness was part of who they were and that they transferred politeness patterns to the TL. Other interactants were not so sure as they felt that Mexican and English-language politeness were not interchangeable. Respondents reported that they often made a conscious effort to employ Mexican polite practices in the TL. For instance, reflecting on whether she promotes her L1 politeness, Claudia said 'Yes, mostly behavior. I try to show people my cultural politeness ways even in a different language' (9.5). Therefore Claudia wanted her addressees to know that she was Mexican and wanted to project that image. Meanwhile, Angelica reflected that it was 'Probably all the time. As I explained before, I am most certain that I transferred much of my Mexican politeness to my English customs' (9.8). Pragmatic transfer of L1 behavioural patterns to the TL was a strong feature of the answers. For instance, Daniel said that 'Definitely I do. Specially, when I´m in formal situations, I always try to be polite and I think how I'm polite in Spanish' (9.17). Meanwhile, Laura has found herself employing Mexican politeness routines in TL social encounters: 'Once I was in a restaurant and offer to everyone else (not Mexicans) from my food, they thought it was odd but kind to offer' (9.28). However, there were participants who said that Mexican and English-language politeness routines were not interchangeable. For instance, Cristina said, 'I don't believe my Mexican customs can be transferable to a non Speaking environment. This in terms of trying to be polite' (9.52). José held the same view 'because both languages use different structures and to some extent English has more polite structures to express politeness' (9.3). The answers generally indicate that respondents felt that Mexican politeness was a resource that could be employed in the TL.

In question 5, respondents were asked whether they noted a lack of politeness in the TL. People generally do not notice when people are polite but rather when it fails to be employed. Respondents particularly noticed when TL practices differ from Mexican practices and especially when relational expectations were not met. Fabiola noticed that Mexican politeness practices such as continuing and extending social encounters were seen impolite in TL interaction: 'Usually what I notice is that Mexicans want to continue with a conversation and might be perceived as insistent' (10.7). Meanwhile, Delia observed TL speakers' forceful conversational practices:

> I have noticed rude language when Americans talk harshly or in a very direct way that contradicts what you just said. Sometimes they

Interpersonal politeness 109

sugar-coat the disagreement with formal words, but either way what they say comes across as rude.

(10.12)

Part of the problem with contrasting views of politeness practices may result from differing expectations. Roberta is particularly aware of this:

> On the one hand, I have felt that people are impolite, but on the other hand, I understand I should not expect them to answer or behave as Mexican people do. A very simple example is that I used to say, "bless you" to a former British colleague every time he would sneeze, but he would never respond, "Thank you". After a million times, I decided not to say, "bless you" anymore, even though we are in Mexico. My colleague would not follow the saying, *When in Rome, do as Romans do...*

(10.23)

Nora had a similar experience where she was expecting her addressee to adhere to Mexican politeness practices:

> Today I had an experience of a professional calling me to ask a question – they didn't introduce themselves nor did they ask how I was and went straight into enquiring about something – I found that impolite and the tone of voice also played a part in the person almost sounding aggressive without meaning to.

(10.32)

Respondents obviously face the challenge of trying to understand whether polite practices are different between Mexican Spanish and the English language or other interactants are being rude or impolite. On the other hand, politeness may not come easy to some people as noted by Dafne:

> Working at a touristy restaurant in Sydney makes me see it every day. People who struggle with the language as well as people who already speak decent English but lack politeness. For example, ordering saying "I want..." instead of "Can I, please, get...?"

(10.29)

Meanwhile, Bernardo noted that in his language class:

> I believe most people who are not in a C1 level or beyond do not understand the many social implications of the language, therefore their politeness can either be non-existing or a complete reflection of politeness from their own culture.

(10.6)

110   *Interpersonal politeness*

[The C1 level reflects proficient language use as defined by the Common European Framework of Reference for Languages (CEFR)].

Discussion

Respondents were very much aware of language and cultural differences between their L1 and the TL and pinpointed areas of individualised interaction that did not necessarily follow TL precepts.

Answers to question 1 indicated that respondents saw interpersonal politeness developing from prosocial politeness. This would suggest that teachers first need to deal with proper, expected and appropriate ways to be polite and help learners to identify societal rules and adhere to social norms of behaviour. This can be achieved through the *Illustration-Interaction-Induction* (i + i + i) mode (Carter, 2004; Carter & McCarthy, 1995; McCarthy, 1998; McCarthy & Carter, 1995) which calls on language users to identify and reflect on communicative patterns and practices (see Chapter 6). FL users are then in a stronger position to engage in interpersonal politeness.

Responses to Question 2 reveal that participants acknowledged that whilst they needed to adhere to TL relational practices and patterns of behaviour, they still sought out their own ways of being polite. The choice was between combined L1 and TL practices or developing their own 'third way' of engaging in relational work. This opportunity allows FL speakers to express themselves through any available communicative resources that can be adapted, constructed or created.

Question 3 revealed that respondents were more than aware of similarities and differences between Spanish and English. Language teachers need to recognise that learners come to the classroom with their own concepts of relational behaviour and these need to be dealt with rather than employing class time on merely focusing on TL ways of expressing politeness. Just as importantly is the fact that interactants see politeness as different concepts in the two languages. This calls for pedagogical intervention so that learners can analyse the phenomenon of politeness as an individualised concept and can be examined through the use of cultural capsules, culture clusters and critical incidents (see Chapter 6).

Answers to question 4 indicate that Mexican politeness was a transferable resource that could and was employed in the TL. Respondents were often proud of their Mexican politeness practices and patterns and wanted to express them in the TL. Consequently, teachers have the opportunity to examine how Mexican politeness practices can be expressed in the TL. At the same time, teachers need to make students aware of those L1 politeness practices that may be employed in the TL but are not truly appreciated and understood and can potentially lead to confusion and misinterpretation.

Interpersonal politeness 111

Question 5 reflects the struggle to understand TL politeness practices especially when one's expectations are based on one's L1 practices or on one's expectations regarding TL politeness. For instance, FL speakers may expect TL interlocutors to be polite as portrayed in language textbooks, films and books. Teachers need to alert students to the problem of positive and negative stereotypes (see Chapter 6) and try to ground politeness expectations in real-life situations and experiences.

Conclusion

Results from the research indicate that foreign language speakers often seek out opportunities to structure, fashion, develop and consolidate social and personal relationships when they engage in meaningful and productive communicative encounters. They will choose to project, develop and construct their own relational understandings in specific contexts by employing interpersonal politeness resources and assets to connect with others, achieve rapport and establish their own positionality.

This means that FL users make conscious decisions regarding their politeness behaviour and how they want interactions to develop, especially since they are more than aware of their relational surroundings. At the same time, FL interactants strongly interrelate TL politeness patterns and practices with their L1 cultural experiences, values and attitudes. Given that interactants are proud of their L1 ways of engaging in interpersonal behaviour, they often want to incorporate these into their TL communicative behaviour. This goal allows interactants to determine and shape their own ways of being polite which may evolve into developing a 'third way.' To effectively allow learners to be 'polite' in their own ways, teachers have to build on the learners' existing knowledge, personal histories and individual experiences when dealing with interpersonal politeness in the language classroom. Rather than merely focusing on TL politeness patterns and practices, teachers need to define how learners can engage in relational work that allows them to connect with others whilst achieving their own communicative goals and, at the same time, allowing them to maintain their individuality and own ways of coming across in the TL.

Engaging in interpersonal politeness presents unique challenges for the FL interlocutors as they relate, engage and position themselves in terms of investment, doing politeness and relational maintenance. Teachers need to help FL users align themselves with others and assess and evaluate developing and ongoing relationships. Consequently, doing FL politeness aims to achieve workable relationships such as affiliation, supportiveness and empathy. However, given the potential communicative clash between L1 and TL politeness practices and patterns, interactants may often reflect on, question and even challenge established TL politeness practices and patterns of behaviour. This is the subject of Chapter 5.

112 *Interpersonal politeness*

References

Arundale, R. (2010). Relating. In M. A. Locher & L. S. Graham (Eds.), *Interpersonal pragmatics* (pp. 137–166). Berlin/New York: de Gruyter.

Arundale, R. (2020). *Communicating & relation: Constituting face in everyday interacting.* New York: Oxford University Press.

Aston, G. (1988). *Learning comity: An approach to the description and pedagogy of interaction speech.* Bologna: Cooperativa Libraria Universitaria Editrice Bologna.

Aston, G. (1989). Solidarity and conflict as metaphors of the discourse process. In L. Curti, L. Di Michele, T. Frank, & M. Vitale (Eds.), *Il muro del linguaggio* (pp. 413–426). Naples: Istituto Universitario Orientale.

Aston, G. (1993). Notes on the interlanguage of comity. In G. Kasper & S. Blum-Kulka (Eds.), *Interlanguage pragmatics* (pp. 224–250). New York: Oxford University Press.

Bayraktaroğlu, A. (1991). Politeness and interactional imbalance. *International Journal of the Sociology of Language, 92*, 5–34.

Bayraktaroğlu, A. (2001). Advice-giving in Turkish: "Superiority" or "solidarity"? In A. Bayraktaroğlu & M. Sifianou (Eds.), *Linguistic politeness across boundaries: The case of Greek and Turkish* (pp. 177–208). Amsterdam: John Benjamins.

Bourdieu, P. (1972). *Outline of a theory of practice.* Cambridge: Cambridge University Press.

Bourdieu, P. (1977). The economics of linguistic exchanges (trans. R. Nice). *Social Science Information, XVI*(6), 645–668.

Bourdieu, P. (1980). *The logic of practice.* Stanford: Stanford University Press.

Bourdieu, P. (1991). *Language & symbolic power.* Cambridge: Polity Press.

Carter, R. (2004). *Language and creativity: The art of common talk.* London: Routledge.

Carter, R., & McCarthy, M. (1995). Grammar and spoken language. *Applied Linguistics, 16*(2), 141–158.

Culpeper, J., & Haugh, M. (2021). (Im)politeness and sociopragmatics. In M. Kádár Haugh, Z. Dániel, & M. Terkourafi (Eds.), *The Cambridge Handbook of sociopragmatics* (pp. 313–339). Cambridge: Cambridge University Press.

Du Bois, J. (2007). The stance triangle. In R. Englebretson (Ed.), *Stancetaking in dis-course: Subjectivity, evaluation, interaction* (pp. 139–182). Amsterdam/Philadelphia, PA: John Benjamins.

Eggins, S., & Slade, D. (1997). *Analysing casual conversation.* London: Cassell.

Englebretson, R. (2007). Introduction. In R. Englebretson (Ed.), *Stancetaking in discourse: Subjectivity, evaluation, interaction* (pp. 1–25). Amsterdam/Philadelphia: John Benjamins.

Fukushima, S. (2019). A metapragmatic aspect of politeness; with a special emphasis on attentiveness in Japanese. In Eva Ogiermann & Pilar Garcés-Conejos Blitvich (Eds.), *From speech acts to lay understandings of politeness* (pp. 226–247). Cambridge: Cambridge University Press.

Grainger, K., & Mills, S. (2016). *Directness and indirectness across cultures.* Basingstoke, Hampshire, UK: Palgrave Macmillan.

Grundy, P. (2000). *Doing pragmatics.* London: Arnold.

Halliday, M. A. K. (1973/1997). Language in a social perspective. In N. Coupland & A. Jaworski (Eds.), *Sociolinguistics: A reader and coursebook* (pp. 31–38). Basingstoke: Macmillan.

Interpersonal politeness 113

Halliday, M. A. K. (1978). *Language as social semiotic.* London: Edward Arnold.

Harder, P. (1980). Discourse as self-expression – on the reduced personality of the second-language learner. *Applied Linguistics, 1*(3), 262–270.

Jaworski, A., & Thurlow, C. (2009). Taking an elitist stance: Ideology and the discursive production of social distinction. In A. Jaffe (Ed.), *Stance: Sociolinguistic perspectives* (pp. 227–249). New York: Oxford University Press.

Johnstone, B. (2009). Stance, style, and the linguistic individual. In A. Jaffe (Ed.), *Stance: Sociolinguistic perspectives* (pp. 29–52). New York: Oxford University Press.

Kádár, D. Z., & Haugh, M. (2013). *Understanding politeness.* Cambridge: Cambridge University Press.

Kasper, G. (2006). Introduction: Special issue on discursive politeness. *Multilingua, 25*, 243–248.

Keisanen, T., & Kärkkäinen, E. (2014). Stance. In K. Schneider & A. Barron (Eds.), *Pragmatics of discourse* (pp. 295–314). Berlin/Boston, MA: Mouton de Gruyter.

Knapp, M. L. (1978). *Social intercourse.* Boston, MA: Allyn and Bacon.

Kramsch, C. (2013). Afterword. In B. Norton *Identity and language learning* (2nd Edition, pp. 192–201). Bristol: Multilingual Matters.

Linguistic Politeness Research Group (2011). *Discursive approaches to politeness.* Berlin/Boston, MA: De Gruyter Mouton.

Locher, M. A. (2004). *Power and politeness in action: Disagreements in oral communication.* Berlin/New York: Mouton de Gruyter.

Locher, M. A., & Watts, R. J. (2005). Politeness theory and relational work. *Journal of Politeness Research, 1*, 9–33.

McCarthy, M. (1998). *Spoken language & applied linguistics.* Cambridge: Cambridge University Press.

McCarthy, M., & Carter, R. (1995). Spoken grammar: What is it and how can we teach it? *ELT Journal, 49*(3), 1–21.

Malinowski, B. (1923/1969). The problem of meaning in primitive languages. In C. K. Ogden & I. A. Richards (Eds.), *The meaning of meaning: A study of the influence upon thought and of the science of symbolism* (pp. 310–352). London: Routledge & Kegan Paul Ltd.

Mills, S. (2011). Discursive approaches to politeness and impoliteness. In Linguistic Politeness Research Group (Ed.), *Discursive approaches to politeness* (pp. 19–56). Berlin/Boston, MA: De Gruyter Mouton.

Mills, S. (2017). *English politeness and class.* Cambridge: Cambridge University Press.

Mugford, G. (2009). La cortesía en conflicto en clases de una segunda lengua. In L. Rodríguez Alfano (Ed.), *La(des)cortesía y la imagen social en México* (pp. 79–107). Monterrey (México)-Estocolmo (Suecia): UANL-EDICE.

Mugford, G. (2011). That's not very polite! Discursive struggle and situated politeness in the Mexican English-language classroom. In B. L. Davies, M. Haugh, & A. J. Merrison (Eds.), *Situated politeness* (pp. 53–72). London/New York: Continuum.

Mugford, G. (2014). Giving Mexican EFL users a social voice: The struggle between conformity and individuality. In S. Marshall, A. Clemente, & M. Higgins (Eds.), *Shaping ethnography in multilingual and multicultural contexts* (pp. 225–249). London/Ontario, Canada: The Althouse Press.

Mugford, G. (2020). Mexican politeness: An empirical study on the reasons underlying/motivating practices to construct local interpersonal relationships. *Russian Journal of Linguistics, 24*(1), 31–55.

114 Interpersonal politeness

Mugford, G. (2022). *Developing cross-cultural relational ability in Foreign language learning: Asset-based pedagogy to enhance pragmatic competence*. New York/ Abingdon, UK: Routledge.

Norton, B. (2013). *Identity and language learning* (2nd Edition). Bristol: Multilingual Matters.

Norton, B., & Toohey, K. (2011). Identity, language learning, and social change. *Language Teaching*, *44*(4), 412–446.

Ogiermann, E., & Garcés-Conejos Blitvich, P. (2019). Im/politeness between the analyst and participant perspectives: An overview of the field. In E. Ogiermann & P. Garcés-Conejos Blitvich (Eds.), *From speech acts to lay understandings of politeness* (pp. 1–24). Cambridge: Cambridge University Press.

Sifianou, M. (1995). Do we need to be silent to be extremely polite? Silence and FTAs. *International Journal of Applied Linguistics*, *5*(1), 95–110.

Spencer-Oatey, H. (2000). Rapport management: A framework for analysis. In H. Spencer-Oatey (Ed.), *Culturally speaking. Managing Rapport through talk across cultures* (pp. 11–46). London: Continuum.

Spencer-Oatey, H. (2008). *Culturally speaking: Culture, communication and politeness theory*. London: Continuum.

Spencer-Oatey, H., & Kádár, D. (2021). *Intercultural politeness*. Cambridge: Cambridge University Press.

Tannen, D. (1981). Indirectness in discourse; Ethnicity in conversational style. *Discourse Processes*, *4*, 221–228.

Tannen, D. (1984). *Conversational style: Analyzing talk among friends*. Norwood, NJ: Ablex.

Terkourafi, M. (2005). Beyond the micro-level in politeness research. *Journal of Politeness Research*, *1*(2), 237–262.

Tracy, K., & Robles, J. S. (2013). *Everyday talk: Building and reflecting identities*. New York: Guildford Press.

Watts, R. J. (2003). *Politeness*. Cambridge: Cambridge University Press.

Watts, R. J. (2008). Rudeness, conceptual blending theory and relational work. *Journal of Politeness Research*, *4*(2), 289–317.

5 Contested politeness

Introduction

Whereas prosocial politeness (Chapter 3) focuses on participating in proper, expected and appropriate ways and interpersonal politeness (Chapter 4) examines ways to construct, shape, expand and maintain personal and social relationships, contested politeness involves interactants reflecting on, questioning and challenging politeness practices. This stance is especially relevant in FL (foreign language) interaction as interlocutors bring their own attitudes, understandings and experiences to the TL (target language) context. Furthermore, interactants may query politeness practices that appear to be insincere, bizarre or just bewildering. As a result, interlocutors may try to behave in more personal and individualistic ways. Personalised behaviour means appropriating politeness practices, creating one's own way of coming across or even adopting a hybrid approach which intermeshes politeness practices from the L1 with the TL.

Traditional approaches to understanding politeness try to identify conventional behaviour, social norms and interactional patterns. Consequently, FL users are expected to adhere to such identifiable practices, particularly, if they want to be accepted into the TL society. However, in adopting a critical stance, FL speakers may choose to respond in a variety of ways when faced with what they believe to be communicatively restrictive practices or even a form of social or personal control. Responses may range from engaging in creative politeness practices to openly opposing and resisting TL norms of behaviour. Responses may emerge from a lack of cultural and social identification with TL norms and practices or from the interlocutor's *habitus* (Bourdieu, 1972, 1980, 1991) i.e. experiences, beliefs, and attitudes that form and affect interactional involvement and social action (Grenfell, 2011).

Contesting TL politeness patterns and practices presents inherent communicative risks for FL interactants as they may resist calls for compliance, conformity and standardised behaviour as is often anticipated and expected in given activity types, frames and genres (see below). Interlocutors may find TL practices contradictory, overpowering and debilitating, particularly

DOI: 10.4324/9781003326052-5

116   *Contested politeness*

if they feel that they isolate, suppress or exclude them. Contesting TL politeness may be reflected through a strong critical cultural dimension if bilingual interactants see a communicative mismatch between what is said and actual behaviour. In response, interactants may value more their own ways of interacting and they may try to carry them out in order to establish, maintain, consolidate and sustain interpersonal relationships. This may result in a much more individualistic and personal touch to FL interaction. In other words, FL users may attempt to access, construct and implement the necessary language resources rather than being limited by socially approved standardised language norms and practices. Whilst opting to transfer assets and resources from their own L1 (see Chapter 4), interlocutors may also decide to construct a 'third place' (Cohen, 2018; Kramsch, 1993) which allows them to take resources from the L1 and the TL and construct their own forms of involvement, engagement and participation.

To examine contested politeness within the context of FL interaction, this chapter is designed in the following way. First of all, I examine the structured nature of politeness which can be examined through Halliday's (1973/1997) textual function and the concept of genres. An understanding of politeness structures provides insights into how FL interactants build on their own experiences, beliefs and histories, i.e. Bourdieu's (1972, 1980, 1991) habitus. FL speakers will attempt to identify their own personal needs and reflect on how, and to what extent, they can express themselves in the TL language. On the contrary, they may find their attempts limited or restricted. In order to respond to their own needs and wants, interlocutors can develop a critical language awareness that enables to assess and react, if necessary, to TL politeness practices and patterns. The development of critical language awareness allows FL users to consider how power and dominance affect interactional and transactional relationships. In understanding the interactional choices when engaging in TL politeness, FL interlocutors are in a position to develop their own individualised practices, engage in creative language use and, if necessary, develop modes of resistance and opposition. FL responses to politeness may result in interactants constructing a 'third place' (Cohen, 2018; Kramsch, 1993) which goes beyond combining L1 and L2 resources and practices by initiating and enacting their own individual approach to TL politeness. Finally, by adopting an emic perspective, I examine if, and how, Mexican FL users' contest TL politeness practices. Answers can reveal the extent to which FL users conform to, and accept, TL politeness norms and practices and the degree to which they create, shape and design their own modes of linguistic and cultural action.

Understanding structured politeness

In questioning, challenging and contesting behavioural patterns, interactants need to examine and identify the organisational structure of

Contested politeness 117

politeness practices and how they are employed to achieve interactional and transactional objectives. Structured politeness can also be understood within Halliday's ideational-interpersonal-textual framework (see Chapter 1 for an overview). (The ideational and interpersonal dimensions were dealt with in Chapters 3 and 4, respectively.) The textual function 'represents the speaker's text-forming potential; it is that which makes text relevant' and 'it is only in combination with textual meanings that ideational and interpersonal meanings are actualized' (Halliday, 1978, pp. 112–113). In other words, the textual function provides a framework within which to express politeness and understand its function. Related to the textual function, the concept of genres offers a way of analysing politeness practices and patterns in specific activity types, frames and scripts (Spencer-Oatey, 2008). Genres can be defined as 'communicative events which are associated with particular settings and which have recognised structures and communicative functions' (Flowerdew, 2010, p. 138). Therefore, the study of genres can help FL interactants understand the specific uses of politeness resources and assets in localised and generalisable situations.

Textual function

Whereas ideational meaning reflects participants' understandings, experiences and the interpersonal dimension considers how people relate to one another whilst expressing their individuality, the textual function organises content and relational positioning to reveal the structural organisation of interaction. Politeness needs to be cohesive and coherent so that utterances are pertinent, purposeful, meaningful and directed. In this vein, Halliday describes the textual as follows:

> The textual component represents the speaker's text-forming potential; it is that which makes text relevant. This is the component which provides the texture; that which makes the difference between language that is suspended *in vacuo* and language that is operational in a context of situation. It expresses the relation of the language to its environment, including both the verbal environment – what has been said or written before – and the nonverbal, situational environment. Hence the textual function has an enabling function with respect to the other two; it is only in combination with textual meanings that ideational and interpersonal meanings are actualized.
>
> (1978, pp. 112–113)

Halliday's definition has important implications for contested politeness practices. First of all, the textual function invites interactants to consider language use with respect to its overall communicative context: the textual function can empower FL users to organise and structure relational talk. It enables them to take control of, and direct, their relational behaviour in

118 *Contested politeness*

given interactional activities such as when gossiping, doing small talk and engaging in self-disclosure. The textual dimension permits interlocutors to appropriate cohesive and meaning-making devices (i.e. coherence) so that they reflect their own goals and objectives. Secondly, the textual dimension allows interlocutors to give prominence or salience to different aspects of relational work as they either foreground or play down their own experiences, histories and attitudes. Thirdly, the textual function emphasises the nonverbal dimension to communication which must be an important consideration in TL use and in analysing and understanding politeness patterns and practices. Lastly, the textual function helps FL interactants to structure their response to politeness norms and conduct in their own way whether it be to query, contest or defy TL politeness practices.

Genres

Key ways of organising texts can be found in the concept of genres as they reflect usually easily distinguishable social conduct and identifiable patterns of interaction. They reveal 'culturally recognised, patterned ways of speaking, or structured cognitive frameworks for engaging in discourse' (Coupland, 2007, p. 15). Spoken genres encompass social action and social practice and may include greetings, goodbyes, arguments, assessments, informal conversations, serious discussions, speeches, interviews, etc. Therefore, to understand how people behave in socially acceptable ways, care for others and present themselves as 'polite' persons (i.e. as seen through prosocial politeness), interactants need to be aware of the relevant genres i.e. 'socially agreed structures' (Bloor & Bloor, 2007, p. 8). Whilst it is fairly easy to give examples of genres, they are more difficult to actually define. For instance, Coupland asks whether banter, small talk, gossip, verbal play are genres. Part of the answer is to be found in the structure of an interaction in the sense as to whether 'it specifies social positions, roles and responsibilities for social actors and usually multiple participants' (Coupland, 2007, p. 15). At the same time, in analysing how interactants establish, consolidate and maintain relationships i.e. interpersonal politeness, 'linguists are able to describe patterns which recur when people use language to... build a relationship through casual conversation' (Feez, 2001, p. 214). Relational examples of genres include self-disclosure, troubles-telling and joking.

In displaying interactional behaviour, genres also reflect the use of 'power dynamics' (Tardy & Swales, 2014, p. 167), since genres may be employed to include or distance other interactants:

> While genres are channels for carrying out communicative and social actions, they can at the same time exclude users who are unfamiliar with their normalized practices or even to those who do not bring the preferred forms of capital to the communicative context.
>
> (Tardy & Swales, 2014, p. 167)

Contested politeness 119

The motivated use of genres may be an important factor with respect to politeness practices when FL users want to integrate into the TL community. Speakers may feel welcome, ignored or rejected by TL behavioural patterns. On the other hand, Bakhtin argues that genres allow for creative language use

> In addition to … standard genres, of course, freer and more creative genres of oral speech communication have existed and still exist; genres of salon conversation, about every day, social, aesthetic, and other subjects, genres of table conversation, intimate conversations among friends, intimate conversation within the family, and so on. … The majority of these genres are subject to free creative reformulation (like artistic genres, and some perhaps, to a greater degree). But to use a genre freely and creatively is not the same as to create a genre from the beginning; genres must be fully mastered in order to be manipulated freely.
>
> (1986, p. 80)

Therefore, reformulation of genres allows FL users to resist and oppose standard politeness practices. Generic structures can influence which aspects are foregrounded and given more prominence and which are downplayed and potentially ignored (Eggins & Slade, 1997). Consequently, an understanding of genres can help interactants understand how politeness is employed to control and manipulate given situations and contexts.

Habitus

In adopting a stance towards TL politeness precepts, norms and stipulations, FL interactants build on their existing schema i.e. their experience of the world. As Widdowson points out, schema is a mental construct of taken-for-granted assumptions about how reality is organised (**ideational schemata**) and how communication is managed (**interpersonal schemata**)' (Widdowson, 1996, p. 132, author's emphasis). Consequently, FL interlocutors are constantly (re)constructing their knowledge of the world through interaction (understanding and analysing utterance meanings) and social action and activity (the lived context in the TL environment).

By processing past and present language use, communicative experiences and interactional knowledge from their schemata, interlocutors start to shape their unique understandings of the world into what Bourdieu (1972, 1980, 1991) terms habitus since

> The individual creates his or her own history, but not randomly: he or she is influenced by past conditions-turned-into-action as well as by present conditions.
>
> (Eelen, 2001, p. 222)

120   *Contested politeness*

Habitus reflects how interactants connect, position themselves and react to the world. This is essentially a very individualised process as each FL interactant is different with their own unique experiences of relational conduct. This may be an especially challenging task for FL speakers when confronting politeness behaviour in the TL and in trying to engage in participative practices:

> In a social model based on habitus, notions of politeness are not simply the result of a passive learning process in which each individual internalizes 'the' societal/cultural politeness system, but rather an active expression of that person's social positioning in relation to others and the social world in general. As such it becomes a social tool of identification and distinction on the basis of which the world is divided into 'normal', 'friendly', 'stuffy', 'well mannered', 'uncouth', 'cool' and other kinds of people.
>
> (Eelen, 2001, p. 224)

As an active process, FL interactants engage with TL politeness behaviour and position themselves according to their beliefs, attitudes, values etc. i.e. their habitus. They may struggle to identify themselves with and fit into TL societal models of politeness. They may feel limited or even stifled when trying to express their individuality:

> Individuals that do not fit in are simply left out, their behaviour is not allowed to contribute to our understanding of politeness. At best it is explained away as 'deficient practice'. As such current politeness theories only explain part of the observed behavioural spectrum they construct theories into which not every individual fits, or at least theories that do not take every individual equally seriously.
>
> (Eelen, 2001, p. 209)

Since conventional and standard TL practices do not appear to accommodate difference or deviance, FL speakers may feel that any attempt at individual expression is labelled as non-standard or in the worst case sub-standard. In such cases, interlocutors are seen to be deficit or deficient language users with a 'reduced personality' (Harder, 1980). At the same time, FL speakers may question normative politeness standard behaviour and norms to which they are expected to rigidly conform whilst perceiving that such norms may not be adhered to by TL speakers. In conclusion, FL users are not afforded individual status and are merely seen as language users, as foreigners, rather than as fully-fledged competent participants and communicators.

Critical language awareness

In order to structure their response to TL relational practices, FL users need to develop critical language awareness that allows them to examine

Contested politeness 121

how power and dominance are exercised in everyday language use. FL learners are submitted to TL politeness practices especially given that 'we live in an age in which power is predominantly exercised through the generation of consent rather than through coercion.' (Fairclough, 2010, p. 531). FL interlocutors are notably expected to 'be polite' rather than engage in 'doing' politeness. Coulmas argues: 'Politeness is inextricably linked with social differentiation, with making the appropriate choices which are not the same for all interlocutors and all situations' (2013, p. 102). In other words, speakers are expected to be passive, submissive and 'respectful' rather than actively engaging in ways of constructing and maintaining interpersonal relationships.

Critical language awareness goes beyond enabling FL users to be successful TL interactants who have an appropriate range of language structures and functions to communicate efficiently and effectively. Critical language awareness involves equipping FL interlocutors with the insights and awareness that enable them to interact on a more equal basis with TL interactants. Therefore, FL users need to be able to access and implement the necessary resources that allow them to interact on a level playing field. This is not a matter of turning language users into surrogate native speakers but rather to enable language users to build their own cultural and linguistic capital. First of all, FL users need to adopt a critical position towards the functions of TL politeness. Prosocial politeness (Chapter 3) and interpersonal politeness (Chapter 4) reflect a non-political view of politeness practices. However, Fairclough (1992) argues that politeness practices within a given culture need to be seen in terms of social and relational variability in that they exemplify, tacitly accept and reproduce specific social and power relations. Politeness practices may, therefore, be more influenced by power relationships rather than by trying to maintain and consolidate interpersonal relationships. Under such a scheme, politeness cannot be seen as neutral. Consequently, FL users' interactional practices may be more motivated by power and domination considerations and, therefore, interactants may seek communicative safety and assuredness in established politeness conventions and norms.

One challenge facing FL interlocutors is identifying perceived instances of politeness as exerting control and dominance. Adhering to Picard (1998), Coulmas argues that politeness reflects one way through which interactants attempt to deal with societal imbalances and avoid altercation:

> Politeness is the evolutionary response to inequality. Gestures of submission and compliance, status assertion and recognition are effective means of social organization and conflict avoidance in the animal kingdom and must be considered as old a part of our heritage as language.
>
> (2013, p. 101)

122 *Contested politeness*

Consequently, in order to acknowledge power differences and avoid subsequent hostility and conflict, interactants will often express politeness through the use of formality (e.g. formal terms of address), indirect language use (e.g. modality), mitigation (e.g. hedges such as *kind of* and *sort of*) and softening adverbials (e.g. *quite* and *hardly*). Submission and compliance may also be seen in the terms of social classes, and marginalised groups may acknowledge this through adherence to standard language use and following adherence to prescribed societal norms of conduct.

> ... the standard-and-dialect continuum is yet another dimension of politeness gradation. Typically, the geographical centre of standard speech is also the centre of power. This being so, indexing a power differential between speaker and addressee is one of the many facets and functions of politeness. To see in linguistic politeness conventions nothing but a means to keep everyone in their place and maintain asymmetric power relation hardly does justice to the complexity of the phenomenon, but this aspect must not be overlooked either.
>
> (Coulmas, 2013, p. 115)

By constructing their own TL capital, FL speakers can place themselves in a stronger position to overcome potentially submissive politeness practices (for a fuller discussion, see Chapter 2). FL users should be able to decide for themselves whether they wish to follow TL norms of politeness, determine the level of politeness and which communicative practices they wish to adopt. This stance lends itself to strategic politeness as interactants decide how to employ politeness conventions, resources and assets to achieve interpersonal and transactional goals rather than being limited by standard practices and conventions.

Creative politeness

Creative language practices in the FL context can be understood through Mead's (1934/1967) concept of the creative *I* and the conforming *me*. These concepts are reflected in the language users' adherence to TL community norms and practices whilst seeking out opportunities to express their individuality:

> The "me" is a conventional, habitual individual. It is always there. It has to have those habits, those responses which everybody has; otherwise the individual could not be a member of the community. But an individual is constantly reacting to such an organized community in the way of expressing himself, not necessarily asserting himself in the offensive sense but expressing himself, being himself in such a co-operative process as belongs to any community.
>
> (Mead, 1934/1967, p. 197)

Contested politeness   123

However, FL users may want to go further in expressing their individuality since 'The "I" is the response of the individual to the attitude of the community as this appears in his own experience' (Mead, 1934/1967, p. 196). If the FL users feel constrained or limited by TL politeness norms and practices, they may look for novel and creative ways to express difference and uniqueness. In response to submissive and dominating aspects of TL politeness, FL speakers may attempt to create their own ways by employing a range of resources which include pragmatic transfer, deviation from accepted norms, language play and repetition in order to express politeness.

As discussed in Chapter 1, pragmatic transfer involves employing L1 resources and assets in the TL. This may be utilised as a sign of resistance as FL users reject TL behavioural patterns and norms. In the case of Mexican EFL speakers, actions may range from emotional displays of supportiveness e.g. face boosting acts (Bayraktaroğlu, 1991, 2001) (See Chapter 1) to specific cultural practices e.g. shaking everyone's hand or kissing on the cheek in every recurring social encounter. At the same time, Mexican interactants may reproduce L1 speech acts in the TL; for instance, they may compliment people on their new purchases (such as when acquiring a new car), or they may give elaborate explanations when apologising, i.e. gushing (Edmondson & House, 1981). Whilst such practices may reflect negative pragmatic transfer, they may also show deliberate deviation from accepted TL relational behaviour.

Contested politeness may also be enacted through language play (Cook, 2000) including manipulating language forms or, semantically, by using archaic language or obscure forms. For instance, Mexican interlocutors use expressions such as *Thanks to God* (from the Spanish *Gracias a Dios*) instead of *Thank God*. On the other hand, they may greet other speakers in English with the phrase *Good morning in the morning* – a literal translation from the jocular Spanish: *¡Buenos días por la mañana!* Language play may also appear in the use of increasingly outdated expressions such as *Take a chill pill, Talk to the hand* and *What's bugging you?*

Creative language use may not always be novel and original and can also emerge through repetition and shadowing. For instance, FL users may repeat stock phrases and idiomatic expressions or engage in shadowing: 'repeating what is being heard with a split-second delay' (Tannen, 1989, p. 88). This can be seen in the extract below as the interactants establish a sense of closeness and solidarity in the TL with the repetition of the word 'somehow'

ESTEBAN: (…) helped even us to get along better, all of us, all the team
    members
ANA: Well
ESTEBAN: Somehow (laughing)
ANA: Somehow… yeah, we… yeah somehow! (laughing)
ESTEBAN: Let's say somehow

124 *Contested politeness*

Besides being able 'to exploit' language rules and 'escape from their confinement' (Widdowson, 1984, p. 242), creative politeness practices allow FL interlocutors to take ownership of their TL relational and appropriate resources and assets that are more akin to their social way of behaving.

Opposition and resistance

Whilst prosocial politeness focuses on reducing tensions and face threats, contested politeness faces up to potential conflicts and seeks out possible ways to resolve them or, at least, to actively confront tensions and frictions. So whilst politeness is inherently a social act and acceptance into a community may depend on embracing group practices and norms (Clark, 2011), FL users may be unable or unwilling to adapt. Furthermore, politeness is often associated with a specific language group or culture:

> Many theorists of politeness assume that it is possible to generalise about the politeness and impoliteness norms of particular language groups, for example, Japanese or Greek (Sifianou 1992). In order to make statements about the language use of a particular culture, most theorists ignore the fact that politeness and impoliteness norms are, by their very nature, contested. As Eelen (2001) argues, politeness is a question of evaluation; those evaluations emanate from groups of people or communities of practice. Therefore, no culture will unequivocally hold a set of norms for what counts as polite and impolite behaviour.
>
> (Mills & Kádár, 2011, p. 21)

Furthermore, FL users may resist the TL community's attempts to 'simultaneously accommodate a newcomer's seemingly transgressive behaviour and protect the community's hierarchical structures' (Clark, 2011, p. 89).

Oppositional choices

Interactants approach the TL with their own views, attitudes and experiences which lead them to make communicative choices:

> Several researchers have noted that nonnative speakers make deliberate, conscious choices about pragmatic strategies and/or features of the target language.... Research has indicated that not all language learners wish to behave pragmatically just like native speakers of the target language.
>
> (Kecskes, 2014, p. 68)

Therefore, FL users may express opposition and resistance in a wide variety of ways. As Giroux (1983) and Canagarajah (1999) argue, a difference needs to be established between opposition and resistance and this is especially relevant to contested politeness:

Contested politeness 125

Giroux distinguishes between *resistance* – which he sees as displaying ideological clarity and commitment to collective action for social transformation – from mere *opposition*, which is unclear, ambivalent, and largely passive.

(Canagarajah, 1999, p. 98)

In other words, when contesting TL politeness practices, FL users may 'voice' their opposition whilst submitting to TL behavioural practices or, on the other hand, repel domination and explore emancipatory and liberating communicative opportunities (i.e. engage in resistance). Opposition and resistance can be described in linguistic and/or cultural terms. In terms of language use, interlocutors may question conventional, appropriate and anticipated behaviour, i.e. Watts' (2003) 'politic' behaviour (See Chapter 1). For instance, interactants may translate their L1 greetings into the TL saying, for instance, *What happened?* (from the Spanish *¿Que pasó?*) instead of the more common English-language expressions *How's everything?* or *How are things?* Mexicans interactants may answer with *Nothing happened* (from the Spanish *No pasó nada*) instead of *Not much.* Culturally, students may address their teacher as 'Teacher' because that is how they address teachers in their L1 even though they know that this may not be conventional practice in TL usage. Regarding conventional politeness practices, language users may resist using what they deem to be exaggerated indirectness when making a request, e.g. *I wonder if there is any chance of you lending me…?* and opt for the more direct *Can you lend me…?* Alternatively, they may display resistance to TL politic behaviour by actively engaging in L1 politic behaviour in the TL. For instance, Mexican interactants may transfer standard politic conduct to TL interaction by actively catering to others' needs (*ser servicial*), helping others without expecting anything in return (*hacer el bien*), demonstrating more than a willingness to help (*acomedirse*) and acknowledging other interactants' social standing (*dar su lugar*). In the TL, such practices may be interpreted as demonstrating over-responsiveness. However, Mexican English-language speakers may be more focused on expressing concern and thoughtfulness than on worrying about how they are perceived by TL interlocutors. Linguistic resistance may centre on rejecting conventional politeness behaviour, standard language use or prestige and imposed language varieties. Therefore, FL users may identify with colloquial language use and slang, and engage in translanguaging, superdiversity and hybrid language practices which allow bilingual speakers to appropriate of TL use (Mugford, 2022; Saraceni, 2015).

Synthetic personalisation

On the other hand, interactants may seek out innovative and divergent ways to go beyond what is expected and anticipated i.e. Watts' (2003) 'polite' behaviour (see Chapter 1). For instance, Mexican interactants may attempt

126 *Contested politeness*

to convey closeness and supportiveness through demonstrating attentiveness (Fukushima, 2011, 2019), engaging in face boosting acts (Bayraktaroğlu, 1991, 2001), endorsing others' wants (Mugford, 2020) and celebrating interactional successes (Aston, 1993) (see Chapter 4). For instance, Mexican interlocutors may express closeness and supportiveness through showing '*confianza*' — 'sense of deep familiarity' (Félix-Brasdefer, 2006, p. 2162); *camaraderie* — interpersonal closeness (Félix-Brasdefer, 2008); *afiliación* — empathy and rapport (Curcó, 2007); *respeto* — respect for the hearer's social status (Curcó, 2007); and *reciprocidad* — mutuality (Curcó, 2011).

Secondly, FL interlocutors may see politeness as a form of hypocrisy through which speakers exhibit insincere and feigned concern and interest for purely transactional motives. This may be apparent through synthetic personalisation (Fairclough, 2010). Synthetic personalisation attempts to individualise ubiquitous routine interactions by making the addressee feel 'valued' and 'special':

> Examples of such practices include offers of assistance ('How can I help you today?') thus potentially implying that the agent wants to help (cf. Márquez Reiter, 2011), the provision of self-identification by the telephone agent typically in the form of his or her first name, thus potentially triggering the consumer to proffer his or her name in return (Sacks, 1992).
>
> (Márquez Reiter & Bou-Franch, 2017, pp. 663–664)

Such interactions may be easily and readily identifiable in the FL interactants' L1 but may be misinterpreted as a genuine sign of affinity and interest in the TL. Misinterpretation may result from the informality and apparent egalitarianism that characterises synthetic personalisation strategies. When friendliness and concern are not sustained, FL interactants may feel deceived by the transactional display of politeness. As a sign of opposition, FL interlocutors may not openly respond to perceived instances of synthetic personalisation.

'Native' speaker pressure

Besides resisting politeness behaviour and discursive practices, FL interactants may resist the actors behind such practices. They may feel that politeness is a way for TL speakers to exert and retain interactional power since FL users are expected to dutifully and blindly conform to prescribed behaviour. FL speakers will often feel the weight of being labelled as a 'non-native' speaker and, therefore, are not on the same communicative level as a so-called 'native speaker'. This may be seen in terms of overt and covert pressure. Overt pressure comes from the following standard language. As Thomas argues:

Contested politeness 127

All too often, however, language teachers and linguists fail to admit the possibility of a foreign student's flouting conventions, in the same way as they fail to allow her/him to innovate linguistically. In fact, the foreign learner is usually expected to be "hypercorrect", both grammatically and pragmatically.

(1983, p. 96)

Covertly, FL users may feel overwhelmed by standard language precepts promoted by language teachers and linguists and feel that they are being constantly judged and evaluated on their adherence (or lack of) to TL politeness norms and practices. Consequently, they do not have the courage to enact their own politenesses patterns

Third Place

A 'third place' offers FL interactants both individual and joint ways to voice opposition and resistance towards TL politeness practices and customs. The concept of a third place (Cohen, 2018; Kramsch, 1993) starts with the premise that individuals from different cultures construct their own cultural behavioural understandings in the TL. This may emerge as an individual or as a joint construction and involves a combination of L1 and L2 resources or, more likely, the emergence of hybridity – the development of novel linguistic and pragmatic resources.

The concept of a third place emerges when individual speakers need to:

give voice to feelings of being forever 'betwixt and between', no longer at home in their original culture, not really belonging to the host culture.

(Kramsch, 1993, p. 234)

Interactants may combine the L1 and L2 but often they feel that they need to develop a space within which they can express themselves on a more personal and individual basis. A third place is not so much about selecting from different languages but rather expressing oneself through whatever communicative resources can be adapted, constructed or created. This can be described in terms of super-diversity, hybridity, translanguaging and metrolingualism (Saraceni, 2015, p. 4).

Super-diversity

Super-diversity goes beyond conventional concepts of language proficiency and language purity and embraces interactants' range of communicative repertoires that emerge from a mass of cultural influences (Blommaert, 2010; Vertovec, 2007).

128 *Contested politeness*

Super-diversity reflects the social, economic and political movement and

> is characterized by a tremendous increase in the categories of migrants, not only in terms of nationality, ethnicity, language, and religion, but also in terms of motives, patterns and itineraries of migration, processes of insertion into the labour and housing markets of the host societies, and so on (cf. Vertovec, 2010).
>
> (Blommaert & Rampton, 2011, p. 1)

In the Mexican context, migratory flows exert a strong influence of English-language practices in Mexico and, therefore, in terms of politeness, behavioural practices and patterns may not be attributable to any one specific discourse community but reflect a kaleidoscopic blending of relational conduct gained from multiple sources and stimuli.

Hybridity

The concept of hybridity transcends established and conventional language boundaries and points forward to the creative emerging power of communicative expression (Saraceni, 2015). It often reflects language appropriation as 'non-native' speakers utilise English to contest, oppose and resist increasingly globalised and homogenised language practices as seen in synthetic personalisation which is 'a way of designing discourse to give the impression of treating people as individuals within institutions that, in reality, are set up to handle people *en masse*' (Cameron, 2000, p. 75) (see discussion above on synthetic personalisation). Therefore, hybridity reflects how interactants develop new and innovative ways of expressing themselves as they take advantage of 'competing values and discourse' (Canagarajah, 1999, p. 182). At the same time, novel approaches to engaging in relational work are constantly emerging due to social, cultural and technological change as witnessed through the ongoing evolution of social media.

Translanguaging

Translanguaging rises above conventional understandings of bilingualism to reflect the wide range of diverse cross-language resources that are available and can be accessed by bilingual interactants (Garcia & Wei, 2014). As a fluid, flexible and intricate practice, translanguaging reflects interactants' appropriation of multilingual resources that allow them to develop their own forms of self-expression and communicative participation. More than reflecting proficient and competent language use, 'translanguaging is viewed as using one's unique linguistic repertoire (idiolect) rather than the traditional socially and politically named languages' (Jones, 2017, p. 202), Breaking away from formal categorisation of language, translanguaging entails the 'ability of multilingual speakers to shuttle between languages,

Contested politeness 129

treating the diverse languages that form their repertoire as an integrated system' (Canagarajah, 2011, p. 401). Repertoire is a key word in translanguaging since it represents the individual speaker's communicative power to choose among desired interactional levels of commitment and affiliation or those of rejection and distancing.

When engaging in FL interaction, speakers reflect their histories, experiences and interpretations by bringing a wide range of cultural and linguistic assets to express their involvement, investment and commitment to the interaction.

> A translanguaging space acts as a Thirdspace [sic] which does not merely encompass a mixture or hybridity of first and second languages; instead it invigorates languaging with new possibilities from a site of 'creativity and power', as bell hooks (1990, p. 152) says.
>
> (Garcia & Wei, 2014, p. 25)

In this way, translanguaging breaks with conventional approaches to bilingualism such as code-switching and code-mixing and recognises bilingual interactants' access to a wealth of discursive and pragmatic resources and assets.

Metrolingualism

Metrolingualism refers to the construction of identity through interaction and communication reflecting i.e. 'creative linguistic practices across borders of culture, history and politics' (Otsuji & Pennycook, 2010, p. 240). As they assert ownership of communicative resources, bilingual interlocutors' 'focus is not so much on language systems as on languages as emergent from contexts of interaction' (Otsuji & Pennycook, 2010, p. 240). Therefore, metrolingualism goes beyond multilingualism and plurilingualism which categorise languages into identifiable entities. Metrolingualism:

> describes the ways in which people of different and mixed backgrounds use, play with and negotiate identities through language; it does not assume connections between language, culture, ethnicity, nationality or geography, but rather seeks to explore how such relations are produced, resisted, defied or rearranged; its focus is not on language systems but on languages as emergent from contexts of interaction.
>
> (Otsuji & Pennycook, 2010, p. 246)

For FL users, metrolingualism represents the active, dynamic and evolving use of resources and assets to express and enact TL relational practices. Whilst often associated with urban areas, metrolingualism reflects contemporary interpersonal contact as opposed to static and idealistic notions of language use. Consequently, FL interactants aim to create relational connections rather than adhere to conventional behavioural practices and patterns.

130 *Contested politeness*

In conclusion, as they seek out ways to establish a third place, FL inter-locutors can only reach their goal through co-construction as they interact with other language users and

> start building mutually acceptable ways of interaction (i.e. building a third culture – patterns of behaviour and ways of thinking that are meaningful to them both.
>
> (Spencer-Oatey & Kádár, 2021, p. 288)

In the final analysis, a third place/way/space/culture rejects the idea that language users have to adhere to TL behavioural norms and patterns and reflects their attempts to communicate their individuality and establish their own cultural practices. Given that there is no one way to be polite, FL users should be given the opportunity to explore and construct their own ways of being polite. This may involve constructing a 'third place' (Cohen, 2018; Kramsch, 1993) which allows bilingual speakers to take ownership of politeness as they express their desired degree of involvement and engagement.

Methodology

In order to understand how FL interactants reflect on, question and challenge politeness practices, I asked participants to respond to the following questions:

1 Do you feel under pressure from native speakers to behave politely when interacting in English? If so, why?
2 Do you think native speakers make allowances for lack of politeness and/or behaviour mistakes made by non-native speakers? Please give details of any incidents that you found to be significant.
3 Do you ever feel that English-language politeness practices clash with your own concept of politeness or the way you are polite? Please give details of any incidents that you found to be significant.
4 Are you ever critical of English-language politeness customs/conventions? Please explain your answer.
5 Do you ever resist following English-language politeness customs/practices? Please explain your answer.

(For full details of the research approach, participants and procedure, see Chapter 1.) As also mentioned in Chapter 1, responses have not been amended or 'corrected' so that the participants' 'voices' can be heard.

Results

The results from the questionnaire attempted to understand whether FL speakers are under pressure to adopt conventional and standardised polite

Contested politeness 131

practices and the degree to which they tried to enact their own understandings of polite behaviour and conduct.

Question 1 tried to identify the pressure that FL users are under when being polite in the TL. Answers indicated that there is a lot of self-generated pressure and the need to demonstrate one's language ability. However, some interactants totally ignored any possible pressure. With respect to self-generated pressures, Angelica noted that she often feels that she wants to create the right impression with TL speakers:

> If it is my first time talking to them then I do feel a bit of pressure to behave politely, but if I'm already well acquainted with them, I don't feel pressure. I guess in the first case I feel under pressure because I want to make a first good impression.
>
> (11.8)

Politeness is, therefore, seen in terms of self-presentation. Paula also puts herself under pressure:

> I think I do, but not because of them. It is more self imposed because I automatically become more aware of my choice of words and sometimes I even go extra polite. I feel it is because I learned the language and we had many tips on how to be polite. I actually feel that there have been times I interact in English where I don't want to sound polite if people are being rude to me and I failed.
>
> (11.10)

At the same time, respondents wanted to demonstrate their FL ability and performance and that they knew how to be polite. For instance, Eva said 'Yes. I personally feel pressured to show politeness when I talk to a native speaker and specially when I meet new people. I think that pressure comes from the need to show language mastery' (11.27). Interactants, therefore, feel that demonstrating politeness is one way to show language proficiency. Elina also recognised that she puts pressure on herself: 'I don't feel like THEY are the ones that are pressuring me. I feel pressure on my own, to fit in, to speak properly, to avoid grammatical mistakes, to use appropriate words, to behave and speak politely' (11.38, Elina's emphasis). However, other interactants did not feel any kind of pressure and opted to be polite in their own way. For instance, Miguel said:

> I act politely in my own way, taking into consideration what I have learnt in Mexico and in other places I have visited. The same way that I will do in my native language. I believe I sometimes I act in a more polite way that some American people I have interacted with.
>
> (11.34)

132   *Contested politeness*

Therefore, Miguel used his knowledge and experience to be polite and does not feel under pressure to follow TL edicts. Samuel also shares the same experience: 'No, I do not feel any pressure whatsoever. I can be myself and express myself as freely as I can. English native-speakers are friendly and I do not have to overdo things' (11.33). The answers suggest that pressure appears to more often than not come from the learners themselves. Women seem to put more pressure on themselves to be polite – or perhaps they are more pressured by society to be 'polite'.

Question 2 aims to understand whether TL speakers make allowances for the FL speakers' lack of politeness and/or behavioural mistakes. Respondents generally felt that TL speakers were tolerant of possible politeness slipups. For instance, Valeria said:

> Yes, I believe that native speakers do make allowances when an L2 speaker lacks politeness or behaviour. I have come across people being understanding and appreciating my effort to speak their language as best as I can, I may have done/said something that was not appropriate or right (I cannot think of a specific example at the moment) but they try to make me be aware of it and realize it without being offensive. This way I will not be in an awkward situation in the future with someone who might not be as understanding.
>
> (12.36)

Positive experiences were recalled by numerous respondents including Amalia, who reflected on personal experience and said:

> Yes, most people are nice enough to understand occasional slips. I remember when I was working as a server and I forgot my "speech" for welcoming. The people at my table were quite understanding and were not upset at all. They even left me a good tip.
>
> (12.44)

These answers indicate that FL speakers are perhaps unnecessarily over-anxious with regard to TL politeness practices. Respondents added that TL speakers' reactions often seem to depend on whether TL interactants had had previous contact with FL users. For instance, Miguel noted:

> If the native speakers are used to interact with people from other places, they quickly realise the lack of politeness is related to a cultural aspect, and they don't make a big deal about it. They sometimes take the time to explain the non-native speakers the situation so they become aware of what happened. I believe it is different when this lack of politeness happens in front of native speakers that are not used to the interaction with people from other places.
>
> (12.34)

Contested politeness 133

Meanwhile, Agustín felt that it depends on individual interactants, and it is difficult to generalise.

> It depends on the person. It depends on how open they are to other cultures or how aware they are of cultural differences. If they are aware or if they have gone through the same situations when traveling abroad, they will most likely make allowances, compared to native speakers who have never left the country.
>
> (12.49)

However, other respondents dissented stating that TL speakers often demonstrated a lack of tolerance. For instance, Nora said:

> I don't think that native speakers make particular allowances, found native speakers perceiving certain languages as harsh and with a lack of politeness and people are not always very receptive to cultural differences that collide with their own.
>
> (12.32)

Nora was particularly aware of possible cultural clashes when it comes to politeness behaviour and interlocutors may not be aware of contrasting cultural behaviour. Pablo highlighted TL speakers' ethnocentric focus claiming that 'Yes, as they expect you to act like them in terms of language, behaviour and way of thinking' (12.46). In most aspects respondents said that TL speakers were tolerant and accepting of different ways of engaging in politeness. However, there was a general agreement among respondents in that they needed to notice and be aware of TL practices and patterns of behaviour.

Question 3 examined conflictive areas between the respondents' L1 and the TL perception of politeness behaviour. Interactants particularly focused on specific behaviours and incidents. For instance, Roberta reflected on the time she was studying in Canada:

> When I stayed with a Canadian family for a month, I noticed their dinner time was very important and they expected me to be there on time. There were a couple of times in which I did not get home for dinner, but I did not call the family to let them know about it, because I did not think that was necessary or important. Both times they complained about my not calling, because they would wait for me. Not being a real family member, I underestimated the importance of my presence during dinner, but after that second time, I learned they thought differently. Next time I was not going to be home for dinner I called, and they were very thankful.
>
> (13.23)

Roberta failed to realise that her Canadian family valued her as a respected member of household. They showed concern and involvement and felt

134 *Contested politeness*

responsible for her. Obviously, she did not see her status in the family in the same way. Meanwhile, Silva reflected on her stay in the UK:

> The common thought and the first impression I had at some point was that English speakers were cold, harsh, blunt indifferent and selfish. However, by empathizing and living in an English speaker country I could understand how they perceive politeness. A huge difference I saw was how English speaking people give great importance to respect (of privacy, time, etc) and this is commonly mistaken as indifference or bluntness.
> (13.20)

Silvia found that the lived experience of being in a TL country with its culture changed her stance towards English-language politeness. It allowed her to examine the values and attitudes of TL interlocutors. At the same time, respondents identified clashes in interactional patterns. For instance, Paula contrasted compliments in Spanish and English: 'In Spanish it is polite to accept compliments and say thank you but in English it is not seen well to do that because it can come across as arrogant' (12.10). Paula needed a way to resolve this cultural clash just like Fabiola who sees a difference regarding directness:

> I have noticed sometimes that my manner can seem too forward. For example, I remember one time a native English speaker asked me if I liked something and I said "No, not at all", and they laughed and said "At least you're honest about it", and it made me wonder whether I should have somehow "softened" my answer, or given an explanation.
> (13.7)

Paula has noticed that mitigation and softeners may be expressed differently between her L1 and the TL. Differences were also highlighted in specific topic areas such as small talk as recalled by Angelica:

> Sometimes when making small talk I forget that there are topics that in English are not polite to talk about, while in Spanish and specially in Mexican Spanish is completely okay to use them. When I went on my exchange I became friends with a girl from Texas, one day we were walking to one of our classes and we were talking and I asked her something related to religion, at first, she seemed surprised but then we continued talking normally.
> (13.8)

Angelica did not appear to be aware of safe topics in the TL and thought that religion was an acceptable and appropriate topic. On the other hand, Delia found it problematic interacting with Americans:

Contested politeness 135

I live in Tijuana, a city that borders San Diego. Many people come from the United States every day to make their shopping, to eat at restaurants or obtain services. Americans are way louder than Mexicans when they speak between themselves. It's like they want everyone to hear what they are doing or what they are thinking. They scream when they talk, but they talk normally when they approach Mexicans. So in this sense, some (very loud) Americans can be perceived as highly disruptive when they enter any space here in Tijuana. I find this veeeery unpolite. And I really can't stand it now. It's like they want to fill the entire space with their sound and their atmosphere, and I think this shows disregard for others that are in the same space as they. So, in this sense, my concept of politeness in these contexts is that we should be deferential to others when we are in a public space, but for them... it seems not.

(12.12)

Delia's perception of Americans clashes with her understanding of appropriate relational behaviour which, for her, should reflect consideration for others, respect, and deference.

Question 4 gave respondents the opportunity to criticise TL politeness norms and practices. Interactants often felt that English conveyed superficiality when it comes to expressing politeness. For instance, Paula said:

Yes, I believe being polite in English is more superficial than in Spanish. People would speak more politely but I don't think it is necessarily that genuine as in Spanish. When I was working in US, a few of my bosses and some co-workers for example seemed to be polite but it was shallower.

(14.10)

Paula seems to have a problem with the lack of perceived sincerity behind TL politeness and feels that it does not express meaningful emotions and feelings. In the same vein, Delia thought that TL politeness lacked emotional closeness and supportiveness: 'I do feel like their politeness strategies are dryer than ours. Like, they don't need to go the extra mile' (14.12). The lack of meaningfulness expressed itself through contrasting values. For instance, Silvia looked for warmth and understanding in relational work saying, 'I can admit that I have criticised the coldness and indifference of people, especially at moments when I was feeling lonely, or in the need of some Latin "love and chiqueos"' (14.20). [In this context, *chiqueo* means being spoiled and looked after.] Renata holds a similar view: 'Mexican culture is warmer, and thus tries to show respect to strangers and authorities' (14.42). Meanwhile, Esteban perceived problems with TL concepts of respect towards one's elders:

136 *Contested politeness*

I believe in the Mexican culture we have a custom of being very polite with elderlies and I don't think this is a part of the English-language politeness customs and I do feel uncomfortable that they don't treat elderlies as politely.

(14.24)

By asking respondents to highlight potential areas of cultural conflict, teachers are in a stronger position to help FL interactants negotiate contrasting values, attitudes and beliefs.

Question 5 asked respondents whether they actually resisted following English-language politeness customs/practices. Generally speaking, few interactants said that they openly 'opposed' TL relational practices. Many respondents said that they had not even thought about doing so. However, reflecting on her politeness practices, Julieta said that:

Maybe the one that I struggle with the most is directness because I do not want to be rude, but at the same time, it is hard when you met new people to know if they are always that direct? If they are joking or being rude? Or if it is normal for them?

(15.1)

Julieta has a problem coping with the use of directness in the TL as, in her case, she is not used to engaging in direct speech. Her analysis is not at a language level but rather at the interpersonal level and she has difficulties in interpreting its use. Meanwhile, Viviana resists politeness practices on a cultural level:

I think when I resist them is mainly because I interact in English in a Mexican context most of the time. For instance, addressing the teachers as "teacher", since in Mexico these situations are totally fine in a school context, and they're not impolite.

(15.15)

Viviana feels that Mexican ways of being polite e.g. addressing the teacher as 'teacher' are acceptable and appropriate in Mexican English-speaking contexts. Therefore, she is willing to express her resistance openly. Agustín offers another example as he resists politeness norms in letter-writing:

Using yours faithfully at the end of a letter/email can be one example. I just don't like using yours, though I know it's completely acceptable and common in English. So, I try to use other ways such as sincerely.

(12.49)

Meanwhile, Pedro resists employing TL politeness norms when faced with rudeness. He appears to use politeness as a weapon:

Contested politeness 137

Only when I believe someone doesn't deserve my politeness, like very rude people.

(12.14)

Therefore, Pedro sees politeness as a mutual arrangement to be withdrawn when it is not reciprocated. Other interactants often do not feel a need to resist because they do not accept TL practices in the first place. For instance, Samuel said: 'I do not have to resist to any customs nor practices because I have my own way of being polite' (15.33). Meanwhile, Francesca makes calculated decisions as to whether she will follow TL politeness norms and practices:

I do my best to be polite but I know I won't always be, so I just try to be and do my things. I went to someone's house one time that they considered rude to go with shoes inside, for me it is rude to be barefoot at someone's place, but it was not my house so I wore socks and I adapted to their own. It doesn't mean that was bad, it was just different and I respected that:).

(15.2)

As Francesca implies, politeness involves a choice i.e. whether to comply, adjust or oppose. In her case, her relational behaviour is decided on a case-by-case basis.

Discussion

Answers to Question 1 indicate that pressure to conform to TL polite practices may be self-generated and that teachers need to examine whether there are ways to achieve a balance between conformity and individuality when it comes to expressing politeness. However, it is important to note that interactants felt that managing politeness was an important way of demonstrating language proficiency. Teachers should exploit this perception so that language performance is not solely judged and evaluated in terms of accuracy and avoiding mistakes.

Question 2 probed how FL interactants felt when engaging in politeness practices. The generally positive responses indicate that speakers are perhaps overly cautious and that TL speakers are aware of different values, attitudes and practices. So, whilst teachers can build on learner confidence, students still need to be prepared to deal with adverse and perhaps even hostile reactions.

Question 3 revealed that politeness practices can be related to very specific instances of cultural clashes and provides opportunities for teachers to discuss and present different ways of viewing politeness. Whilst it may not be possible to resolve different perspectives, awareness and understanding can lead to acceptance and accommodation.

138   *Contested politeness*

In Question 4 by asking respondents to be critical of TL practices, teachers are encouraging open and frank discussion regarding not only politeness practices but the values and motivations behind them. Often interactants will ignore the insincerity and pretence of their own practices whilst criticising those of others. Whilst it is not their role to defend TL practices, teachers can go some way to explaining the reasoning and motivation behind such practices.

Responses to Question 5 indicated that there was little opposition to TL politeness norms. Those respondents who did express a certain level of resistance were uncomfortable with TL practices and often wanted to maintain their Mexican way of undertaking relational work. Whilst teachers should respect speakers' choices, it is important that they alert learners to the consequences and implications of their actions. They also need to demonstrate how politeness can be used to enhance or restrict interpersonal relationships since FL users themselves can decide how they wish to employ politeness practices.

Conclusion

This chapter has examined contested politeness and tried to ascertain how interactants reflect on, question and challenge politeness practices. Teachers should not be encouraging students to oppose and resist TL practices but ascertaining whether FL speakers feel that their language resources and assets can help them achieve their communicative goals and objectives. Respondents' replies indicated that there was often a conflict between their own attitudes, understandings and experiences and TL ways of doing and expressing things. Furthermore, interactants commented that politeness practices often appeared to be less meaningful or sincere in the TL. As a result, some interlocutors try to behave in more personalised and individualistic ways which often reflect their L1 relational behaviour. At the same time, FL interlocutors will often appropriate politeness practices, create their ways of interacting and even interconnect L1 politeness practices with those from the TL.

Respondents' answers indicate that there is a fundamental need for a critical dialogue regarding TL politeness practices. Pressure to conform often comes from the language users themselves rather than from TL interactants. FL learners may feel under pressure to respect normative politeness patterns and practices as they feel that they are held to a higher standard than native speakers who are given more interactional freedom. Such a discussion may lead FL interlocutors to struggle for a greater freedom of action regarding relational practices and behavioural patterns. Teachers have a key role to play in helping learners deal with this self-imposed pressure. Discussion may even lead to answering key questions regarding the 'ownership' of politeness and who can dictate relational behaviour. This may be especially pertinent when interactants feel that

Contested politeness 139

they cannot effectively express their feelings and emotions in the TL. Teachers can help learners find and develop the necessary resources that will allow them to engage in more expressive relational work rather than making learners adopt existing conventional politeness resources.

References

Aston, G. (1993). Notes on the interlanguage of comity. In G. Kasper & S. Blum-Kulka (Eds.), *Interlanguage pragmatics* (pp. 224–250). New York: Oxford University Press.

Bakhtin, M. M. (1986). *Speech genres & other late essays.* Austin: University of Texas Press.

Bayraktaroğlu, A. (1991). Politeness and interactional imbalance. *International Journal of the Sociology of Language, 92*, 5–34.

Bayraktaroğlu, A. (2001). Advice-giving in Turkish: "Superiority" or "solidarity"? In A. Bayraktaroğlu & M. Sifianou (Eds.), *Linguistic politeness across boundaries: The case of Greek and Turkish* (pp. 177–208). Amsterdam: John Benjamins.

Blommaert, J. (2010). *The sociolinguistics of globalization.* Cambridge: Cambridge University Press.

Blommaert, J., & Rampton, B. (2011). Language and superdiversity. *Diversities, 13*(2), 1–21.

Bloor, M., & Bloor, T. (2007). *The practice of critical discourse analysis: An introduction.* London: Hodder.

Bourdieu, P. (1972). *Outline of a theory of practice.* Cambridge: Cambridge University Press.

Bourdieu, P. (1980). *The logic of practice.* Stanford: Stanford University Press.

Bourdieu, P. (1991). *Language & symbolic power.* Cambridge: Polity Press.

Cameron, D. (2000). *Good to talk.* London: Sage.

Canagarajah, S. (1999). *Resisting linguistic imperialism in English teaching.* Oxford, UK: Oxford University Press.

Canagarajah, S. (2011). Codemeshing in academic writing: Identifying teachable strategies of translanguaging. *The Modern Language Journal, 95*(3), 401–417.

Clark, J. (2011). Relational work in a sporting community of practice. In Bethan L. Davies, Michael Haugh, & Andrew John Merrison (Eds.), *Situated politeness* (pp. 88–107). London/New York: Continuum.

Cohen, A. D. (2018). *Learning pragmatics from native and nonnative language teachers.* Bristol: Multilingual Matters.

Cook, G. (2000). *Language play, language learning.* Oxford: Oxford University Press.

Coulmas, F. (2013). *Sociolinguistics: The study of speakers' choices.* Cambridge: Cambridge University Press.

Coupland, J. (2007). *Style.* Cambridge: Cambridge University Press.

Curcó, C. (2007). Positive face, group face, and affiliation: An overview of politeness studies on Mexican Spanish. In Maria Elena Placencia & Carmen García (Eds.), *Research on politeness in the Spanish-speaking world* (pp. 105–120). Mahwah: Laurence Erlbaum.

Curcó, C. (2011). El papel de la imagen positiva en la expresión de la cortesía en México, Conferencia Magistral, Segundo Coloquial Regional del Programa EDICE-México, Universidad Autónoma de Nuevo León.

140 Contested politeness

Edmondson, W. & House, J. (1981). *Let's talk and talk about it*. München: Urban & Schwarzenberg.

Eelen, G. (2001). *A critique of politeness theories*. Manchester: St. Jerome.

Eggins, S., & Slade, D. (1997). *Analysing casual conversation*. London: Cassell.

Fairclough, N. (1992). *Discourse and social change*. Cambridge, UK: Polity Press.

Fairclough, N. (2010). *Critical discourse analysis: The critical study of language*. Harlow, England: Pearson.

Feez, S. (2001). Curriculum evolution in the Australian Adult Migrant English Program. In D. R. Hall & A. Hewings (Eds.), *Innovation in English language teaching* (pp. 208–228). London: Routledge.

Félix-Brasdefer, J. C. (2006). Linguistic politeness in Mexico: Refusal strategies among male speakers of Mexican Spanish. *Journal of Pragmatics, 38*(12), 2158–2187.

Félix-Brasdefer, J. C. (2008). *Politeness in Mexico and the United States: A contrastive study of the realization and perception of refusals*. Amsterdam/Philadelphia: John Benjamins.

Flowerdew, J. (2010). *Discourse in English language education*. London/New York: Routledge.

Fukushima, S. (2011). A cross-generational and cross-cultural study on demonstration of attentiveness. *Pragmatics, 21*(4), 549–571.

Fukushima, S. (2019). A metapragmatic aspect of politeness; with a special emphasis on attentiveness in Japanese. In E. Ogiermann & P. Garcés-Conejos Blitvich (Eds.), *From speech acts to lay understandings of politeness* (pp. 226–247). Cambridge: Cambridge University Press.

Garcia, O., & Wei, L. (2014). *Translanguaging: Language, bilingualism, and education*. Basingstoke, UK: Palgrave Macmillan.

Giroux, Henry A. (1983). *Theory & resistance in education: A pedagogy for the opposition*. New York: Bergin & Garvey.

Grenfell, M. (2011). *Bourdieu, language and linguistics*. London: Continuum.

Halliday, M. A. K. (1978). *Language as social semiotic*. London: Edward Arnold.

Halliday, M. A. K. (1973/1997). Language in a social perspective. In N. Coupland & A. Jaworski (Eds.), *Sociolinguistics: A reader and coursebook* (pp. 31–38). Basingstoke: Macmillan.

Harder, P. (1980). Discourse as self-expression – on the reduced personality of the second-language learner. *Applied Linguistics, 1*(3), 262–270.

hooks, b. (1990). *Yearning*. Boston: South End Press.

Jones, B. (2017) Translanguaging in bilingual schools in wales. *Journal of Language, Identity & Education, 16*(4), 199–215.

Kecskes, I. (2014). *Intercultural pragmatics*. New York: Oxford University Press.

Kramsch, C. (1993). *Context and culture in language teaching*. Oxford: Oxford University Press.

Márquez Reiter, R. (2011). *Mediated business interactions. Intercultural. Communication between speakers of Spanish*. Edinburgh: Edinburgh University Press.

Márquez Reiter, R., & Bou-Franch, P. (2017). (Im)politeness in service encounters. In J. Culpeper, M. Haugh, & D. Z. Kádár (Eds.), *The Palgrave Handbook of linguistic (im)politeness* (pp. 661–687). London, UK: Palgrave Macmillan.

Mead, G. W. (1934/1967). *Mind, self and society from the standpoint of a social behaviorist*. Chicago: University of Chicago Press.

Mills, S. & Kádár D. (2011). Politeness and Culture. In Kádár, D. & Mills, S. (eds.), *Politeness in East Asia*, (pp. 21–44). Cambridge: Cambridge University Press.

Contested politeness 141

Mugford, G. (2020). Mexican politeness: An empirical study on the reasons underlying/motivating practices to construct local interpersonal relationships. *Russian Journal of Linguistics, 24*(1), 31–55.

Mugford, G. (2022). *Developing cross-cultural relational ability in foreign language learning: Asset-based pedagogy to enhance pragmatic competence.* New York/Abingdon, UK: Routledge.

Otsuji, E., & Pennycook, A. (2010). Metrolingualism: Fixity, fluidity and language in flux. *International Journal of Multilingualism, 7*(3), 240–254.

Picard, D. (1998). *Politesse, savoir-vivre et relacions sociales.* Paris: Presses Universitaires de France.

Sacks, H. (1992). *Lectures on conversation,* vol. 1, ed. G. Jefferson. Oxford: Basil Blackwell.

Saraceni, M. (2015). *World Englishes: A critical analysis.* London: Bloomsbury.

Sifianou, M. (1992). *Politeness phenomena in England Greece.* Oxford: Oxford University Press.

Spencer-Oatey, H. (2008). *Culturally speaking: Culture, communication and politeness theory.* London: Continuum.

Spencer-Oatey, H., & Kádár, D. (2021). *Intercultural politeness.* Cambridge: Cambridge University Press.

Tannen, D. (1989). *Talking voices: Repetition, dialogue, and imagery in conversational discourse.* Cambridge: Cambridge University Press.

Tardy, C. M., & Swales, J. M. (2014). Genre analysis. In K. Schneider & A. Barron (Eds.), *Pragmatics of discourse* (pp. 165–187) Berlin/Boston: de Gruyter Mouton.

Thomas, J. (1983). Cross-cultural pragmatic failure. *Applied Linguistics, 4,* 91–112.

Vertovec, S. (2007). Super-diversity and its implications. *Ethnic and Racial Studies, 30*(6), 1024–1054.

Vertovec, S. (2010). Towards post-multiculturalism? Changing communities, contexts and conditions of diversity. *International Social Science Journal, 199,* 83–95

Watts, R. J. (2003). *Politeness.* Cambridge: Cambridge University Press.

Widdowson, H. G. (1984). *Explorations in applied linguistics 2.* Oxford: Oxford University Press.

Widdowson, H. G. (1996). *Linguistics.* Oxford: Oxford University Press.

6 Foreign language politeness pedagogy

Introduction

Whilst teachers can prepare FL learners to engage in relational work, it is an open question whether they can actually 'teach' politeness. Without getting into such a hotly contested debate, which was touched on in the Introduction (Chapter 1), I argue that teachers can help speakers identify and make communicative choices regarding how they want to interact relationally with other interlocutors. These choices can be described in terms of conformity, connection and creativeness. Interlocutors may want to conform and adhere to societal behavioural norms and consequently follow prosocial politeness practices (Chapter 3). Interlocutors who seek to 'connect' with other interactants aim to construct, shape, expand and maintain not only social relationships but also to develop more personal relationships and will subsequently employ interpersonal politeness practices (Chapter 4). Speakers who resist TL normative behaviour and want to create their own ways of interacting and coming across in the TL may select contested politeness patterns of behaviour (Chapter 5). The choice of a particular practice depends largely on the language users themselves, their communicative objectives, their interactional motivation and how they view a specific context or situation.

Whilst encountering opportunities and running risks in following a specific line of behaviour, FL interactants rely on their existing L1 knowledge and understandings, i.e. habitus (Bourdieu, 1972, 1980, 1991). At the same time, they will develop and build on their expanding range of TL interactional encounters and experiences. In this developmental process, language teachers have a key role to play in helping learners:

a) identify and be aware of different relational context types (e.g. transactional, interpersonal, etc.);
b) decide how they want to present themselves (Goffman, 1959), interact with other interlocutors, and involve themselves in relational work (Locher & Watts, 2005);
c) recognise how other TL interlocutors engage in politeness behaviour; and

DOI: 10.4324/9781003326052-6

Foreign language politeness pedagogy 143

d) construct and employ relevant pragmatic assets and resources (e.g. pragmalinguistic and sociopragmatic knowledge (Leech, 1983; Thomas, 1983).

Teachers can help learners to gain access (perhaps when interacting under communicative pressure) to the most effective and suitable resources to use in a given situation. However, in the final analysis, it must be an individual speaker's decision regarding how they want to approach and participate in a particular interaction. Nevertheless, teachers can raise students' (critical) awareness, help them identify interactional possibilities, realise the implications behind adopting a particular course of action and understand possible communicative constraints. In doing so, teachers can support FL interactants so that they participate in the way they want to rather than being overly restricted to a limited range of language resources.

To examine how teachers can help learners engage in relational work, the present chapter is structured in the following way. First of all, I outline how Halliday's (1973/1997) ideational, interpersonal and textual language functions can provide a broad framework for examining speaker choice when engaging in relational work. This is based on the concepts of conformity, connection and creativeness. I examine then how language users view and approach TL politeness and discuss how a critical approach to teaching and learning TL politeness can respond to students' stated personal communicative objectives. Subsequently, I consider how teaching can approach and deal with prosocial, interpersonal and contested politeness patterns and practices. Finally, I examine the cultural and nonverbal dimensions to learning TL politeness.

Choice and TL politeness

Language learners may feel that the only reason that they are 'taught' to be polite in the TL is because it represents conventional and expected behaviour. Within such a framework, students engage in, perform and rehearse extremely mechanical practice routines which seem to have been read off on a checklist of polite phrases and modal constructions to signal politeness. Examples may include *Excuse me / Sorry / Please...* and *Can / could / might ... you pass me the salt?* A more productive approach centres on the use of politeness resources and assets to achieve ideational, interpersonal and textual meanings (see Chapter 1). As interlocutors are normally focused on achieving satisfactory and meaningful interaction, Halliday's (1973/1997) ideational, interpersonal and textual language functions offer FL interlocutors focused ways of understanding, highlighting, strengthening and reinforcing the relational dimension. Halliday's language functions are intimately connected and supportive of each other and offer interlocutors communicative choices rather than giving one function more prominence than another. Whether chosen consciously or unconsciously, Halliday's

144 *Foreign language politeness pedagogy*

functions allow FL users to focus on their own realities, experiences and histories (the ideational function), social and personal dimensions (the interpersonal function) and communicative contexts in terms of activity types, frames and genres (the textual function).

The ideational function centres on speakers' cultural and individual experiences (Halliday, 1978, p. 112) and the expression of both implicit and explicit meanings. Enactment of effective politeness practices and patterns can help FL interlocutors structure their participation with regard to ways of narrating experiences, how they are conveyed, and how communicative objectives can be achieved. This

> involves looking at what topics get talked about, when, by whom, and how topic transition and closure is achieved, etc.
>
> (Eggins & Slade, 1997, p. 49)

Therefore, the ideational function can help learners identify relational work in everyday communicative activities, such as doing, saying, sensing and being (Martin & Rose, 2003, p. 71). The ability to understand and tackle TL politeness practices may present serious challenges for FL users navigating unfamiliar communicative territory.

The interpersonal function focuses on interactional and personal relationships and can help FL users express their own personalities whilst engaging in social interplay. This function is vital for language users who want to express both their individuality and sociocultural background in the TL. It allows FL users to reflect on how they present themselves and come across in the TL whilst thinking about how they want to establish, maintain and expand on TL relationships. Importantly, it reflects the speaker's meaning potential (Halliday, 1978, p. 112) and underscores what can (and cannot) be achieved in TL interaction. The interpersonal function highlights roles and relationships with a

> focus on the interpersonal meanings: this involves looking at what kinds of role relations are established through talk, what attitudes interactants express to and about each other, what kinds of things they find funny, and how they negotiate to take turns, etc.
>
> (Eggins & Slade, 1997, p. 49)

The textual function allows FL interlocutors to consider how they want to structure their contributions and how they are perceived by others. At the same time, it allows FL users to consider how others structure their own contributions. This may be crucial in understanding how activity types (e.g. classroom participation and work interviews), frames (e.g. routine greeting sequences) and genres (e.g. informal conversations and social media messaging) are structured and enacted. FL learners may want to consider how politeness resources can add cohesiveness and coherence so

Foreign language politeness pedagogy 145

that utterances are pertinent, purposeful, meaningful and directed. The textual function allows interactants to examine how politeness is expressed through activity types, frames and genres:

> [T]his involves looking at different types of cohesion used to tie chunks of talk together, different patterns of salience and foregrounding, etc.
>
> (Eggins & Slade, 1997, p. 49)

Understanding the textual function can become especially important when identifying relational work in gossip, small talk and self-disclosure. FL users are often not aware of the structured nature of casual conversation in terms of relational behaviour, such as participatory practices and topic choice.

Since ideational, interpersonal and textual meanings emphasise different aspects of relational meaning, teachers can help learners exploit language functions so that relational work is more directed and successful. Choice will depend on how FL users perceive and want to engage in relational work. Consequently, a teaching approach needs to commence with the learners' own understandings, functions and perceptions of politeness.

Responding to learners' wants

When engaging with the TL, learners have expectations concerning how their interactions will go, along with perceptions regarding how other people will interact. Interlocutors will often adopt predetermined positions (or stances) regarding TL politeness patterns and practices. These may be based on existing knowledge, previous experiences, ongoing interactions, personal observations and second-hand reports. At the same time, these may emanate from positive and negative stereotypes and generalisations about the TL and/or TC. To build on students' ideas and perceptions, the starting point for 'teaching' politeness should not commence with presenting and practising social formulae, conventional expressions and grammatical structures. Rather, teachers should attempt to discuss relational work directly with learners. People generally have very firm opinions about im/polite behaviour, and often they are more than willing to talk about these. By contrast, people may not be so interested or willing to talk about their views on grammar, vocabulary, pronunciation, etc. Therefore, head-on overt as well as covert conversations in the classroom about politeness can identify learners' beliefs, attitudes and values. It can help detect and formulate learners' relational wants and even help them to build up relational confidence. Rather than ignoring, downplaying or even dismissing learners' perceptions, teachers might want to start with how learners actually see and interact with the world: 'Sweeping generalisations and public stereotypes, mediated in popular culture and mass media and ubiquitous on the internet, are the realities of people's cultural currencies'

146 *Foreign language politeness pedagogy*

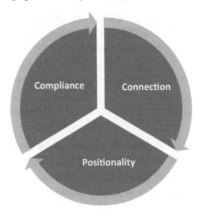

Figure 6.1 Mexican EFL speakers' relational objectives.

(Culpeper, O'Driscoll & Hardaker, 2019, p. 175). Consequently, learners' realities need to be dealt with by teachers in a direct, up-front and uncompromising manner.

Discussions regarding politeness may centre on what interactants want to achieve. Based on the results of the questionnaires discussed in previous chapters, Mexican EFL speakers' relational objectives can be summarised as follows (see Figure 6.1):

1 **Compliance**: Conforming to social rules; showing respect; being helpful and considerate; interacting smoothly and fluently; being a 'good' member of society, etc. (Chapter 3).
2 **Connection**: Demonstrating familiarity; establishing and maintaining relationships; supporting others; showing sympathy and empathy; building confidence, etc. (Chapter 4).
3 **Positionality**: Opposing and resisting norms by questioning practices (e.g. use of directness); confronting confusion and rejecting apparent superficiality; criticising TL practices (e.g. perceived coldness and indifference of people); etc. (Chapter 5).

By identifying learners' needs, teachers can enable students to make politeness work for them rather than seeing politeness as submissive and docile behaviour. Just as importantly, teaching should not present politeness as a one-size-fits-all strategy and take into consideration individual, social, cultural variations as argued by Liddicoat & McConachy:

> Within the process of learning, it is through concrete engagement in processes of interpretation and reflection that learners come to see politeness not as an inherent feature of the linguistic system per se, but as an interpersonal resource that can be constructed and interpreted in a variety of ways. Interpretative processes involve the learner in an

Foreign language politeness pedagogy 147

active process of attributing degrees of politeness (or conversely, lack of politeness) to the use of linguistic forms in context, considering not only the speaker intentions but the uptake of the listener and how perception of interpersonal roles, rights and responsibilities influence the construction of meaning.

(2019, p. 24)

Therefore, the study of politeness involves reflection and action. FL users need to understand communicative activity and interaction and, subsequently, decide how they want to participate in a given context. This may mean active involvement as an engaged participant or more passive participation in monitoring, evaluating and assessing the ongoing interaction. Within this context, teachers can help learners make choices so that they can:

1 enact their own favoured and desired way(s) of being polite;
2 achieve desired levels of mitigation, forcefulness, involvement, etc.; and
3 attain the preferred levels of formality / informality, directness / indirectness, closeness / detachment.

These choices can help give FL interactants a greater degree of control over their participation and in trying to achieve personal goals in transactional and interactional relationships as they attempt to deepen, maintain or even weaken social ties and relationships. By employing such a framework, FL users are in a stronger position to influence the outcomes in personal, social and business encounters.

Furthermore, the concept of choice alerts interlocutors to the fact that politeness is not a stable and fixed concept but can be used to varying degrees depending on the situation, addressees, bystanders and the importance given to the interaction. In other words, politeness is often constructed locally and incrementally, developing step by step. Politeness reflects a gradual, ongoing and often shaky process of making and understanding interpersonal and transactional connections. At the same time, learners can be helped to realise that an absence of politeness can cause serious communication problems. Whether it reflects a lack of prosocial or interpersonal politeness, missing interactional contributions and reactions can undermine, put into question and even threaten relationships.

Explicitness vs implicitness

In trying to respond to learners' wants, teachers need to decide whether to approach politeness explicitly or implicitly. This dilemma has been discussed by Leech:

148 *Foreign language politeness pedagogy*

[T]here has been much consideration (Kasper and Rose, 2002; Koike and Pearson, 2005, Felix-Brasdefer, 2008) of whether pragmatic competence including "politeness competence" in an L2, is best attained by students who are explicitly instructed in pragmatics, being made aware of the devices and strategic means for achieving politeness in English, or whether the acquisition of pragmatic competence can be achieved more informally and implicitly, for example by exposing students to suitably selected conversational learning materials, but not making them overtly aware of the pragmatic choices to be made. Most studies have indicated first that study in the native-language environment is advantageous, and second that it is also advantageous for students to receive explicit instruction in the pragmatics of the L2.

(2014, p. 269)

Leech's argument suggests that learners should first be made aware of politeness practices in their L1 and then they should study and examine TL conduct and behaviour. This process calls for a degree of explicitness. However, it is crucial to point out that language awareness teaching does not necessarily mean adopting a teacher-centred pedagogy that promotes explicitness, as argued by Bolitho, Carter, Hughes, Ivanic, Masuhara and Tomlinson:

It is important to distinguish between a teaching approach which advocates giving explicit knowledge to the learners, and a Language Awareness approach, which is actually a reaction against such top-down transmission of language knowledge. Language Awareness is not taught by the teacher or by the coursebook; it is developed by the learner. Language Awareness is an internal, gradual, realization of the realities of language use. It is driven by the positively curious learner paying conscious attention to instances of language in an attempt to discover and articulate patterns of language use.

(2003, p. 252)

Key to developing a language awareness approach is understanding how to interact in the TL. This may involve explicitly recognising one's own politeness routines and practices and matching them with TL patterns and practices. In developing an understanding of one's own routine, FL users can examine the resources and assets that can be transferred to the TL. Learners may then want to reflect on what they think and know about TL politeness. In the process, students may have to 'unlearn' certain L1 practices. For instance, in Mexican Spanish, a speaker might ask for a glass of water by saying: *Regálame un vaso con agua, por favor* (literal translation: "Gift me a glass of water, please"). The crux of the issue lies not so much with the verb *regalar* (gift/give a present) but rather the use of the imperative, which reflects an imposition rather than a request. In this respect, Leech contrasts the use of imperatives between English and other languages:

Foreign language politeness pedagogy 149

[T]he imperative mood is used considerably more in other languages than in English. This is true not only of Polish but of Spanish, of Japanese, and of many other languages. In fact, it appears to be a near universal of relations between other languages and English, which shows up regularly in ILP [interlanguage pragmatics] studies of requests: learners of English as an L2 have to "unlearn" the more liberal use of imperatives of their mother tongue in order to adjust to the English habit of avoiding direct directives, as a typical manifestation of the Tact maxim*.

(2014, p. 276)

* "The Tact maxim aims to: (a) Minimize cost to *other* (b) Maximise benefit to *other*" (Leech 1983, p. 132, author's emphasis).

FL users will often use their L1 bearings to understand TL politeness. Therefore, this approach favours the explicit treatment of politeness in the FL classroom as it promotes noticing and raising awareness (Schmidt, 1995) (see the discussion below).

After having identified how FL interactants want to employ politeness practices and patterns, teachers can also help learners interpret the politeness practices of other interactants. Given that concepts of politeness are based on our own experiences of the world, learners need to be made aware of other ways of experiencing the world and of engaging in relational work. For instance, small talk may not be a feature of a given discourse community or of particular individual interactants. Furthermore, just because certain TL speakers do not follow the FL speaker's L1 practices, it does not necessarily mean that they are being impolite or rude.

Critical pedagogy

Before examining the possible content of a politeness teaching 'programme,' teachers need to consider their approach to helping students activate and gain access to their existing L1 and TL knowledge. The teachers' aim must be to construct TL assets so that learners can be actively engaged in social and transactional encounters. Critical language awareness approaches can help bilingual users understand how linguistic politeness is used to celebrate relationships, reinforce feelings of camaraderie and supportiveness as well as overcome potential interpersonal challenges, difficulties and confusions. In other words, politeness resources and knowledge can help FL interlocutors achieve a range of social, interpersonal and personal objectives. These can be seen in both linguistic and cultural terms.

[L]earning politeness in a given language – to the extent that this makes any sense – cannot be reduced to memorising specific vocabulary items along with certain syntactic patterns and a particular intonation. Other important factors to be considered include non-verbal

150 *Foreign language politeness pedagogy*

behaviour, intersubjective relationships, situation and speech types, context of utterances, and individual subjectivities.

(de Penanros, 2019, p. 69)

Developing language awareness follows a student-centred approach to understanding TL politeness practices: 'A key element of a Language Awareness approach is that learners "discover language for themselves"' (Bolitho, Carter, Hughes, Ivanič, Masuhara & Tomlinson, 2003, p. 251). Therefore, learners need to take charge of their own learning and determine which direction it should take and decide for what purposes they wish to employ their politeness knowledge, skills and assets.

Any attempt to 'teach' politeness needs to reject what Freire (1993) has described as the 'banking' approach. The banking approach assumes that *tabula rasa* learners need to be filled up with language resources which have to be memorised and reproduced when required. Learning is achieved because 'the teacher has the knowledge and deposits it in the empty heads of the learners' (Winks, 2011, p. 55). In contrast, Freire argues for a teaching approach based on learners' realities which involves a critical dialogue between teachers and learners. In terms of teaching politeness, a critical stance 'goes beyond mere correlations between language and society and instead raises more critical questions to do with access, power, disparity, desire, difference, and resistance' (Pennycook, 2001, p. 6). As part of a participatory process, such teaching aims to raise learners' awareness of opportunities, possibilities, constraints and limitations.

A first step involves raising learner awareness regarding how politeness is enacted as well as noticing TL politeness practices and patterns. Awareness and noticing, along with attention to language form, fosters pragmatic development (Schmidt, 1993; Culpeper, Mackey & Taguchi, 2018). Such an approach calls for a deliberate and mindful approach to learning about politeness as opposed to picking up politeness patterns and practices by merely interacting with TL interlocutors. It is important to bear in mind that language proficiency does not necessarily correlate with pragmatic ability. For instance, advanced students, say in grammar, may not necessarily be advanced in pragmatic competence (Flores-Salgado, 2011). Indeed, foreign language fluency may not be reflected in language competence.

The i + i + i approach

Rather than adopting a teacher-led approach to raising awareness and engaging in noticing activities, learners can be encouraged to adopt Carter and McCarthy's *Illustration–Interaction–Induction* (i + i + i) mode (Carter, 2004; Carter & McCarthy, 1995; McCarthy, 1998; McCarthy & Carter, 1995). With respect to relational behaviour, this scheme invites learners to identify and reflect on politeness patterns and practices and relate them to actual TL interaction. (Figure 6.2).

Foreign language politeness pedagogy 151

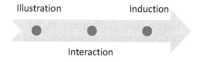

Figure 6.2 Illustration–Interaction–Induction (i + i + i) mode.
(Carter, 2004; Carter & McCarthy, 1995; McCarthy, 1998; McCarthy & Carter, 1995).

The concept of *illustration* calls for learners to observe and note real-life uses of language. McCarthy explains that '[i]llustration means looking at real data where possible, or at the very least texts carefully concocted on the basis of observations of real data' (1998, p. 67). Learners can be encouraged to adopt an ethnographic approach to TL politeness as they build up their own data bank of observations and experiences. This means that they will record instances of relational work and consider the contexts in which politeness resources are employed.

Meanwhile, the concept of *interaction* calls for the active examination of, and reflection on, politeness practices: 'Interaction means talk among learners and teachers about language (carried out in L1 if necessary), sharing and forming views' (McCarthy, 1998, p. 67). *Interaction* opens up possibilities and opportunities for learners to accept diverse insights into understandings of TL relational work. In doing so, learners may be able to avoid ethnocentric interpretations that uncritically compare TL practices with those in the L1. Multiple interpretations means that 'interaction stands for discussion, sharing of opinions and observations' (Carter & McCarthy, 1995, p. 155).

As the final component of the i + i + i mode, *induction* involves working out how language is actually used and 'drawing conclusions about the way the L2 realises its discourse patterns and genres and the means encoded in particular instances of lexicogrammar' (McCarthy, 1998, p. 67). *Induction* helps FL users to construct a viable working framework with which to participate in TL politeness practices. FL interactants observe and reflect on other interlocutors' language practices since 'induction stands for making one's own, or the learning group's, rule for a particular feature, a rule which will be refined and honed as more and more data is encountered' (Carter & McCarthy, 1995, p. 155). *Induction* allows FL users to take 'ownership' of their own politeness practices whilst taking into consideration TL patterns of use.

In summary, the i + i + i mode provides FL users with a framework for engaging in TL relational work. Rather than indiscriminately accepting TL practices, FL users can observe and reflect on their direct experiences of language use and decide on the position they wish to adopt:

a) uncritically embrace, and adhere to, TL norms;
b) establish localised interpersonal relationships;

152 *Foreign language politeness pedagogy*

c) reject and oppose unfamiliar practices; or
d) develop a 'third' place where learners take L1 and TL resources and construct their own forms of involvement, engagement and participation. (see Chapter 5).

'Teaching' politeness

By selecting a critical approach to dealing with politeness, teachers can help students develop their own ways of negotiating prosocial, interpersonal and contested politeness patterns of behaviour. They can do this by giving learners a range of pragmatic resources and assets from which to strategically choose. In the following discussion, I offer different approaches to engaging in prosocial, interpersonal and contested politeness rather than offering a list of possible classroom activities.

Prosocial politeness

Given that prosocial politeness emphasises expected, promotional, compliant and cultural behaviour, FL users need to be able to access a range of pragmalinguistic resources that can be employed appropriately (see Chapters 1 and 2). Learners can be alerted to prosocial politeness by examining a) expected behaviour; b) self-image; c) compliant conduct; d) cultural actions:

- **Expected behaviour** reflects anticipated and conventional expressions i.e. politic behaviour (Watts, 2003). Relational work may be expressed through politeness markers (e.g. *Please*), social formulae (e.g. *How are you?*) and conversational gambits (*Can I have a word?*). It may also involve indirectness through the use of embedded speech constructions (e.g. *I was wondering....* or *Would you be so kind as to...?*)
- **Self-image** involves 'presenting' oneself (Goffman, 1959) as a 'polite' person and showing oneself to be well-mannered, courteous, considerate and being on one's best behaviour. Linguistically, it is reflected through relational style e.g. formality / familiarity, respectfulness / casualness, etc. On a personal level, interlocutors may want to project a self-image of conformity, orthodoxy, assertiveness, self-deprecation, or even submissiveness.
- **Compliant conduct** involves adopting and adapting to societal practices such as by adhering to conversational routines (Coulmas, 1981), compliment formulas (Manes & Wolfson, 1981) and keeping to 'safe' topics (e.g. talk about the weather). Discursively, interaction involves following turn-taking practices (Sacks, Schegloff & Jefferson, 1974), the use of preferred responses (Schegloff & Sacks, 1973) and adjacency pairs (Paltridge, 2006).

Foreign language politeness pedagogy 153

- **Cultural actions** express social values, forms of participation and inter-action practices. Prosocial actions may reflect linguistic and cultural sensitivity as interlocutors show respect (e.g. use of appropriate forms of address), distance (e.g. acknowledging other interactants' right to privacy), etc. Cultural actions may also be expressed through the use of body language: closeness and distance (proxemics), body move-ments e.g. gestures and facial expressions (kinesics), eye contact e.g. gaze and avoidance, and even touching (haptics).

As previously mentioned, prosocial politeness offers a well-trodden rela-tional path which typically produces fairly predictable communicative results that can be especially helpful in building up the confidence of uneasy and anxious FL interactants.

Interpersonal politeness

Interpersonal politeness entails investment as FL interactants seek to establish, develop and maintain interactional and transactional relation-ships. It involves achieving convergence, finding common ground and doing agreement (Aston, 1988). Learners can examine interpersonal politeness in terms of a) relating; b) engagement; and c) positionality. Importantly, it involves exchange between interactants:

- relating involves investing in relational work as interactants probe, construct, craft, link and continue interpersonal relationships (Arundale, 2010, 2020). However, relating is a two-way street: interac-tants need to reveal information about themselves in order to find common ground e.g. self-disclosure (Coupland, 2000) and reveal that they are listening to the other interlocutors e.g. backchannelling (Cutting & Fordyce, 2021) – See Chapter 2. To encourage other inter-locutors to interact with them, FL interactants can help addressees establish themselves through asking presentation-eliciting questions (Svennevig, 1999).
- engagement reflects affinity, congruence and comity (Aston, 1988) and this can be developed through affiliation (e.g. identifying interpersonal connections, sharing common interests and building on others' opin-ions and perspectives), supportiveness (e.g. connecting with others' feelings and putting oneself in other people's shoes) and empathy (e.g. feeling the same ways as others and having a solid understanding of how others' feel). It can also be described in term of solidarity and 'likemindedness or similar behaviour dispositions' (Brown & Gilman, 1960, p. 258).
- positionality reflects the active decision-making as interlocutors con-verge and align themselves with others linguistically interactionally and culturally and build on each other's stance through dialogue and

154 *Foreign language politeness pedagogy*

intersubjectivity (Du Bois, 2007). It reflects localised social actions and reflects 'participants' joint construction of evaluations, attitudes, affective stances etc. in dialogic interaction....' (Rauniomaa, 2007, p. 221).

Interpersonal politeness reflects a much more individualistic, co-constructed and localised approach to politeness. In contrast to prosocial politeness, interpersonal politeness is developed through joint understandings in an ongoing interaction as interlocutors express camaraderie, supportiveness, empathy and solidarity.

Contested politeness

When reflecting on, questioning and challenging politeness practices, FL speakers have a choice (or even multiple choices) since they can engage in opposition and resistance to TL practices and patterns. They may seek counterhegemony, 'a more political, theoretical, and critical understanding of both the nature of domination and the type of active opposition it should engender' (Giroux, 1988, p. 162). However, contested politeness may also be expressed through proactive appropriation or individual agency:

- **Opposition** reflects non-compliance with existing norms and practices and implies adopting a passive and ambivalent response in TL practices (Canagarajah, 1999). FL users may refuse to conform to existing patterns of relational behaviour which appear to them to reflect submission and acquiescence. For instance, FL interactants may ignore TL turn-taking practices (e.g. that only one speaker talks at one time), time management (e.g. punctuality) and proxemics (e.g. keeping an appropriate physical distance from other interactants).
- **Resistance** involves taking a stance regarding 'the need to struggle against the social nexus of domination and submission' (Giroux, 1983, p. 107). It may be reflected through 'non-native' speakers refusing to accept their subordinate status with respect to 'native' speakers by resisting being given the allocation of a 'reduced personality' (Harder, 1980). In response, learners may seek to achieve intelligibility and comprehensibility rather than wanting to adhere to standard language usage (McKay & Brown, 2016; Munro & Derwing, 1999).
- **Appropriation** sees learners employing language in their own way rather than closely following the dictates of TL speakers. It 'allows students to speak from their own histories, collective memories, and voices while simultaneously challenging the grounds on which knowledge and power are constructed and legitimated' (Giroux, 1997, pp. 157–158). For instance, FL users may employ their own ways of greeting and saying goodbye. Appropriation, therefore, may involve constructing a 'third place' (Cohen, 2018; Kramsch, 1993) (see Chapter 5).

Foreign language politeness pedagogy 155

- **Agency** allows FL users to express their identity, social and transactional roles and ideological subjectivity (Canagarajah, 2004). Agency permits FL interactants to establish themselves as legitimate language users. Furthermore, it 'contributes to making possible a variety of social forms and human capacities which expand the range of social identities that students may carry and become' (Giroux, 1997, p. 158). Therefore, FL users do not have to accept their 'assigned' relational roles and can decide how they want to be 'polite.' Indeed, by giving interactants a voice, agency 'suggests learners approach learning with their own agendas and purposes' (Hall, 2011, p. 242).

Contested politeness, therefore, helps FL users not only to resist TL politeness norms and practices but also to take a more individualistic and critical stance. However, FL interactants need to take into consideration the overall communicative context when contesting politeness; considerations will include societal pressures to conform, other interactants' stances and attitudes and ultimately, the (prevailing) power dynamic that makes interactants conform.

Pedagogical resources

As proposed in the i + i + i mode, FL learners can garner relational resources through observation and participation in TL encounters and experiences. This enables FL speakers to monitor and understand authentic politeness practices and patterns of behaviour rather than having to rely on textbook examples and teacher admonitions regarding the 'correct' use of politeness structures. This can have an empowering effect on FL users, as argued by Kramsch:

> The thrill at being able to use forms of speech that are only reserved to native speakers, such as slang or highly idiomatic gambits, are ways in which learners can gain power within a system that by its nature reminds them how powerless they really are.
>
> (1993, p. 243)

All too often FL interactants are under pressure to conform to TL norms and practices, as observed by Thomas: '[T]he foreign learner is usually expected to be "hypercorrect", both grammatically and pragmatically' (1983, p. 96). Indeed, FL teachers have a choice to make here between teaching learners to adhere to orthodoxy, conformity, and conventionality *or* to expose learners to genuine, real and legitimate language contexts which allow them to decide on their own course of action.

To help learners decide how they want to interact in the TL regarding relational work, teachers can encourage learners to 'notice' the TL features and characteristics and understand the challenges and potential difficulties

156 *Foreign language politeness pedagogy*

involved in TL encounters. Noticing and understanding starts with the L2 students' observation of TL language use over a range of contexts so that they can base their understandings of politeness on principled observation, structured participation and critical reflection. Here Schmidt underscores the importance of noticing and understanding:

> I use "noticing" to mean conscious registration of the occurrence of some event, whereas "understanding," as I am using the term, implies recognition of a general principle, rule or pattern. Noticing refers to surface level phenomena and item learning, while understanding refers to deeper level abstraction related to (semantic, syntactic or communicative) meaning.
>
> (1995, p. 28)

To help students 'notice' and develop a deeper understanding of TL politeness practices and patterns, teachers can present politeness situations that call for reaction, reflection and action. To achieve this, teachers can invite learners to examine:

1. Illustrative events – studying teachers' own relational experiences
2. Cultural capsules – examining TL politeness practices
3. Culture clusters – analysing TL themes or events
4. Critical incidents – understanding problem situations

These approaches can be exemplified as follows:

Illustrative events

Termed 'cross-cultural experiences' by Ishihara (2010), illustrative events invite students to examine teachers' personal stories that reflect pragmatic routines, norms and strategies which highlight differences and similarities between the L1 and TL with the aim of developing students' awareness. Such stories give learners the opportunity to reflect on real-life experiences of relational behaviour and allow students to compare and contrast relational work across two or more languages. With specific reference to politeness studies, Georgakopoulou (2013) proposes 'studying im/politeness-in-interaction on the basis of small stories as a framework for narrative and identity analysis' (2013, p. 55). This involves 'stories about short (fragmented, open-line) tellings about self and other of ongoing, future or shared events, allusions to tellings, deferrals of tellings, etc.' (2013, p. 58).

Cultural capsules

Cultural capsules involve scripts that look at a particular TL practice or phenomenon and offer a 'summary description and explanation of the

Foreign language politeness pedagogy   157

cultural difference' (Taylor & Sorensen, 1961). For instance, Omaggio-Hadley, in discussing the context of U.S. students, depicts a cultural capsule as 'a short description, usually one or two paragraphs in length, of one minimal difference between an American and a target-culture custom' (1993, p. 394). Cultural capsules can provide insights into TL relational practices and patterns. For example, FL interlocutors examine relational work, at a micro level, regarding how interlocutors engage in troubles talk, share gossip and participate in small talk. This provides the opportunity to examine the use of mitigation devices (e.g. hedging and downtoners) as well as supportive moves (e.g. engaging in rapport and finding common ground).

Culture clusters

Culture clusters build on cultural capsules by focusing on a theme and examining different components that may be reflected through cultural capsules (Omaggio-Hadley, 1993). For instance, 'greetings, invitations and arrivals at a host's house for dinner ... could be easily converted into a culture cluster... with a culture-capsule narrative description of (1) greeting behavior, (2) extending invitations, (3) setting the table and (4) arriving at a host's home for dinner and appropriate guest etiquette' (Omaggio-Hadley, 1993, p. 396). Culture clusters give FL learners the opportunity to examine prosocial and interpersonal politeness behaviour at both micro and macro levels within an activity type.

Critical incidents

Focused on problem solving, '[t[he critical incident technique consists of a set of procedures for collecting direct observations of human behavior in such a way as to facilitate their potential usefulness in solving practical problems and developing broad psychological principles' (Flanagan, 1954, p. 327). An examination of critical incidents in the classroom can prepare students for possible difficult and confusing situations and provides them with a range of pragmalinguistic and sociopragmatic resources (Leech, 1983; Thomas, 1983) with which to tackle awkward situations. Critical incidents in relational work may emerge when expected prosocial and interpersonal behaviour does not go as expected especially when attempting to identify common interests, enrich friendly relations, reinforce interpersonal bonds and celebrate convergence.

The above-mentioned pedagogical activities play an important role in helping learners understand and prepare themselves for TL relational work. All too often politeness teaching focuses on the detail rather than the overall intention, performance, etc. (Schauer, 2009). The activities discussed above reflect both top-down and bottom-up approaches to examining and reflecting on relational work. They help FL users make principled

158 *Foreign language politeness pedagogy*

choices when faced with difficult decisions and assist learners in developing adroitness and adeptness when engaging in unexpected and unrehearsed politeness behaviour. They aid interlocutors in confronting TL politeness practices that appear to be confusing and ambiguous. Furthermore, such activities can help learners critically examine generalisations and stereotypes regarding TL interactants and their behaviour.

Nonverbal politeness

Nonverbal politeness is an important but often neglected dimension in the teaching–learning of FL relational work. It includes expected prosocial politeness conduct and, at times, the absence of certain behaviour as is argued by Eelen:

> The commonsense definition of politeness in terms of 'proper behaviour' points out that politeness is not confined to language, but can also include non-verbal, non-linguistic behaviour. Most people will be familiar with examples of politeness such as holding the door open for someone, greeting someone with a wave of the hand or a nod and so on. Politeness may manifest itself in any form of behaviour, and even the absence of behaviour: on many occasions, not returning a greeting or simply remaining silent may be interpreted as impoliteness, whereas in a library or church, talking aloud may also be regarded as impolite and politeness involves refraining from speech.
>
> (2001, p. iv)

Eelen raises an important point here in that 'absence of behaviour' may be interpreted as a lack of politeness. Therefore, it is essential that politeness is understood in both linguistic and nonlinguistic terms. This includes corporal movements:

> Other non-linguistic behavioural options such as bodily proximity, gazing behaviour and so on may all be interpreted in terms of (im) politeness. Staring at a stranger for too long, or peering extensively into someone else's home through a window, may quickly elicit hostile reactions. So the scope of politeness stretches well beyond purely verbal choices, and includes the whole spectrum of behaviour, as is clearly illustrated by another stock example of politeness: table manners, which include guidelines for verbal as well as non-verbal behaviour.
>
> (Eelen, 2001, p. iv)

Furthermore, it is often challenging to separate linguistic from nonlinguistic forms. For instance, when identifying instances of nonverbal politeness, Scollon and Scollon argue that 'it is very difficult to know where to

Foreign language politeness pedagogy 159

separate verbal and non-verbal forms of communication' (1995, p. 142). As discussed in Chapter 1, nonverbal conduct covers the use of physical space, e.g. closeness and distance (proxemics), body movements, e.g. gestures and facial expressions (kinesics), eye contact, e.g. gaze and avoidance, and even touching (haptics).

From a pedagogical perspective, the i + i + i mode can be especially useful in helping learners understand the politeness dimension to TL-TC nonverbal politeness as they carry out their own observations of TL-TC behaviour. Indeed, FL interactants need to be ethnographers in their own right and avoid simplistic generalisations or stereotyping regarding TL speakers. For instance, the tendency to analyse cultures as being high-context or low-context may lead to generalisations about all members of a given society. High-context cultures rely on implication and indirectness (Spencer-Oatey & Kádár, 2021) whilst low-context cultures reflect clarity and straightforward linguistic decoding. Bowe, Martin and Manns explain the difference between high- and low-context cultures as follows:

High-context cultures are those in which much of the meaning exchanged in a context is done so without or with relatively few words. The messages communicated in such societies are more subtle, indirect and often non-verbal.... Cultures considered high-context include many Asian cultures and the African American and Native American cultures.

Low-context cultures, conversely, are those in which detailed verbal messages are favoured. Individuals from these cultures share less background information and intimate information about one another and consequently can rely less on non-verbal contextual cues. The messages conveyed in these cultures tend to be direct and verbose and these cultures value people who 'speak up' and 'say what's on their mind' (Samovar et al., 2013). These societies are typically less 'traditional' and include North American, German and Scandinavian cultures

(2014, p. 6)

Such labelling runs the risk of ignoring individual and localised speech community practices. So for, instance, defining the United States as a 'low-context' culture does not mean that all members of that society engage in directly observable nonverbal forms of behaviour. Speakers of English in the U.S come from a wide variety of cultural and ethnic backgrounds, and, consequently it is difficult and misleading to try to place them universally within the low-context category. Indeed, Bowe, Martin and Manns notably identify African American culture as high-context in the passage above.

Whilst teaching and learning politeness rightly focuses on language use, a great deal of relational work is conveyed through non-verbal communication. For instance, Scollon and Scollon note:

160   *Foreign language politeness pedagogy*

The way a person dresses for a meeting may suggest to other participants how he or she is prepared to participate in it. In fact, we can use virtually any aspect of our behavior or our presentation which others can perceive as a means of communication. This would include our posture, our movements, our attire, our use of space, and our use of time.

(1995, p. 143)

This means that FL interactants need to observe how interlocutors manage interpersonal distance and engage in physical contact including under what circumstances. Any interpretation of nonverbal language needs to be understood on a localised move-by-move basis rather than jumping to summary conclusions. Furthermore, there is no one-to-one correspondence between nonverbal language and a single meaning. For instance, a smile may indicate amusement and friendliness or bemusement and embarrassment.

In picking up clues from other interactants, speakers need to take into account three groups: a) addressees; b) other participants; and c) eavesdroppers and overhearers, or what Kádár and Haugh (2013) refer to as ratified (addressees and other participants) and unratified (eavesdroppers and overhearers). It is important to recognise that unratified participants may help FL interactants understand the meanings being conveyed by ratified participants. Consequently, FL interlocutors need to observe, register and evaluate the relationship between language and non-verbal communication within the overall situation and not just between the immediate speaker(s) and addressee(s). In given instances, nonverbal language such as eye contact (e.g. gazing and staring), and facial expressions (e.g. smiling and frowning) may reveal more than the verbal message itself. Consequently, FL speakers need to observe the degree of nonlinguistic behaviour that accompanies, for instance, greetings and departures, e.g. the wave of the hand, a handshake or a kiss on the cheek. Such conduct can be studied in terms of communicative actions and reactions. At a speech act level, learners can monitor nonverbal actions that accompany an invitation, a compliment or a greeting. Nonlinguistic clues may highlight sincerity / hypocrisy, seriousness / flippancy or closeness / coolness. For example, when greeting, the firmness of the handshake or the type of kiss may reveal the strength / uncertainty of an interpersonal relationship. Therefore, evaluating addressees' reactions through nonverbal language may uncover the underlying message behind rejections, refusals, etc. Simultaneously, it is important to alert FL interlocutors to the fact that they may be inadvertently sending unintended communicative messages through their nonverbal behaviour.

Conclusion

Just as Kasper (1997) reflected on teaching pragmatics, any attempt to teach politeness needs to take into consideration learners' histories,

Foreign language politeness pedagogy 161

existing knowledge and experiences. FL interactants know how to be 'polite' in their first language, but enacting politeness in the TL may be problematic. The role of the teacher is to understand what resources and assets are transferable from the L1 to the TL and where any adjustments, if any, need to be made. Secondly, as pointed out by Siegal, '[s]econd language learners do not merely model native speakers with a desire to emulate, but rather actively create both a new interlanguage and an accompanying identity in the learning process' (1996, pp. 362–363). Therefore, teachers can play a key role in helping learners to construct and develop their understandings of TL politeness and practices. FL interlocutors may attempt to emulate TL practices or seek to establish intelligibility and comprehensibility. In doing so, teachers can offer students a safe space or environment in which to experiment with TL politeness practices. They can also help learners decide how far they want to go with politeness whether it be in terms of prosocial, interpersonal or contested politeness since not every user is looking for the same degree of involvement and commitment. Most of all, teachers can help learners identify the choices, their implications and the opportunities to engage in establishing, developing, consolidating, maintaining, and terminating both social as well as transactional relationships.

References

Arundale, R. (2010). Relating. In M. A. Locher, & L. S. Graham (Eds.), *Interpersonal pragmatics* (pp. 137–166). Berlin/New York: de Gruyter.

Arundale, R. (2020). *Communicating & relation: Constituting face in everyday interacting.* New York: Oxford University Press.

Aston, G. (1988). *Learning comity: An approach to the description and pedagogy of interaction speech.* Bologna: Cooperativa Libraria Universitaria Editrice Bologna.

Bolitho, R., Carter, R., Hughes, R., Ivanič, R., Masuhara, H., & Tomlinson, B. (2003). Ten questions about language awareness. *ELT Journal, 57*(3), 251–259.

Bourdieu, P. (1972). *Outline of a theory of practice.* Cambridge: Cambridge University Press.

Bourdieu, P. (1980). *The logic of practice.* Stanford: Stanford University Press.

Bourdieu, P. (1991). *Language & symbolic power.* Cambridge: Polity Press.

Bowe, H., Martin, K., & Manns, H. (2014). *Communication across cultures: Mutual understanding in a global world.* Cambridge: Cambridge University Press.

Brown, R., & Gilman, A. (1960). The pronouns of power and solidarity. In T. A. Sebeok (Ed.), *Style in language* (pp. 253–277). MIT Press & New York/London: Wiley.

Canagarajah, S. (1999). *Resisting linguistic imperialism in English teaching.* Oxford, UK: Oxford University Press.

Canagarajah, S. (2004). Multilingual writers and the struggle for voice in academic discourse. In A. Pavlenko & A. Blackledge (Eds.), *Negotiation of identities in multilingual contexts* (pp. 266–289). Clevedon: Multilingual Matters.

Carter, R. (2004). *Language and creativity: The art of common talk.* London: Routledge.

162 Foreign language politeness pedagogy

Carter, R., & McCarthy, M. (1995). Grammar and spoken language. *Applied Linguistics, 16*(2), 141–158.

Cohen, A. D. (2018). *Learning pragmatics from native and nonnative language teachers.* Bristol: Multilingual Matters.

Coulmas, F. (1981). *Conversational routine: Explorations in standardized communication situations and prepatterned speech.* Mouton: The Hague.

Coupland, J. (2000). Introduction: Sociolinguistic perspectives on small talk. In J. Coupland (Ed.), *Small talk* (pp. 1–25). Harlow, Essex: Pearson.

Culpeper, J., Mackey, A., & Taguchi, N. (2018). *Second language pragmatics from theory to research.* New York/London: Routledge.

Culpeper, J., O'Driscoll, J., & Hardaker, C. (2019). Notions of politeness in Britain and North America. In E. Ogiermann & P. Garcés-Conejos Blitvich (Eds.), *From speech acts to lay understandings of politeness* (pp. 177–200). Cambridge: Cambridge University Press.

Cutting, J., & Fordyce, K. (2021). *Pragmatics: A resource book for students.* Abingdon, UK: Routledge.

de Penanros, H. (2019). When politeness is in the detail: The case of an imperative in Russian. In T. Szende & G. Alao (Eds.), *Pragmatic and cross-cultural competences: Focus on politeness* (pp. 69–113). Brussels: Peter Lang.

Du Bois, J. (2007). The stance triangle. In R. Englebretson (Ed.), *Stancetaking in dis-course: Subjectivity, evaluation, interaction* (pp. 139–182). Amsterdam/Philadelphia, PA: John Benjamins.

Eelen, G. (2001). *A critique of politeness theories.* Manchester: St. Jerome.

Eggins, S., & Slade, D. (1997). *Analysing casual conversation.* London: Cassell.

Felix-Brasdefer, C. (2008). Pragmatic development in the Spanish as a FL classroom: A cross-sectional study of learner requests. *Intercultural Pragmatics, 4*(2), 253–287.

Flanagan, J. C. (1954). The critical incident technique. *Psychological Bulletin, 51*(4), 327–358.

Flores-Salgado, E. (2011). *The pragmatics of requests and apologies.* Philadelphia/Amsterdam: John Benjamins.

Freire, P. (1993). *Pedagogy of the oppressed.* New York: Continuum.

Georgakopoulou, A. (2013). Small stories and identities analysis as a framework for the study of im/politeness-in-interaction. *Journal of Politeness Research, 9*(1), 55–74.

Giroux, H. A. (1983). *Theory & resistance in education: A pedagogy for the opposition.* New York: Bergin & Garvey.

Giroux, H. A. (1988). *Teachers as intellectuals: Towards a critical pedagogy of learning.* New York: Bergin & Garvey.

Giroux, H. A. (1997). *Pedagogy and the politics of hope: Theory, culture and schooling: A critical reader.* Boulder, CO: Westview.

Goffman, E. (1959). *The presentation of self in everyday life.* London: Penguin.

Hall, G. (2011). *Exploring English language teaching: Language in action.* Abingdon, UK /New York, NY

Halliday, M. A. K. (1973/1997). Language in a social perspective. In N. Coupland & A. Jaworski (Eds.), *Sociolinguistics: A reader and coursebook* (pp. 31–38). Basingstoke: Macmillan.

Halliday, M. A. K. (1978). *Language as social semiotic.* London: Edward Arnold.

Harder, P. (1980). Discourse as self-expression – on the reduced personality of the second-language learner. *Applied Linguistics, 1*(3), 262–270.

Foreign language politeness pedagogy 163

Ishihara, N. (2010). Lesson planning and teacher-led reflection. In N. Ishihara & A. D. Cohen (Eds.), *Teaching and learning pragmatics: Where language and culture meet* (pp. 186–200). Harlow, Essex, England: Longman/Pearson Education.

Kádár, D. Z., & Haugh, M. (2013). *Understanding politeness*. Cambridge: Cambridge University Press.

Kasper, G. (1997). Can pragmatic competence be taught? (NetWork #6) [HTML document]. Honolulu: University of Hawai'i, Second Language Teaching & Curriculum Center. Retrieved [November 19th, 2021] from the World Wide Web: http://www.nflrc.hawaii.edu/NetWorks/NW06/

Kasper, G., & Rose, K. (2002). *Pragmatic development in a second language*. Malden, MA: Blackwell.

Koike, D. A., & Pearson, L. (2005). The effect of instruction and feedback in the development of pragmatic competence. *System, 33*, 481–501.

Kramsch, C. (1993). *Context and culture in language teaching*. Oxford: Oxford University Press.

Leech, G. (1983). *Principles of pragmatics*. London: Longman.

Leech, G. (2014). *Pragmatics of politeness*. Oxford: Oxford University Press.

Liddicoat, A. J., & McConachy, T. (2019). Meta-pragmatic awareness and agency in language learners' constructions of politeness. In T. Szende & G. Alao (Eds.), *Pragmatic and cross-cultural competences: Focus on politeness* (pp. 11–25). Brussels: Peter Lang.

Locher, M. A., & Watts, R. J. (2005). Politeness theory and relational work. *Journal of Politeness Research, 1*, 9–33.

McCarthy, M. (1998). *Spoken language & applied linguistics*. Cambridge: Cambridge University Press.

McCarthy, M., & Carter, R. (1995). Spoken grammar: What is it and how can we teach it? *ELT Journal, 49*(3), 1–21.

McKay, S. L., & Brown, J. D. (2016). *Teaching and assessing EIL in local contexts around the world*. New York: Routledge.

Manes, J., & Wolfson, N. (1981). The compliment formula. In F. Coulmas (Ed.) *Conversational routine: Explorations in standardized communication situations and prepatterned speech* (pp. 115–132). The Hague: Mouton.

Martin, J. R., & Rose, D. (2003). *Working with discourse*. London: Continuum.

Munro, M. J., & Derwing, T. M. (1999). Foreign accent, comprehensibility, and intelligibility in the speech of second language learners. *Language Learning, 49*(S1), 285–310.

Omaggio-Hadley, A. (1993). *Teaching language in context* (2nd Edition). Boston, MA: Heinle & Heinle.

Paltridge, B. (2006). *Discourse analysis*. London: Continuum.

Pennycook, A. (2001). *Critical applied linguistics: A critical introduction*. Mahwah, NJ: Lawrence Erlbaum.

Rauniomaa, M. (2007). Stance markers in spoken Finnish: Minun mielestä and minusta in assessments. In R. Englebretson (Ed.), *Stancetaking in dis-course: Subjectivity, evaluation, interaction* (pp. 221–252). Amsterdam/Philadelphia, PA: John Benjamins.

Sacks, H., Schegloff, E., & Jefferson, G. (1974). A simplest systematics for the organization of turn-taking for conversation. *Language, 50*, 697–735.

Samovar, L., Porter, R., McDaniel, E., & Roy, C. (2013). *Communication between cultures* (8th Edition). Boston: Wadsworth Cengage.

164 Foreign language politeness pedagogy

Schauer, G. A. (2009). *Interlanguage pragmatic development: The study Abroad Context*. London: Continuum.

Schegloff, E. A., & Sacks, H. (1973). Opening up closings. *Semiotica, VIII*(4), 289–327.

Schmidt, R. (1993). Consciousness, learning and interlanguage pragmatics. In G. Kasper & S. Blum-Kulka (Eds.), *Interlanguage pragmatics* (pp. 21–42). Oxford: Oxford University Press.

Schmidt, R. (1995). *Consciousness and foreign language learning: A tutorial on the role of attention and awareness in learning*. Honolulu, Hawai'i: University of Hawai'i, Second Language Teaching and Curriculum Center.

Scollon, R., & Scollon, S. (1995). *Intercultural communication*. Oxford: Blackwell.

Siegal, M. (1996). The role of learner subjectivity in second language sociolinguistic competency Western women learning Japanese. *Applied Linguistics, 17*(3), 356–382. Oxford University Press.

Spencer-Oatey, H., & Kádár, D. (2021). *Intercultural politeness*. Cambridge: Cambridge University Press.

Svennevig, J. (1999). *Getting acquainted in conversation: A study of initial interactions*. Amsterdam: John Benjamins.

Taylor, H. D., & Sorensen, J. L. (1961). Culture capsules. *The Modern Language Journal, 45*(8), 350–354.

Thomas, J. (1983). Cross-cultural pragmatic failure. *Applied Linguistics, 4*, 91–112.

Watts, R. J. (2003). *Politeness*. Cambridge: Cambridge University Press.

Wink, J. (2011). *Critical pedagogy: Notes from the real world*. Boston: Pearson.

Index

Pages in *italics* refer figures and pages in **bold** refer tables.

addressee-focused politeness 48
Aston, G. 76

Bakhtin, M. M. 119
bilingualism 128
Bolitho, R. 41, 148
Bourdieu, P. 38, 73, 116, 119
Bowe, H. 159
Braine, G. 61
Brown, P. 20, 42, 48–50, 66, 68, 71–72

Canagarajah, S. 124
Carter, R. 41, 148, 150
Clark, H. 11
colloquial language 62
Common European Framework of
    Reference for Languages (CEFR) 23
contested politeness 6–7, 116; creative
    politeness 122–124; critical language
    awareness 120–122; genres 118–119;
    habitus 119–120; hybridity 128;
    methodology 130; metrolingualism
    129–130; native speaker 126–127;
    oppositional choices 124–125;
    synthetic personalisation 125–126;
    textual function 116–118; third place
    127–128; translanguaging 128–129
contesting TL politeness 115–116
conventional behaviour 62, 69
Coulmas, F. 121
creative politeness 115, 122–124
critical incidents 157
critical language awareness (CLA) 8,
    120–122
cross-cultural approach 37
cross-cultural experiences 156
Culpeper, J. 46, 77, 103

cultural capital 36–38
cultural capsules 156–157
cultural conventions 63
cultural currencies 145
cultural politeness 40
culture clusters 157

data collection approach 24–25
declarative cultural knowledge 38–40

Edmondson, W. 42, 45
Eelen, G. 46, 124, 158
Eggins, S. 103
English as an International Language
    (EIL) 8
English-language politeness 134
English 'negative politeness,' 72
English social politeness 71–72

face-boosting acts (FBA) 12
Face-Threatening Acts (FTAs) 20, 48
Fairclough, N. 42, 121
Fillmore, L. W. 76
first-language (L1): experiences 61, 68;
    and L2 resources 127; relational
    behaviour 138; *vs.* TL 134; *vs.* TL
    cultures 79
FL *see* foreign language
FL speakers 66–67, 76, 116, 120, 123,
    130, 132, 138; native speaker 126;
    Question 1: A polite person 78–79;
    Question 2: politeness with culture
    79–80, 84; Question 3: participants
    to reflect on motivation 80–81, 85;
    Question 4: polite behaviour 81–82,
    85; Question 5: own experiences with
    TL politeness 83–84

166 Index

FL users 60, 69–70, 78, 85, 115–117, 119–125, 144, 147; experiences of politeness 65–66; metrolingualism 129; motivation 61, 86; native speaker 126–127; observation and scrutiny 63; politeness 66–67, 86; structure of conversation 63; TL modes of enacting politeness 68

foreign language (FL): ability 131; cognitive and social strategy 76, **76**; interactants 63, 67, 69–71, 84–85, 115–116, 119–120, 126–127, 129, 142, 147; interlocutors 61, 65, 86, 116, 119, 121, 124, 130, 138, 144; learners 138; learning 76–77; speakers *see* FL speakers; teachers 61–62, 71; users *see* FL users

foreign language (FL) politeness: automatisation and procedural knowledge 40–41; bilingual learners 32; and culture 1, 2; defining 9–10; degrees of 33–36; five key components 11–12; individual projection 4–5; interlocutors 51; interpersonal and transactional language use 32; learners 16–17; patterns and practices 18–19; positioning 46–52; positioning politeness 31; principles *4*; relational work 3; social contact 4; speakers 2, 43; teachers 14–16; teaching and learning 12–14; teaching and learning contexts 32; types of 5–7; understandings of TL culture 32

Fox, K. 63
Fraser, B. 47
Freire, P. 150

Gabbott, M. 44–45
genres 118–119
Georgakopoulou, A. 156
Giroux, Henry A. 124–125
Goffman, E. 48, 52
Grainger, K. 43, 46
Guillermo 83
Gumperz, J. J. 77
Gu, Y. 68

habitus 119–120
Hall, E. 45
Halliday, M. A. K. 2, 22, 25, 60–61, 64, 90, 92, 116–117, 143
Halliday's ideational function 60–61, 64

Harder, P. 17
Haugh, M. 10, 46, 52, 77, 103, 160
Hogg, G. 44–45
House, J. 42
Hughes, R. 41, 148
hybridity 128
Hymes, D. H. 77

Illustration–Interaction–Induction (i + i + i) mode 150–152, *151*
independence politeness style 95
interactional/affiliative politeness 50–52
interpersonal politeness 6–7; achieving satisfactory relationships 96; employing prosocial politeness 97; engaging 94–95; engaging in relational work 105; FL interlocutors 99; FL speakers 104; investing 97–98; involvement and commitment *99*; lack of politeness in TL 108–110; language and cultural differences 110–111; language function 90–91; Mexican politeness resources in English 108; Mexican Spanish and English expressions, similarities between 106–108; positionality 95–96; prosocial politeness practices 93, 104; relating 93–94; relational maintenance 100–103, *101*; understandings of 91–93

interpersonal relationships 10
involvement politeness style 95
Ishihara, N. 156
Ivanić, R. 41, 148

Jefferson, G. 69–70

Kádár, D. Z. 2, 10, 12, 38, 46, 101, 160
Kasper, G. 160
Kramsch, C. 7, 98, 155

Lakoff, R. 20, 42, 47, 64
Leech, G. 42, 48–49, 55–56, 147–148
Levinson, S. 20, 42, 48–50, 66, 68, 71–72
Liddicoat, A. J. 146
linguistic politeness 40
Locher, M. A. 96

Manns, H. 159
Martin, K. 159
Masuhara, H. 41, 148
McCarthy, M. 150–151

Index 167

McConachy, T. 146
McCroskey, J. 44
Mead, G. W. 122
metrolingualism 129–130
Mexican: bilingual speaker 24; English-speaking contexts 136; interactants 125–126; interlocutors 126
Mexican culture 71, 84, 136
Mexican English-language 22
Mills, S. 38, 43, 47
motivations 73–74
Mugford, G. 21, 61

native speaker 126–127
negative politeness 72
networks 77
nonpoliteness 35–36
nonverbal politeness 44–46
normative politeness 34–35
Norton, B. 73–74, 98

oppositional choices 124–125

Payne, S. 44
Picard, D. 121
polite culture 36
politeness 117, 121; competence 148; contested 154–155; and culture 71–73; in English 83–84; in everyday conversation 63; harmonious relationships 62; interpersonal 153–154; nonverbal 158–160; prosocial 152–153; in social behaviour 63; in Spannish 83–84
politeness principle (PP) 48
positive politeness 72
pragmalinguistic knowledge 13–14, 55
procedural knowledge 40
prosocial politeness 6; concept of investment 73–74; establish safe 'ground,' 74–77; experiences of 78; lay perspectives of 64; linguistic, social and cultural dimensions 60; motivations to be polite 73–74; participants to respond 78; patterns of behaviour 74; structuring 64–65; TL culture 68

rationality 66
repertoire 129
resistance 125
Richmond, V. 44
risk politeness 35

Robles, J. S. 32
Roever, C. 40
Rubio Michel, C. 61

Sacks, H. 69–70
Schegloff, E. 69–70
schemata 119
Schmidt, R. 43
Scollon, R. 36, 45, 159
Scollon, S. 36, 45, 159
self-disclosure 118
self-identification 126
self-interest 81
self-presentation 131
Siegal, M. 161
Sifianou, M. 65, 72
Slade, D. 103
social harmony 62, 69
socialisation 81
social norm politeness 46–48
societal norms, of conduct 122
sociopragmatic knowledge 14, 143
solicitousness 67
Spencer-Oatey, H. 2, 101
super-diversity 127–128
sweeping generalisations 145
synthetic personalisation 125–126

Taguchi, N. 40
target culture (TC) 27
target language (TL): behavioural patterns 119; communicative norms 2; community 84, 124; conduct 78; critical language awareness 149; cultural and language practices 32; cultural behaviour 21; identifying concepts and politeness 77; i + i + i approach 150–152; interaction 67, 83, 85, 125; interactional encounters and experiences 142; interlocutors 62, 69; interpersonal encounters 2; interpersonal skills and abilities 20; language 116; language awareness approach 148; language realities 2; Mexican EFL speakers 146; normative behaviour 68; norms and practices 136–138; politeness 61, 78, 83, 85–86, 121, 123, 135–136, 143–145; politeness patterns and practices 21–22, 145; relational behaviour 62–65; relational interaction 22; relational practices 129, 136; relational work 23; relational work and politeness 43–44;

168 *Index*

societal expectations 32; speakers 21–22, 131–133; use 118
target-language culture (TC) 13
teaching programme: politeness commitment 53–54; politeness resources 54–56; presentation of self 52–53
Terkourafi, M. 66
textual dimension 118
textual function 116–118
third place 127–128
Thomas, J. 17, 50, 155

TL *see* target language
Tomlinson, B. 41, 148
Toohey, K. 98
Tracy, K. 32
transition-relevance place (TRP) 69; and turn-taking practices 70
translanguaging 128–129
Truss, L. 64
Turn-Construction Units (TCUs) 69

Watts, R. J. 9, 17, 32, 35, 96, 125
Widdowson, H. G. 119